be in info bill row

the people

ANC, says Kasrils

Zuma, say sorry to Khwezi'

- KASRILS URGES PRESIDENT TO MAKE AMENDS WITH RAPE ACCUSER'S MOM
- MALEMA PLANS TO VISIT HER FAMILY TO APOLOGISE FOR POST-TRIAL REMARKS

REPORTS ON PAGE 5

ight', says Kasrils

rogant, dictatorial'

To Oisin,

A

Simple

Man

A fellow African.

Remie Kosils

A Simple Man

Kasrils and the
Zuma Enigma

Ronnie Kasrils

First published by Jacana Media (Pty) Ltd in 2017

10 Orange Street
Sunnyside
Auckland Park 2092
South Africa
+2711 628 3200
www.jacana.co.za

ISBN 978-1-4314-2577-8

Editing by Russell Martin
Proofreading by Lara Jacob
Cover design by publicide
Design and layout by Shawn Paikin
Set in MrsEaves 11.5/15
Printed and bound by CTP Printers, Cape Town
Job no. 003087

See a complete list of Jacana titles at www.jacana.co.za

Dedicated to the Man in the Green Blanket and the Girl in the Green Scarf — Mgcineni 'Mambush' Noki and Fezeka Kuzwayo — who fearlessly stood their ground against power in the most corrupt of times

Little did we suspect that our people, when they got the chance, would be as corrupt as the apartheid regime.
— NELSON MANDELA

The final disillusionment will come, of course, when the repressive apparatuses of the state ... turn their weapons on the masses to protect the interests of the capitalist class.
— NEVILLE ALEXANDER[1]

Contents

Foreword

THIS IS THE STORY of the hidden death of a beloved African myth. It is a story told as only an insider could tell it. The meticulous detail makes it a unique record of how close comrades, having been involved in decades of struggle for an immensely ambitious project of transformation, once in power made political choices which enriched a new class at home, made state patronage and corruption a new norm, and in foreign policy frequently evaded principle. It reads like a thriller, with characters and happenings stranger than fiction and Shakespearean in depth. How did all this happen in full view of a world which mostly chose not to see?

South Africa's freedom had been so long delayed, so hard won, so drenched in blood and sacrifice that at home and abroad people greeted it as a miracle which was going to change everything, not just at home, but in the standing of the continent in the wider world. The towering stature of Nelson Mandela alone was believed to be enough to ensure internal harmony for the future.

Many factors ended the dream of harmony. One of them, never so clearly illustrated, was the personal characteristics of some of the leadership from the outset. An opening scene here of a moment long ago in 1982 in the high-risk world of the clandestine armed struggle outside the country's borders reveals the shadow of what was to come.

The author's response that night was a long private reflection, a questioning of his own responsibility, and a new ambivalence and wariness about his comrade — traits which would carry him decades later to choose open collision rather than collusion with his old associate, whose own traits that night began to display that he was far from being a simple man of the people.

It was twenty-odd years after that night that the two contrasting visions of politics, revolution and morality it had foreshadowed came into the open, at least between party cadres though not yet before the country.

Ronnie Kasrils, in the years of underground work from London, Angola and Mozambique, and, later, on the run inside South Africa and then in the government ministries he headed, built teams of men and women cemented by mutual respect, which endured long after their inception. Principles for safeguarding the country from the abuse of power were regularly reiterated by him to his colleagues. Jacob Zuma, meanwhile, built patterns of personal patronage on ethnic ties, ruthlessly sacrificing valuable colleagues with a different profile. And the memorable women's parts in his story are not of trusted colleagues but of figures of tragedy: one of Zuma's many wives who committed suicide and left a devastating note, and a young woman abused by a man she had known as her father's comrade in the years of armed struggle, as Kasrils was too. She considered them her uncles. How telling it is that the first person she phoned after her traumatic experience with Zuma was Kasrils.

That occasion when she alleged rape and its aftermath form one strand of the complex tale of corruption and power dominance laid bare here. Against all evidence and logic Zuma, speaking in court only in his own dialect and invoking local cultural norms, won the rape case against him. Outside in the streets, vulgar displays of ANC male chauvinism and female adulation for Zuma shamed everything the party had stood for. The victim was treated like a medieval witch, and Kasrils was accused of involving her as a 'honey trap' to harm Zuma's career, as part of a 'conspiracy'.

Other conspiracies, however, were all too real. Here is an extraordinary series of complex tales of real corruption, faked emails, leaked phone conversations, conmen and criminals, betrayals within the several intelligence services, laughable incompetence, and diligent forensic work by professionals. Only someone living deep inside this web could unravel the strands to show clearly what happened and how he was misled by his own staff, and defamed as a traitor by people who should have known better. Along the way there were many trials, many sentences, lies, defamation and, above all, confusion in people's minds at all levels in the country. Good men and women made bad choices in good faith, he writes. The judiciary's role veered wildly between blatant partisan ruling and impeccable upholding of the rule of law. In this prepared atmosphere the ANC, backed by the SACP and the trade unions, removed the dignified, bookish president, Thabo Mbeki. Kasrils was among the ministers who went with him.

Jacob Zuma had won a thirty-year ambition. He and Ronnie Kasrils had been formed together over years in the ANC and SACP. But that night incident on the Mozambique border reveals the roots of Zuma's turning away from party ideals onto a trajectory of linking power and money. The symbol would be his ostentatious spending on a rural mansion complex, which became a national scandal. Kasrils, whether in or out of party and power, lived modestly with the ideological choices forged by the international fraternity of the Cubans and others in the years of secrecy, disruption and discipline. Aesop's fable says it all for the two of them: 'A man is known by the company he keeps.'

Many academics and journalists have written from many angles on the southern African liberation movements' incompetence and slide into corruption and repression once they were in power in their various countries. Exiles from other African countries have written bitter accounts of the failures of new post-independence regimes back home. Many are interesting, but limited in their contribution to understanding the processes of change that happened, seemingly mysteriously. A new generation deserves a key to understanding how a country can be brought low by structural factors and some legacies of exile and underground years steeped in paranoia and suspicion, combined with ruthless ambition to gain power at all costs and the hubris that could convince a man like Jacob Zuma that he was untouchable by the law. They have just such a key here.

It takes a brave and principled man to write openly of the unravelling world in which he was a key participant for so long. The myth of South Africa's success became just a PR trick, which much of the world chose to swallow. Ronnie Kasrils has lived with the deepest of disappointments in the collective failure to keep faith with the millions of families living lives of shameful deprivation whom he and his colleagues risked their lives for over and over again in the hopeful armed struggle years. The defeat has many external factors — the socio-economic environment and multinational corporate and political power — as well as the weakness or self-interest of so many colleagues who chose to follow the siren song of Jacob Zuma on the road to personal power, status and ostentatious wealth over the interest of the country's masses.

But history is not over. Those same deprived and angry men and women were once the key to independence, and they and their next generation still trust the likes of Ronnie Kasrils personally today. He has made no secret of his continuing commitment to their rights — as he showed so clearly in his instant response to the Marikana Massacre, in which Zuma's police shot down in cold blood thirty-four striking miners in 2012. His optimism and burning belief in the collective power of ordinary men and women to change the world remain undimmed, as is shown graphically in this outstanding book. South Africa's future will be in the hands of a new generation who have much to learn from this story.

Other visionaries of another African generation, such as Nkrumah, Nyerere, Cabral, Lumumba, Neto and Lúcio Lara — from Ghana, Tanzania, Cape Verde, Democratic Republic of Congo and Angola — have gone now, but their common ideals still drive the conviction of a man like Kasrils that transformation in Africa can be real, not just a myth.

Victoria Brittain
London, June 2017

Preface

THE IDEA FOR THIS BOOK began in my favourite coffee shop in Kalk Bay soon after I moved there in 2008 after resigning from government as the minister for intelligence services. That portfolio has nothing to do with high IQ but rather the murky world of 'spies' – the derogatory term normally used by one side to describe the other. (All spy agencies always call their own spies 'agents' and the other side's agents 'spies'.) At the coffee shop the engaging Jacana Media trio – Bridget Impey, Maggie Davey and Russell Martin – tried to persuade me that I would be the ideal author of a book about South Africa's spies or, rather, agents.

I was flattered but not keen then. It was far too soon into retirement – although I came to call my new status 'refirement', as I soon got busy making more enemies for myself by raising awkward questions in the media about the increasing secrecy and corruption in government. I also needed time to reflect and relax a bit with my companion of forty-eight years in our new abode overlooking False Bay. Tragically, Eleanor died within a year, and in tribute I wrote a book about her, *The Unlikely Secret Agent*, which Jacana published and which won the Alan Paton Sunday Times award for the best non-fiction of 2011.

Almost a decade after the coffee shop meeting Bridget Impey asked whether I was ready to write a book, not simply about spies, but about what had brought the country from a hopeful beginning in 1994, and impressive achievements to the brink of ruin under Syndicate Zuma and the Guptas. Much mud had passed under the bridge, which actually served to clarify things by the accumulation of clues in the sewage, and I was more than ready to take up the pen. In fact, the book had been writing itself in my subconscious all those years. I wanted to answer the question put to me by many friends: what were the factors that transformed Zuma the freedom fighter, and ostensibly a simple man of the people, into a corrupt and disreputable figure who surrounded himself with a load of creepy kleptocrats? But I also wanted to understand more than that. For our problems have not started with Zuma or Zupta, for he is a consequence of errors made during the transformational arrangements of the early 1990s – what I have previously called the Faustian pact. How to make sense of all this?

At the time of writing, what appeared to be a settled political post-apartheid transition, albeit one marked by the profound persistence of racial inequalities inherited from the past, was rapidly unravelling not least with irreconcilable conflicts bursting out within each element of the liberation movement's Tripartite Alliance (ANC, SACP and Cosatu) and across it as a whole. It is apparent that this has been provoked and particularly expressed through the corrupt presidency of Jacob Zuma and the hopes some placed on it, culminating in the current bizarre pretence that he is the champion in the fight against 'white monopoly capitalism' (WMC) for radical economic transformation (i.e. anything that favours him and his cronies must be for the public good even though it is ultimately and even immediately dependent upon a system based on WMC).

Yet this is not just a momentary episode or a single grossly flawed administration but an outcome of the path followed over the entire post-apartheid period – the Faustian pact – with danger signs at earlier points but bursting into the open with the 2012 Marikana Massacre. This means that the present must be traced through its journey from the past, even over such a short, if complex, period, which has too much detail to be covered in a single book. I was party to these events and I strive to bring that journey to life through select accounts from my own experience, enriched by post facto reflection and research, and thereby forge the connection between where we are and how we got here, within my book.

The reader may be interested to know how I am able to recount the past with any degree of accuracy and how reliable my memory is. As any visit to my archive at Wits University will reveal, I have always maintained copious and scribbled notes, diaries, news cuttings, letters and photographs. These are essential items for the reconstruction of the past. My main weapon, however, is a facility to recollect experiences in visual form. This I put down to the thousands of hours I spent at the local Yeoville bioscope when I was growing up. I suppose it is a little like the photographic memory some people have who can reel off page after page of printed matter. I cannot do that. My memory sparks off a mental image, which I am able to recall, and then a hidden button in my mind begins to unreel the happening. Once I have achieved a fairly good recall of events, I check my version with others who might have been present and also through interviews where possible. Research is necessary, but most of all I revel in being able to write from the mind.

One factor I have had to take into account is ensuring that I have not fallen foul of the Secrecy Act. That has required care, and I have therefore avoided the use of classified documents. The purist will claim this means that my narrative consequently cannot provide a completely accurate account of anything in the field of secrecy. My own intention, however, is to provide no more than an honest account of events, as I have seen and experienced them, without revealing classified information. What I seek to offer readers is a narrative from my own viewpoint, focusing on important details that may not have been noticed and connecting the dots. This cannot be a definitive account of the past. More recently, a number of role players, such as Vusi Pikoli, Frank Chikane and Khulu Mbatha, once close to the action, have provided their own personal accounts, which can be read alongside mine. Researchers in the future will find these — and, I trust, my own book — of value. Hopefully, classified information will also be available to them too — unless a police state curtain of secrecy clangs down.

Readers will ask why I did not reveal some of this material, especially my doubts about Zuma, in *Armed and Dangerous*. That memoir came out in 1993 at a point in history when it did not seem appropriate to reveal all, owing to the attacks and smears we were then facing from our enemies. Neither was it apparent that Zuma could become so powerful and do so much damage to the democratic project. It is always a question of judgement and timing. In this book I do not hold back but tell the story — warts and all. The time is long overdue not only to deal with such leaders as Jacob Zuma but equally to analyse, where things have gone so terribly wrong. My intentions are not personal or malicious, and I do not spare myself from sharing the blame.

The situation is dire but I refuse to bow down to the worst. This book points out the nightmare that may await us all if the thieves and racketeers get their way. But I believe in the possibility of people's power and the abiding hope that the gathering momentum will become decisive sooner rather than later. I am neither an optimist nor pessimist in this regard although I subscribe to Gramsci's dictum 'pessimism of the intellect but optimism of the will'. The corollary of that is Fidel Castro's urging that in these challenging times what is vital is to keep alive the spirit of revolutionary hope.

The reader will ask, 'What is to be done?' I do not claim to know the answers, which must be found by a younger generation. I believe veteran fighters have a duty to keep a flame burning for developing ways of thinking about the human condition. A way of understanding its nature and genesis, learning from the lessons of the past in constant changing conditions. By maintaining the flame, and passing it on to the next generation, we can do our best to ensure that a form of understanding survives. This is a hope that by analysing where we have come from we may shine some light on the path ahead.

Acknowledgements

My APPRECIATION TO Bridget Impey, who has as ever been a joy to work with. Thanks to Russell Martin for his splendid editing, and to Maggie Davey and all at Jacana Media, particularly Lara Jacob for her meticulous proofreading of the book, Stavi Kotsiovos and Shawn Paikin, for assisting me while working through the editorial process and book design; and Janine Daniel and Neilwe Mashigo for the marketing. Thanks to Zanele Mbuyisa for specialist legal advice. Special gratitude to David Niddrie, who has kept me from going insane by helping me assemble the book on my computer. I managed to lose only one chapter of the book and some paragraphs here and there, but I lost that material so thoroughly that not even David or my young relative, Jamie Francis, could manage to retrieve them. David has been more than a computer buff; he has been an excellent adviser and discussant on various aspects of the book, as well as assisting me in getting the manuscript into an acceptable form and suggesting editing changes and refinements.

My thanks to numerous comrades for ideas, suggestions and comments not only while writing but over the years, in assessing and analysing developments in South Africa. I am especially grateful to Vishnu Padayachee and Ben Fine for the economic insights they have provided; to Moeletsi Mbeki, who tirelessly campaigns for a technologically modern South Africa; to my close friend Pallo Jordan for his efforts to keep me aligned and my apologies for differing but always gaining from the association; to Carlos de Cossio, the Cuban ambassador, always ready to respond to my queries about his inspiring country; to Gabi Mohale, who looks after my archive at the Historical Papers research archive at Wits university's Cullen Library and is always ready to assist in locating any item; and to fellow subversives of the Sidikiwe Campaign, such as Nosiviwe Madlala-Routledge, Louise Colvin, Barney Pityana, Vish Satgar and a hundred others who helped to remind the ANC that the gravy train days were numbered unless they remedied their ways.

A special salute to Patrick Bond, academic activist, with a tremendous zest for justice and the truth, and his many writings (not the least of which are his book *Elite Transition* and essay 'Was Mandela pushed or did he jump?'). And to Sampie Terreblanche in ackowledgement of his slim volume, *Lost in Transformation*, which prompted my concept of a 'Faustian Pact'.

Deep appreciation to my legal team: Advocates Dali Mpofu and François Grobler and my attorney Jenny Friedman, who prepared the ammunition (as her father and mentor, Rowley Arenstein, had taught her) to fire in winning my defamation case against the chairperson of the MK Military Veterans Association and salvaging the name of Fezeka Kuzwayo and my reputation; for Louise Colvin and Ivan Pillay for assisting with arrangements to ensure the care of Fezeka's mother; and to Nokuthula and Thokozani Mtshali for coming to the rescue. Hugs to Kimmie Msibi, the lifelong friend of the late Fezeka Kuzwayo, who stood up to Jacob Zuma for the women of our country. Zola Ngcakani, the former inspector general, and Imtiaz Fazel, who investigated the fake emails, afforded me the time I needed to jog my memory; as did Frank Dutton, the country's top detective (retired), who was the Scorpions' initial leader; and Laurie Nathan, who wrote the Matthews Commission Report recommending reforms of the intelligence services and who helped me struggle against the almost ingrained culture of 'bending the rules'. Unforgettable was my engagement with the press ombudsman, Johan Retief, the public advocate, Latiefa Mobara, and all at the Press Council for enabling me to extract an unprecedented apology from the *Sunday Times* for publishing false allegations about me. Special appreciation to comrade and former president Kgalema Motlanthe for the time he afforded me. Profound thanks to David Bell for the stimulating discussions we had as I explained the purpose of this book to him.

I will not name most of those in government positions and especially MK veterans, as the book is not going to be popular with the powers that be; but my thanks to them for they know what and they know why. In this respect I need to acknowledge the useful insights provided by 'Chico', 'Rosie' and 'Chancey' over time.

Thanks to Victoria Brittain for her encouragement and to John Rose, who for several years has nagged me to write about my years in government; to my sons Andrew and Chris for their encouragement and support, and Andy's alter ego, the Admiral, for encouraging chats over many lunches. Gratitude to Liz Francis for her devotion to the memory of Eleanor and visits to the Kirstenbosch tree growing out of the soil where we buried her ashes. Special mention of Angie Kapelianis, the 'Harrow Road heroine', who drove like a bat out of hell to save us from a hijacking and obtained for me various out-of-print books.

Most important of all, boundless appreciation to my dearest wife, Amina, who has shown such patience and provided the support and love with which this book could not have been started or concluded. She effortlessly kept me going with masala chai and good cheer, well beyond the call of duty.

Crossing the Border

Mozambique–Swaziland border, 1982

THEIR VISION IMPAIRED by soft rain and mist, two shadowy figures lurk in the bush, peering through binoculars into the descending gloom, as they scan the border fence.

'Just the weather for violating the frontier, eh Baba [Father],' one mutters to the other, and they quietly chuckle (as lads do) at the sexual connotation.

'*Yebo*, mFana'kithi [Yes, Homeboy],' agreed the one addressed as Baba, 'like *amaRussia* used to say: bad weather is the guerrilla's best friend.'

'Some would rather be in bed with the "blanket",' Homeboy responds; and the two chuckle at the army slang for the comforts of a sweetheart.

'Let's hope the Swazi men are doing the "thing" on a night like this,' says Baba, 'instead of sniffing around the border,' which gets them chuckling again.

'Sniffing the blanket!' and the two struggle to control their laughter.

The levity had the purpose of assuaging the tension. There was no sign of the dusk patrol along the frontier strip, a formidable no man's land some twenty-metres wide cleared of vegetation, flanked by two parallel lines of strong, high fencing along the Mozambican–Swaziland border.

They were on the Mozambican side, which was friendly territory where their movement, the African National Congress (ANC) had a relatively secure base in the capital of Maputo. They were in a particularly dangerous area, for the South African border was but a few kilometres north of where they stood, and by daylight a listening post with gigantic satellite dishes was clearly visible on a prominent koppie, monitoring radio traffic across a vast area.[1] As a result they literally operated in the dark, without any form of radio communication: if they had had any, they would instantly give their position away and be tracked down by a South African reaction unit.

They had been dropped off an hour before dusk near the border village of Namaacha, where they avoided the local Frelimo troops, and slipped away into thick bush. Both men, in their early forties, were well clad for the weather, in waterproof anoraks with hoods, jeans and boots, each armed with Makarov pistols tucked into their belts. They were well-built, fit-looking, and in good shape. Baba was bearded and wore a balaclava cap. Homeboy was of lighter complexion, bearded too, the hood of his waterproof coat covering his head. Despite Baba being the respectful Zulu term for 'father', he was the younger of the two. But he had a tribal air of authority about him and enjoyed the form of deference, whether used by his equals or underlings. To be sure, he used it when addressing others as well with an air of levity, a pronounced chuckle and flashing smile which showed his fine white teeth. One never quite knew whether he was serious about affected patriarchy or simply wryly patronising, for he loved to joke.

The frontier posts, cheek by jowl, had shut down for the night; the villages astride the boundary were silent; there was no traffic, no sign of patrols.[2] The border was enveloped in the kind of atmospheric hush that only fine rain and mist can produce. It was time for the crossing.

Crouching low, they moved swiftly and silently into the open, Baba to the fore, Homeboy running close behind, hefting his knapsack onto his back. The first man clambered quietly up the fence, slipped

dextrously over the top, and sprang lightly down. The second man
followed and, despite the knapsack, was over the top in agile fashion
and leapt into no man's land. As he landed, his foot came down on
a rock, twisting viciously and propelling him headlong. He hit the
ground with a thud and stifled groan.

Baba turned with a start, and came back to assist his comrade
writhing in pain.

Homeboy cursed through clenched teeth, struggling to stand up.
He stood gingerly on his foot, both men looking anxiously around to
see if they had been spotted. Leaning on his companion's shoulder,
he staggered across the twenty metres of open ground, where they felt
naked and vulnerable, to the second barrier. There was no question
of retreating back into the safety of Mozambique.

'I'm OK, it's not broken, let's keep going,' Homeboy whispered,
but he could not hide the pain.

Baba, his face tight, helped his partner ascend the second fence,
this time much more slowly and with greater difficulty, and carefully
guided him down the other side into the uncertainty of Swazi territory.
He had taken the knapsack, filled with arms, and was surprised at the
weight. No wonder Homeboy had fallen so heavily.

They moved slowly, the one leaning on the other. After a couple
of kilometres of slow going, cloaked in the dark damp, they found the
road without trouble, and halted at a rendezvous point where they
expected to be picked up.

Homeboy was grateful to sit down, which he did slowly, back against
a tree, to examine his aching ankle, while Baba went about the business
of placing two empty Coke cans alongside the road, ten metres apart,
as a stopping signal for the car that would be coming for them.

'How's the ankle?' he enquired.

The injured man put on a brave face: 'Probably no more than a bad
sprain. I'll manage.'

They had not lost time, for the pick-up from the distant Swazi town
of Manzini, a hundred and fifty kilometres away, had been arranged
for nine o'clock. That meant an hour's wait.

It began to rain harder. They were grateful for their anoraks and the two plastic sheets which Homeboy produced from his knapsack. He laid one on the ground for them to sit on and the other they propped over their heads to keep as dry as possible. They were close together, breathing in tandem, their body warmth generating heat, a musky aroma in their nostrils, 'joined at the hip', a phrase Baba liked to use about close comradeship.

Homeboy's ankle was throbbing. It was well past nine o'clock and the rule was never to remain at a rendezvous point such as this for longer than half an hour. The rain had turned gentle again, but the mist was thicker and cold seeped through their bones. There had been no traffic on the road whatsoever. They stared and stared, anticipating the sound of an engine and the hoped-for sight of a car travelling with lights dipped. But the long, empty road just stared back at them. By eleven o'clock they decided to give up waiting. It was clear their lift was not coming. They braced themselves for the trek back to the Mozambican side, a good hour's distance. Again Baba supported Homeboy, who leaned heavily on him, wincing every time he stepped, no matter how gingerly, on his injured ankle.

The pair then brazenly made their way, as though they were a couple of late-night drunks, along the national road, veering around the desolate Swazi frontier post and, with difficulty and huge relief, successfully surmounted the two fences that separated the Kingdom of Swaziland from the People's Republic of Mozambique.

Namaacha on the Mozambican side, with its small *cantinas* and stores, was as quiet as the village of Lomahasha on the Swazi side. They made their way down narrow lanes, crossed an alleyway, and knocked on the door of a house. It was opened by a woman who looked at them in surprise. She was Isabella, one of Baba's women from Maputo: half-Zulu, half-Mozambican. He knew Brother had a 'thing' going with her. '*Boa noite* [Good evening],' Homeboy, ever the polite one, greeted her. She ushered them in and sat them down in a tiny lounge, with pictures of Jesus and Samora Machel, Mozambique's president, in military uniform, on the wall. Homeboy struggled to untie his boot. The ankle was hideously swollen and purple in colour. Isabella brought him some aspirin and a glass of water and found a bandage, which she wrapped tightly around Homeboy's ankle. 'It needs support,' she said with a Portuguese accent. She and Baba disappeared into the kitchen where she began to prepare coffee. 'Rest a little,' they suggested.

Homeboy tried to relax on an overstuffed couch, propping his injured leg up on a cushion. The pain was excruciating, and he was lost in thought about getting to hospital in Maputo first thing in the morning. Baba would be organising a car to take them back that night. He tried to focus his mind on something other than his ankle and studied the religious picture of the Last Supper. He had seen a similar print in Isabella's Maputo home, where Baba had once given a hilarious interpretation of the scene.

Baba had pointed to the twelve disciples in turn as they sat with Jesus at the centre of a long table. 'This one here,' he pointed out, 'you can imagine this disciple thinking of Jesus: "Is he really a Zulu?"' At once he had engaged Homeboy in the game. 'See these two whispering to one another,' he pointed. 'This one is confiding to the other: "But he doesn't look like a Zulu."' By now Homeboy was mesmerised, and Baba, enjoying the attention, continued: 'Likewise the two over here, clearly gossiping, "If he can't prove he's a Zulu, he can't lead us."' The two guffawed together. 'This one here, looking directly at Jesus, I think he's looking quite slyly, he is thinking, "I'll watch how he eats. It will show whether he is Zulu or Shangaan."' Homeboy by then was in stitches. 'Likewise the six on the other side of the table.' Baba pointed to each in turn: '"Eish! I think this man is a stranger from Timbuktu!"; "That one resembles a Xhosa"; "We must watch him carefully, can't be sure he is one of us."' And then the denouement: 'See this one here,' Baba commanded, and Homeboy totally captivated, watched closely: 'This one is Judas. Judas Iscariot. You know, the Zealot! What's he say?' Homeboy was all ears: 'Judas is thinking: "Is he selling us out to the Romans? If he is not true, I will turn him in."'

As Homeboy lay there, looking at the picture, the words '*umlungu*' and '*mampara*' filtered through in undertones from the kitchen. He was at once attentive, thinking he was mistaken. But it was clear. Baba was complaining about him to Isabella, referring to him as a 'stupid white man' who was responsible for that night's setback.

He felt momentarily ashamed at the thought of having let his colleague down. He reflected again on his mishap. Was that really cause for him to be regarded as stupid; as a stupid white man at that? And this in stark contrast to Baba's engaging manner, his empathy — 'joined at the hip', indeed! Was 'stupid white man' what Baba, when irritated, really thought of him? Did it come down to that? Was comradeship that skin-deep with him?

Baba was back in the room with a mug of steaming coffee.

'Have the aspirins helped my brother?' he enquired with a generous smile.

'The coffee is good,' Baba continued rapidly, 'will help ... Car's coming now-now ... we'll get back to our beds in Maputo very soon.'

Ah, this was the Baba known to all in the movement: trustworthy and considerate.

Except that Homeboy had heard the unkind tone, whispered behind his back, whispered in a tongue he was not proficient in, but the words 'umlungu' and 'mampara' were unmistakable. Homeboy was shaken and worried, in a way that went deeper than the pain in the ankle. Could Baba be a two-faced Judas? Did his middle name Gedleyihlekisa really mean what Baba had once explained to Homeboy: 'he who stabs you in the back while smiling'?[3] Whatever the literal translation, that's how he has come to be regarded.

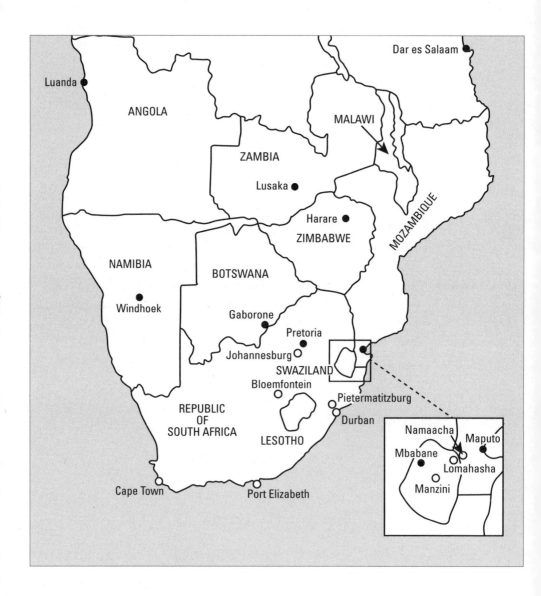

PART ONE

President and Deputy

1999–2005

Every good tree bringeth forth good fruit;
but the corrupt tree bringeth forth evil fruit
— Matthew 7:17

CHAPTER I

Update
South Africa, 1990–2004

THAT RAINY NIGHT IN 1982, when the two of us – 'Baba', or Jacob Gedleyihlekisa Zuma, and I, 'Homeboy' (mFana'kithi, one of my many noms de guerre) – slipped across the border into Swaziland still stands out in my memory, not only because I fell and sprained my ankle. Whenever the weather grows cold, the ankle still protests a little and I relive that night's mishap. But the incident marked, too, the start of a gradual rupture with my friend Jacob Zuma, whom I had till then considered to be a straight-cut, simple man of the people. For if I had not overheard him soon afterwards referring to my mishap in a two-faced manner, then my memory of the event would not be clouded by feelings of ambivalence, and all I would recollect would be my leaning on his shoulder for support as he guided me safely back across the border into Mozambique.

Twelve years after that incident, our whole world had changed. South Africa had been politically free since the first national elections in 1994, which saw the elevation of Nelson Mandela as president. Mandela himself was succeeded by his deputy, Thabo Mbeki, in 1999, and Zuma in turn became Mbeki's deputy while I served alongside them both in the cabinet. Zuma's original rise to prominence in the country owed much to Mbeki. They were both born in the same year, the one into a leading struggle family of intellectuals, the other coming from an impoverished rural background. While Mbeki had the advantages of a university education in Britain, Zuma had little formal education, was largely self-taught as a child, herding cattle whilst his friends went to school, and may be perceived as harbouring a degree of resentment for 'clever' blacks. The duo began a second term in 2004 after that year's general election when the ANC's popular vote rose to within a whisker of 70 per cent, the highest it had achieved till then.

It appears that Zuma was not Mbeki's first choice as deputy president in 1999. Mangosuthu Buthelezi, leader of the Zulu-based rival of the ANC, the Inkatha Freedom Party (IFP), says Mbeki approached him but he turned down the offer. This was possibly because the powers of the position had been greatly reduced since Mbeki's tenure, when he was a virtual prime minister under Mandela. For many years the ANC, short of Zulu leaders though not of Xhosa ones, had been keen to ensure their presence in leadership, and Thabo Mbeki was no exception. I thought that Mbeki's initial preference for Buthelezi might have distressed Zuma. On an election campaign in the run-up to the 1999 national elections I was present when Zuma made a speech glibly explaining that it was the ANC's tradition that a deputy president always succeeded a president when the latter's term of office came to an end. It occurred to me at the time that this kind of ambition could cause problems. It crossed my mind again when I learnt from a source close to his family that he was already saying in 2000 that Mbeki would block him from ever becoming president. Resentment and ambition were already brewing.

Mbeki and Zuma had once been extremely close. They originally worked for a year as a team in Swaziland in 1975–6, forging links with contacts inside South Africa sympathetic to the ANC. Later, Zuma joined a trusted quartet led by Mbeki that was involved in secret talks with representatives of the apartheid regime in the late 1980s. He was certainly hand-picked by Mbeki for this role, which greatly aided his political profile. This channel paralleled Mandela's historic talks as a prisoner with his jailers, the dual initiatives eventually merging and flowing into the formal negotiations between the ANC and the white government for a political settlement.

The negotiations process was accompanied by violence and killing on a scale that was not matched even in the strife-torn 1980s. It was in this violence-prone period that Zuma made a positive mark for himself, and impressed Mandela and many more besides. He was deployed to his turbulent home province of Natal, later KwaZulu-Natal, which was controlled at the time by Buthelezi's IFP. In the 1980s the IFP had literally fought off the United Democratic Front (UDF), which was strongly pro-ANC. The IFP had become aligned to the National Party, and some two hundred of its members had been secretly trained in the Caprivi Strip by the police and South African Defence Force (SADF) as a counter to the ANC.[1] Natal had come to resemble a killing field with so-called black-on-black violence stoked by apartheid security forces and led by a shadowy policeman, General Jack Buchner, who was police commissioner in the Zulu homeland.

In this situation Zuma's background and shrewdness were impressive qualities, assisted by his knowledge of the region, his fluency in the language, and his affinity with the rural people and their culture. He got on well with the Zulu monarch, King Goodwill Zwelithini, like him a polygamist and always requiring ever more funds. It would be an exaggeration to say that it was Zuma alone who managed to neutralise much of the enmity between the role players, including the king, and win over considerable numbers of supporters to the ANC ahead of the 1994 elections, but he nonetheless proved an adept leader in those circumstances and built up a personal following from that time. It was Zuma's relationship with the likes of Schabir Shaik and other ambitious businessmen that began to raise eyebrows and concern about his fallibilities and constant need for a handout, whatever the source. There were ANC militants like Harry Gwala and Blade Nzimande who frowned on Zuma's approach to peace-making, which they viewed as far too conciliatory.[2]

Long before Mbeki stepped down as president, relations between him and Zuma had become increasingly strained. Indeed, as I shall explain, Mbeki had dismissed Zuma from his position as deputy president in a move that would later rebound on him and lead to his own dismissal by the party. This fraught relationship between the two came to reflect a bitter and divisive schism within a proud and historic liberation movement that had always prized its unity as its greatest source of strength. In a wicked twist Mbeki was destined not to serve out his full term of office as president of the ANC and of the country partly owing to the rift between Zuma and himself and to growing factionalism within the movement, which began to tear it apart.

In the meantime I had served Mandela as deputy minister of defence, and was appointed minister of water affairs and forestry by his successor, Thabo Mbeki. Incidentally it was in that position that I once had the occasion to be in the company of Deputy President Jacob Zuma and King Zwelithini. They treated me like a hero on a day in 2000 when I renamed the Chelmsford Dam, near Newcastle, in KwaZulu-Natal, after the Zulu general Ntshingwayo, who had annihilated Lord Chelmsford's invasion column at the Battle of Isandlwana in 1879.

The promotion to a full cabinet position by Mbeki had surprised me as I had never been particularly close to him. I was historically more aligned to the military grouping of Joe Slovo and Chris Hani, and the South African Communist Party (SACP) leadership of Slovo, rather than any Mbeki grouping. We considered both Mbeki and Zuma moderate and less inclined to mass action, and did not quite trust Zuma. To my surprise Mbeki appointed me minister of intelligence services in May 2004, a senior post carrying considerable responsibility. I was aware he had become concerned about the ineffectiveness and pro-Zuma politicisation of the security and intelligence sector, and I felt he had become more confident in my ability owing to my loyal service in government. By then he too had certainly lost confidence in Zuma.

At the cabinet appointments Mbeki was accompanied by the secretary general of the ANC, Kgalema Motlanthe, a man of dignified bearing whom I greatly respected. That gave me a comfortable feeling, as it conveyed a synergy between government and the political movement.[3]

I also had high regard for Motlanthe as a seasoned revolutionary. He was five years younger than Mbeki and Zuma, had been leader of the powerful National Union of Mineworkers (NUM), a Robben Island prisoner, and, like Mbeki and Zuma, a former member of the SACP. The careers of the trio were to feature together dramatically in the years ahead.

CHAPTER 2

Spooks

Pretoria and abroad, 2004

INTELLIGENCE WAS A DIFFICULT PORTFOLIO although, given its perceived power, it was much sought after. Some may have thought that Mbeki had handed me a poisoned chalice, for the office had huge problems. The loyalty of the ANC old guard in the sector was geared to the Zuma group, which had faithfully served him in exile and on returning home. By mid-2004 if not far sooner, Mbeki, I believe, had become increasingly wary of his deputy. When I transferred from defence into my first full ministerial position, water affairs and forestry, I thought of it as passing from fire to water. But moving to my new post in intelligence seemed akin to jumping into a sizzling frying pan.

The first six months of my tenure went quietly enough. I was briefed by the three main structures that I would oversee as their executive head. These were the National Intelligence Agency (NIA), responsible for domestic security issues; the South African Secret Service (SASS), whose remit was foreign intelligence gathering; and the National Intelligence Coordinating Committee (NICOC). The last-mentioned was responsible for assessing the intelligence reports submitted not only by NIA and SASS, but also by both police and military intelligence, and preparing a final document for cabinet. In practice these structures jealously hung onto their best intelligence material and only submitted watered-down versions to NICOC. Their heads were inclined to make a beeline for the president, whom they treated with their most impressive information, for his ear only. A serious problem was the politicisation of ANC officers in the public service and growing factionalism within the organisation. The politicisation issue had been understandable enough when after 1994 it was a question of amalgamating former regime personnel with those from the liberation movement. After a decade, however, government and state should have moved beyond that phase, and a stable environment should have been created. But the struggle for ascendancy within the ANC meant otherwise.

Other structures I was responsible for were the top-secret Communications Interception Office (CIO), which required judicial authority for tapping phone lines, and an Intelligence Academy. When I first visited the academy I asked a class of new recruits how they were finding the training. An enthusiastic youngster replied that he loved the world of James Bond. That set me off lecturing them about the role of the spies (*amakhangela* or *iintlola*)[1] deployed by the indigenous armies of our country in the wars of resistance to colonialism, as sources of inspiration. I commissioned a sculptor to produce a fine figure of one such warrior, which we erected at the services headquarters next to one of the Boer *fietsryers* of the Anglo-Boer War,[2] which had stood there for years.

I had my time cut out meeting the various heads of subdivisions and touring the country to acquaint myself with NIA structures in the nine provinces. The extent to which problems abounded was brought home to me when the liaison officer assigned to accompany me around the provinces went AWOL on the third day. An excuse that he was ill was presented to me, but I soon ascertained for myself that his absence was owing to an alcoholic binge. He was a highly intelligent operative known to me in the dangerous Swaziland days, who was quite probably suffering from post-traumatic stress disorder which had never been diagnosed. A combination of factionalism within the services and the ANC, rivalry for positions, and difficulty in coping with responsibilities, including family stress, in a transforming environment was the likely explanation for the mess he, and many others, found themselves in.

All the same I began to form the opinion that most of the former ANC operatives were relying on an outer show of competence that hid inner deficiencies and fear of failure. This was understandable, for most of our people had lacked work and life experience – experience that could not be made up through a six-month training course in a socialist country – and they had limited technical and managerial skills. As a result they tended to apply what they had learnt in training in a mechanical and dogmatic manner. They were at a decided disadvantage when compared to the apartheid-era spooks, who, whatever their deficiencies, were highly skilled and efficient managers. ANC people tended to use their political knowledge as a compensatory weapon, which meant they would often talk until the cows came home to impress the gullible. Their formal training abroad was very good but they unfortunately picked up an exaggerated suspicion bordering on paranoia from their instructors in the Soviet Union and East Germany. While the communists in those countries had ample reason to be vigilant about Western plots against them, and we had an extremely ruthless adversary ourselves, it was one thing to be on the lookout for enemy infiltration and quite another thing to be sensible and balanced, which required a maturity not learnt overnight. I make a critical observation of socialist countries, but there are notorious cases of ultra-paranoid Western spy masters in the atmosphere of the Cold War and the current war on terrorism.

President Mbeki complained about the poor quality of the intelligence reports. He invariably knew far more of what was going on in Africa than those who were meant to be providing him with useful information, given his contact with heads of state and other strategic links from exile. I found the country's intelligence services in a poor state. The officers were of questionable ability and had politically compromised allegiances. Crying wolf had become for them a virtual *raison d'être,* justifying their existence.

I reported to Mbeki that in my view our security and intelligence agencies suffered from 'immaturity', which militated against professional objectivity. I used the word not in the sense of belittling their status but rather owing to their lack of life experience and sophistication, which led to their jumping to conclusions, ignoring the many shades of grey.

Back in the old days there had been a case of undue suspicion cast on Jane Bergerol, née Wilford, who came from an upper-class English background. She was a fearless journalist who covered the Angolan conflict from inside that country in 1975 and became a loyal supporter of the People's Movement for the Liberation of Angola (MPLA) government then establishing itself in Luanda. When the ANC was accommodated there after liberation, she strongly supported us and was well received, so much so that when Oliver Tambo visited Angola he would choose her as his interpreter. There was some jealousy over this, from both MPLA and ANC security organs, who believed they should mutually provide such a service, and consequently resentment of Jane grew behind the scenes. Tambo was none the wiser. It was when our security people discovered that Jane's father was the British ambassador in Japan that things began to go awry. To them, that meant she must be spying for the United Kingdom. It took some effort to get them to understand that it was not uncommon for upper-class English people to be genuinely anti-apartheid, irrespective of their parents' position.

To my dismay I discovered that in all the years such naïve and primitive reasoning persisted in the services. Anyone of Western association critical of the ANC leadership was damned as a 'foreign agent' serving a 'counter-revolutionary' agenda. Such paranoia later came to suit Jacob Zuma's conspiracy theories to the letter. Those appointed to sensitive security positions stridently sang that same tune.

My wariness for many of the old Imbokodo ('grinding stone') of the ANC's external security department stemmed from the days of exile, when I was head of military intelligence. Suspicion was ingrained in them from their training although I must point out that it was not from the East Germans or the Russians that some in Imbokodo derived their proclivity for brutality — paranoia about imperialist plots, yes; but use of force, no. Those agencies stressed the need to use the mind in interrogation. Force would only encourage the person being questioned to admit to anything you wanted to hear, which was of absolutely no value.

On a visit to Germany in 2005 I was shown around the Stasi complex in former East Berlin by my hosts. When I asked about the Stasi's measures of interrogation, those former West German officials readily informed me that their hated adversaries did not use torture. I was told that mental pressure, which could become a form of torture, was what the East Germans had relied on. This could involve suggestions that if you did not cooperate your and your children's career opportunities would be unfulfilled. Not very pleasant of course, but not a physical beating in such cases.

ANC security was uneasy, on pins and needles, with MK leadership. We of MK looked after our own personal security; cherished our own secrets; did not care for prying eyes; sought to protect our operatives — they were the ones who did the risky work — and did not gladly suffer fools who knew little of combat work. We were consequently wary of Imbokodo's suspicions about MK combatants and would withhold judgement until allegations could be verified. MK rank-and-file soldiers resented them for never having been on combat missions and for the undue attention they often posed to their activities.

Travel abroad was a normal part of the job as minister of intelligence services and was necessary to acquaint myself with the work of SASS, our foreign intelligence service. Establishing relationships with international intelligence agencies was as essential to the job as the work of the country's foreign relations department. In a sense, obtaining sensitive information globally is a strategic reinforcement of any country's diplomatic relationships and understanding of the international arena. Consequently I had to meet foreign secret service agencies with notorious records. Just as I had to accustom myself to interacting with them, so they had an interest in assessing me. While there might be immense political differences, there were also areas of common interest such as knowledge pertaining to security threats, transnational crime, weapons of mass destruction, and certainly the growing threat of international terrorism. The last problem gave me a chance to engage on the skewed way that Western agencies perceived the Muslim religion and to raise the warning that growing Islamophobia only played into the hands of the fanatics. In a parliamentary address I argued that terrorism could only be dealt with by going beyond its manifestations to understanding and paying attention to its root causes. I expressed concern that the 'global war on terror had opened a Pandora's box which veered towards a dangerous phobia about Islam, one of the world's most venerated and respected religions'.[3]

On a trip to Malaysia I settled down to receive a security briefing from the country's various heads of department. It was a genial atmosphere, as the occasions inevitably were, with quite a degree of banter. The chief of police intelligence, after introducing his colleagues, pointed to one of many portraits of previous chiefs lining the conference room. 'Minister, you may be interested to know,' he said, pointing to a portrait above me, 'that man was assassinated by the communists in 1966.' After laughter, he added, 'at that very door you came in through.' More laughter. Everyone watched for my reaction. 'Well, I trust you're not going to make me pay for the crime,' I replied, and all laughed yet again.

When I visited the Central Intelligence Agency (CIA), at its Langley headquarters outside Washington DC, I was besieged by a score of senior officials asking me to sign copies of my memoir, *Armed and Dangerous*. It happened to be a 2004 edition with a photograph on the back cover of me presenting Fidel Castro with a copy. I had no illusions about the CIA, MI6 or any of the agencies, and found it unsettling to think that the genial and sophisticated people I met were guilty of brutal human rights abuses.

From the Malaysian meeting I took advantage of being in the region to take a short private holiday with Eleanor at the offshore island of Langkawi at the northern end of the Strait of Malacca. One morning relaxing around the hotel pool I got into a discussion with a couple of English tourists. We retreated into the poolside bar to down the local Tiger lager and debate football. Eleanor came to inform me that all the water in the bay had rushed out and that people were picking up marooned fish. I told her I would join her later. Half an hour of football chat is no time at all. Eleanor rushed in a second time to report that an enormous wave had filled the bay to capacity. No damage had been caused. It was only some hours later that we learnt of the tsunami that had struck the region that Boxing Day in 2004. Langkawi was sheltered by Banda Aceh, directly to its west, and our resort had the added protection of a steeply rising beach and mangrove swamps although twenty fishermen were drowned on the other side of the island. However, we had almost booked into a Thai resort where almost everyone was swept out to sea. We had changed bookings on a whim at the last minute. The head of SASS, Tim Dennis, spent hours on the phone from South Africa trying to check whether we were safe and, until we were in touch, assumed the worst. Who would have thought that before long the word 'tsunami' would become part of South Africa's political lexicon to highlight the threat to a sitting president's position?

CHAPTER 3

A Suitable Man

Communist Party headquarters, Johannesburg, July 2005

WE HAD GATHERED AT PARTY headquarters in downtown Johannesburg for a regular executive committee (Politburo) meeting on an upper floor offering a sweeping view of the city, but since insufficient members had turned up the gathering was postponed. While we chatted in a convivial mood over coffee, discussing when to reconvene, I suggested that instead of dispersing, we use that morning to informally discuss the situation that had arisen over Mbeki's recent dismissal of Zuma as the country's deputy president. That had occurred on 14 June 2005 and was announced by Mbeki in an address to a combined session of the two houses of parliament. Mbeki had been unanimously applauded for his firm stand against corruption, and the media likewise was in agreement that he had no other option, owing to a High Court judgment of 2 June, handed down by Judge Hilary Squires, which found that Zuma had benefitted from his financial adviser Schabir Shaik's crimes. Shaik was found to have paid over R1.3 million to Zuma between 1995 and 2005, and allegedly solicited a bribe for him of R1.5 million from the French arms company Thomson-CSF (later renamed Thint Holdings). In return, the company allegedly expected to receive favourable treatment and protection from Zuma regarding its bid in South Africa's arms acquisition programme. Shaik was sentenced to fifteen years' imprisonment, of which he served just over two before gaining parole.

I had initially met Schabir Shaik in his hometown of Durban after clandestinely slipping into the country in 1990 just before Easter to join Mac Maharaj, Siphiwe Nyanda and Janet Love on an ANC–SACP mission codenamed Operation Vula. They had been in the country for two years doing exceptional work in establishing a senior leadership presence. My involvement, and that of several others, came late in the day (the ban on the ANC and SACP had been lifted in February 1990). Even with negotiations looming, the realistic possibility that the De Klerk regime might negotiate in bad faith meant the ANC needed to retain its insurrectionary capacity. Schabir Shaik, who came from a notable family of brothers, appeared to be paying the rent for an office we were using. While Operation Vula landed Maharaj, Nyanda and a score of others, including Billy Nair and Pravin Gordhan, in detention, both Janet Love and I missed arrest by sheer luck, ducking and diving for a year, until we all received indemnity by June 1991. This was in time for the ANC's first legal national conference in the country since the 1950s.

While we set about the monumental tasks of organisational renewal, strategising for negotiations and winning electoral power, there was a primary need for funds. This was not only intended for the organisation's coffers but to assist exiles and former prisoners to find their feet and continue with their honest lifetime toil of serving the ANC and the people. The organisation became a magnet, drawing all sorts of carpetbaggers and vultures to feast for flesh and favours. Insiders like Schabir Shaik were quickest off the mark. With the uncanny instinct of the predator, the weakest targets were easy to identify.

My one-time friend Jacob Zuma had returned home to a previous wife in rural Zululand, and at least two wives from exile, with nine children between them,[1] and several other offspring fathered over the years. He was a leader, he was influential and bound to rise to higher office. He had no property, no bank account, no savings, but many mouths to feed. He was helpless at balancing his books and gullible. Schabir Shaik became his initial financial adviser and confidant.

By no means all freedom fighters behaved like Zuma, but those who did would justify their behaviour on the basis of sheer entitlement: they had suffered in the struggle, hence they were poor; their needs were great; it was their time to feed — the country owed it to them. In exile Zuma seemingly had not revealed such a side of his nature. Now with power- and favour-seekers on hand, masks slipped. It is said that power corrupts. I believe power reflects one's character, for it can be wielded for positive and negative purposes depending on the nature of those who possess it. In those early days, before his corruption trial, Schabir Shaik was conveniently available to fill Zuma's car with petrol, buy him fancy shirts, pay his children's school fees and his rent, and settle his debts. Zuma appeared not to give such charity a second thought. These favours were described by Shaik as 'loans to a friend', and who can say that he had no such regard for Zuma? Mandela hoped to save Zuma's dignity by raising R1 million for his needs, but even that did not suffice. It failed to have the desired effect on Zuma and it simply aroused the appetite of the greedy in the movement who felt they should similarly benefit. For some there is nothing that arouses the appetite for more money than getting some money. It is like the alcoholic and drink, the gambler and the winning stakes — there is never enough. Not even when, as in the case of Jacob Zuma, your wife is a minister with a handsome income and you are a provincial economic affairs minister and, later, deputy president:[2] powerful positions which come with free accommodation, a retinue of servants, official vehicles, drivers, protectors, overseas travel, a swarm of benefactors, gifts and expense accounts. How useful, then, if you can manipulate your political power for private benefit.

Zuma was extremely fortunate that the country's National Prosecuting Authority (NPA) had declined to proceed against him after Shaik's conviction even though NPA officials stated there was a prima facie case for so doing. They had identified 783 individual potentially corrupt actions. Bulelani Ngcuka, head of the NPA, stated that the NPA did not feel they had a winnable case – but this was most likely a ploy to avoid embarrassment to the ANC and the government. Mbeki had wanted Zuma to voluntarily resign from office but Zuma had refused, arguing that if he did it would be an admission of guilt. An overly polite Mbeki, in my view, was snagged in a trap, and had no other recourse than to fire his deputy. Zumaites in the ANC, some with their own axes to grind against Mbeki for allegedly failing to call off investigations into their own malfeasance, were on an unprecedented warpath, and a huge schism developed. The SACP and the trade union ally, Cosatu, both of whom had been frostily ignored by Mbeki on unpopular issues of policy, sided with Zuma as a preferred candidate for leadership of the ANC. Their main opposition to Mbeki related to the government's economic policies, which they deemed a decided shift to the right, and to allegations that he was concentrating too much power in the Presidency at the expense of the liberation alliance.

The disgraced Zuma, who had never disagreed with Mbeki's policies, raised the spectre of a conspiracy against him hatched by 'counter-revolutionaries', and his supporters seized that idea with alacrity. If, as Karl Marx famously said, religion was the opiate of the masses, then to smear a comrade as 'counter-revolutionary' without concrete facts was a sure way to convince the shallow-minded and also provide good enough reason for opportunists needing a cause. In my view the accusation is the first and last refuge of the scoundrel. Those in the SACP and Cosatu opposed Mbeki on ideological grounds, and although some had personal reasons too, I did not lump them into the same group as those I characterise as crony capitalists. The fact that the comrades at SACP headquarters supported Zuma for the top leadership spoke volumes about the extent to which he had succeeded in exploiting their antagonisms to Mbeki and their belief that he was a suitable man for the left and for the country. The situation was ugly and fraught with unforeseen consequences. A National General Council had been held by the ANC in June 2005, shortly after Zuma's dismissal that year, and the mood towards Mbeki had been hostile. It was soon thereafter that we of the SACP were taking stock of the situation when we gathered at the Party headquarters in Johannesburg.

In the SACP offices I studied the group of battle-hardened communists, comrades with whom I had worked for several years to change South Africa and the world. Foremost among them were the Party general secretary, the feisty Blade Nzimande; the chairperson, Gwede Mantashe, a weather-beaten former mineworkers leader who did not mince his words; and the gently spoken poet and ideologue, Jeremy Cronin, whom I had once trained in London for underground work. His activity had led to a ten-year prison sentence. As I was not just a comrade, the old 'ANC Khumalo' and MK veteran, but an Mbeki appointee and the intelligence minister at that, I could feel for sure that despite obvious respect they showed me, there was an element of doubt about my motives.

I was relieved at the opportunity to speak my mind. The underlying tensions had festered for too long. I had been so engaged in ministerial matters that I had neglected political work to my detriment.

CHAPTER 4

A Long Shadow

Communist Party headquarters, Johannesburg, July 2005, continued

As I GATHERED MY THOUGHTS at the Communist Party meeting, the long shadow of Jacob Zuma occupied my mind. Almost twenty-five years — a generation — had passed since that event on the Mozambique–Swazi border when I'd damaged my ankle.

Hindsight is said to give one 20/20 vision. Yet the past is never easy to unravel, to grasp in all its complexities and dimensions with anything approaching certainty. Consequently, debate and interpretation rage on and on, even among those of a shared worldview.

It was not just the insight I gained by Zuma's reaction to my fall at the border fence, the dismissive, two-faced utterance of 'stupid white man' by someone who projected geniality and comradeship. It was not that I judged him on that single incident once and for all. Within a day or two I had dismissed my suspicion, not wishing to hold anything against someone I was going to have to work with for a length of time. Our relationship even grew to some extent. I had taken to Zuma when I joined him in Mozambique from Angola in 1980. He led a frugal lifestyle; was content to drive a small car around Maputo's streets; was a non-smoker who never touched alcohol; appeared a simple dresser invariably in neat slacks, sandals and ethnic shirts; was popular on the streets and charmed the women. I took to him alright.

We worked on a daily basis in his apartment on Avenida Julius Nyerere, studying reports and meeting countless comrades. Zuma enjoyed cooking samp and beans (*ngqush*) and delighted in adding pieces of meat spiced with chilli. When we took a lunch break he loved putting on his Jaluka tapes, telling me that '*jaluka*' meant 'sweat' in Zulu, and explained who South Africa's popular musicians Johnny Clegg and Sipho Mchunu were. He spared no effort in tutoring me in my Zulu high kicks, which I had picked up in the Angolan camps. We joked about what we would like to do when freedom came. He stated with his broad grin that his desire would be to wear a whistle around his neck and train a football team.

But the niggling incidents and insights mounted as time passed. I came to see that broad smile and chuckle of a down-to-earth rural man as a mask hiding dimly lit flaws. Zuma had enormous energy when it came to chatting to people. Invariably, at the end of the day as I left his apartment a line of comrades began to form, like patients in a consulting room. And consult he often did well into the evening. He would engage in one-on-one discussions and sometimes with groups. His popularity and readiness to assist comrades resolve personal problems were the hallmarks of a natural leader. Yet I began picking up remarks from those who had seen this before. Why were those attracted to him invariably from his home province of Natal? Comrades did not like to mention the 'Z' word but implied they were mainly Zulu and represented an ethnic faction. 'Well,' I argued in his defence, 'many of those around were from the province.' The cynical would shrug their shoulders in a 'you wait and see' attitude. There were certainly accusations that he was building his own fiefdom, to which I responded that if you were going to become a leader you needed a constituency. But a feeling of unease began to gnaw. He never talked about the late-night meetings, which had no place in the structural arrangements and responsibilities of the movement. Why the need for secrecy within secrecy? To hell with it, I told myself, stop being so paranoid!

I did learn from Joe Slovo and Joe Modise, commanders of MK, that the year prior to my arrival in Maputo they had decided to dissolve a structure that Zuma commanded infiltrating weapons into Natal. It appears Zuma had failed to report certain of their activities, which he had also concealed from non-Zulu members of the structure, and they found that unacceptable.

I later divulged my initial observation of distrust to Jeremy Cronin, who arrived in Lusaka in the late 1980s to reinforce our underground machinery. He and his wife Gemma and infant son Ben lived in a rented house and security was precarious. Zuma, by then a newly appointed head of ANC intelligence, a position in which he revelled, used their telephone to speak to his various contacts — a highly dangerous practice, for calls were easily traceable to source, putting the family at risk. It caused me to warn Jeremy about such recklessness. I recounted the incident on the border when I sprained my ankle and Zuma's underhand reaction.

Other causes of concern accumulated. When Chris Hani joined us in Maputo in 1982, retreating from assassination fears in Lesotho, I worked on plans for him to meet the members of the Swazi underground structures, who were thrilled at the prospect. Behind my back Zuma cancelled the trip on the basis of security warnings he claimed to have received. When a disappointed Chris and I discussed the cancellation, we suspected the reason originated in Zuma's rivalry with him. We may have been wrong about that, but the very fact that we contemplated the possibility reflected the existence of doubts about Zuma's integrity.

The most abiding concern was the case of Thami Zulu (real name Muziwakhe Ngwenya), who at one time commanded MK's highly active Natal operations from Swaziland. By 1987 Zuma was operating from Lusaka, although his focus had seemingly slipped into counter-intelligence and the rooting out of spies. The MK command of which Chris had become chief of staff under Joe Modise, with me as MK intelligence chief, was highly impressed with Thami. We were also becoming increasingly angry over the number of MK cadres being removed from operational duty without consultation, owing to suspicions emanating from Zuma's counter-intelligence structure that they were enemy agents. While the ANC, including MK, rooted out many elements found to have been sent to infiltrate our ranks, there were a number of others who remained in detention without any conclusion being reached to their cases. When Thami Zulu suffered this fate, the MK command was suspicious that his removal from his post had more to do with the fact that he had never been recognised as 100 per cent pure Zulu because he came from the urban melting pot of Soweto. True, many of his operatives had been ambushed while infiltrating into South Africa but we did not accept that Thami had betrayed them, since we had been pressing him to step up operations. That meant the need to take risks. By the time we managed to have Thami released from detention he was a sick and dying man. It appears he was poisoned in Lusaka within days of his release. The ANC set up commissions of inquiry which were critical of irregularities in our military camps and in our treatment of detainees, but mysteries and suspicions concerning agents high up in our ranks remained and were never satisfactorily resolved. An ANC Commission of Inquiry was unable to come to any conclusive findings in the Thami Zulu case.[1]

In 1991, shortly before the ANC's first national conference at home, Mandela asked me what I thought of Zuma. I was in the company of Raymond Suttner and I told the old man that distrust towards him had been evident in exile. I restricted myself to an opinion that he was too ethnically inclined and conservative, and ultra-suspicious in security matters. I was sure Mandela would have elicited the views of those of more consequence than me, such as Joe Slovo and Chris Hani, and since he did not persevere with his questions, I left it at that. Given the violent situation in Natal at the time and the problematic role of the IFP, Mandela was compelled to rely heavily on Zuma, who in fact did achieve considerable success in winning support for the ANC. He was always going to operate best among his 'own people'. He enjoyed close affinity with sections of them and prided himself on the traditional Zulu culture, which he interpreted according to his own personal needs. This was to become evident with time and unabashedly displayed before a bemused nation, even when he was striving to answer questions in parliament or justify himself to the media. In the long shimmering shadow he cast from our Swaziland days I came to discern his flaws in greater clarity. I felt too that in time to come his fallibilities would be revealed to others in the glare of public activity.

CHAPTER 5

Working–Class Hero

Communist Party headquarters, Johannesburg, July 2005, continued

I REGAINED THE THREAD of my exposition. 'Comrades, let's be perfectly open with one another,' I requested of the group at Party headquarters. 'I'm going to open my chest, and although this discussion should be confidential, if what I say gets to Zuma, I couldn't care less.'

I certainly had their full attention and resolved to keep my cool. I had eyeballed the secretary of the Young Communist League (YCL), Buti Manamela, an up-and-coming youth leader, who was pro-Zuma, and wondered just how far he would be swallowed by personal ambition. The Cosatu president, the heavily bearded Willie Madisha, shuffled perceptibly, and looked down. I guessed he was unhappy with the growing adulation of Zuma and was in the process of falling out with Blade, who had a tight grip on the Party.

'Comrades,' I continued, 'I want to address aspects about Jacob Zuma, such as tribalism; the question of morality; the fact that he is no working–class hero; and the issue of conspiracy and security.'

Blade nodded with puckered mouth, beckoning me to proceed. Outside, the city hummed under a bright winter sky. Through our upper-floor windows we had a commanding view of downtown

Johannesburg's skyline: skyscrapers, mining houses and financial centres long past their glory days. The capitalist values that once had their fountainhead in the City of Gold had taken flight to the new capital of Mammon — the gleaming towers of Sandton City on Johannesburg's northern edge. I wondered whether we communists could adjust to the times.

'Comrades, with all due respect, I have known JZ from his recruitment into MK in Durban, 1962 when he was a promising young activist and well thought of.' Apart from Jeremy, who had joined while studying abroad at the Sorbonne in Paris in 1972, the others were products of the internal struggle of the 1980s and only knew him after 1990. 'Jeremy knows him from Zambia. I worked with him very closely in Maputo from 1980.' I gestured in a friendly way at Blade. 'General secretary, you were at loggerheads with him, you and Harry Gwala' — I evoked the deceased SACP firebrand from Pietermaritzburg — 'from the time he returned from exile, you warned about Zuma as a conservative, a traditionalist, a tribalist who was too close to Inkatha and the Zulu monarch.'

'You comrades might not be aware that Joe Slovo and Joe Modise dissolved an MK structure he commanded in Maputo in 1979 because they were unhappy with the way he was working and withholding reports,' I continued. 'When I arrived in Maputo to work with him in a new structure I was discreetly warned about that, but decided to take my own time and judge him from personal experience.'

I was warming to the topic. 'You know he's no working-class hero. A man who immediately quit the Party the moment the ban was lifted in 1990 and we became public. Actually, comrades, quite different from Mbeki in that respect, whom the leadership saw as future president of the ANC and who in that position could not be a member of the Party.'

In retrospect, I recognise that the Party's support for Zuma was more about its negative attitude towards his one-time close comrade, Thabo Mbeki, than about Zuma himself. Attitudes towards Mbeki by both the ANC's Alliance partners, the SACP and Cosatu, had hardened by 2005 into outright antagonism, rooted in dislike of Mbeki's personal style and views, and towards the policies they believed he had foisted on the ANC and on South Africa.

As deputy to President Mandela from 1994 to 1999, when he played a central role in policy development characteristic more of a prime minister, and as president from 1999, Mbeki built on the compromises the ANC had felt it had to accept in the pre-democracy negotiations to consolidate acceptance of a largely market-driven liberal economic policy. While there was a need for stability in the traumatic 1990–4 period, some argued that this no longer applied by 1996 when the pro-market Gear (Growth, Employment and Redistribution) programme was instituted. The question was no longer one of maintaining stability because of the political violence and tensions. Instead, the rationale became economic issues.

At the core of this move to the right was the assumption that market stability was primary, and that rapid growth of the South African market economy would see benefits accruing to the black majority. This would ease the poverty experienced by the bulk of the population.

In retrospect, this was clearly wrong, as events were to prove. From 1996, when Mandela unveiled Gear, to 1999, inflation fell faster than the policy predicted, and government spending was slashed. But while GDP edged up, it did so well below Gear predictions, and employment levels plummeted while cuts in government spending meant there was ever less to distribute to poor and jobless South Africans.

Not only did the policy alienate the SACP and Cosatu, but Mandela's often haughty decision-making style and the general perceptions of Mbeki as arrogant and as wanting to break up the alliance added personal bad blood to the mix. In addition, the 1999 defence procurement programme (the 'arms deal') strengthened the ANC allies' sense that the organisation had lost its way. Ironically, it also produced a champion around which opposition to the ANC's policies, and to Mbeki's presidency, could coalesce. Almost as simultaneously as Mkeki discovered Aids Denialism, apparently on the internet, Cosatu joined the Treatment Action Campaign (TAC) appeal for free medicine.

Just as we were meeting, Mugabe was sweeping 700,000 urban

dwellers out of the cities – mainly opposition supporters – and in South Africa, community protests against inadequate service delivery was on the rise. The Party and Cosatu had lost patience with what they regarded as Mbeki's treachery.[1]

My argument to my colleagues in the SACP was less about the pros of Mbeki than about the cons of Zuma. He was a wily operator and had by the mid-1990s recognised that Party and Cosatu antagonism to Mbeki and his market-driven policies could be useful to his career. He wooed both the Party and Cosatu, and although he was politically and ideologically aligned to Mbeki, he successfully painted himself as a viable alternative to Mbeki, able to rebuild the ANC as the ideological vehicle it had been pre-1994.

'But comrades, let's face it,' I continued, 'it's Zuma's corruption, his lack of morality, which has landed him in the soup and brought our movement into disrepute. I don't have to go into the litany of corruption, whether we consider the Schabir Shaik relationship, starting with all the petty favours and leading to bigger things such as the arms purchase benefits; the talk about benefactors and crooked tycoons; all the gossip swirling about his head ever since he put his foot back in the country.'

I could have added perhaps the single most depressing thing, the suicide in 2000 of one of his wives, Kate Mantsho, while he was deputy president, and the note she left behind: 'Life had been hell' living with him; 'bitter' and 'painful', she wrote.[2] Everyone knew about that unspoken episode though it had been brushed under the carpet. Mbeki's director general, Frank Chikane, had prevented the media from getting hold of the suicide note and the Presidency had gone to inordinate lengths to protect Zuma – rather than conspiring to destroy his career.

I thought of those seemingly innocent far-off days in Maputo, being driven by Zuma through the busy streets, stopping to pick up a pretty young woman, niftily dressed in an Airways uniform: tight skirt, blouse, scarf, high-heel shoes, a figure you whistled about. She smiled sweetly as she got into the back seat and he introduced me to her as Kate.

CHAPTER 6

A Question of Morality

Party headquarters, July 2005, late afternoon

THE THOUGHT OF KATE FLASHED through my head as I paused for breath and then Gwede Mantashe interrupted, shaking his head. 'No, on that question of morality,' he growled, 'I don't accept the fuss going on in the mainstream media. What morality?'

Buti Manamela, of the YCL, nodded in agreement, also wishing to contest that one.

'Oh, come on,' I interjected, 'comrades Gwede, Buti, if you are speaking of bourgeois morality, the word you're looking for is hypocrisy. But don't imply there's no such thing as morality. What we are about, from Marx to Lenin to Che Guevara, is revolutionary morality. We are not the corrupt bourgeoisie hypocritically attacking Zuma over his morals. As revolutionaries we should be in the fore, taking him to task as a corrupt and immoral leader and consequently the corrupter of others. He is a dangerous man.'

The younger comrades were keeping quiet. Among them were Yunus Carrim and Ben Martins, both, like Blade, with roots in Pietermaritzburg, close to him but to some degree independent-minded and, in my experience, extremely principled.

I had missed something though. And it was Gwede who weighed

in, not to be easily dismissed. In his gravelly voice, he expounded on the double standards of the white media, which focused only on black corruption. They were in a frenzy about Zuma, he argued, but it was the old apartheid system and white business who were the kings of corruption. Blade and Jeremy in particular argued powerfully about the racist capitalist system as it had developed, elaborating on its intrinsic structural and systemic corruption.

'Comrades, of course that is right, the heart of corruption arose in front of our eyes.' I waved at the city scene through the windows of our boardroom. 'But we dare not use corrupt business by way of comparison or to divert attention from our faults, our lapse into corrupt practice, because we are a revolutionary movement.'[1]

'Zuma has become the role model of those who say it's our turn to eat,' I continued shaking my head disapprovingly. 'They eat out of the pockets of big business while the masses starve. Come on, how shameful and obscene. We used to say we struggled and sacrificed for the people, and is that not what we are still about?'

I did not want to go on too long. I was only too aware that my colleagues viewed Mbeki and his close circle as having a pro-business agenda, which spelt out the very corruption I was assailing — and betrayal to boot. For me, however, this was a completely different kettle of fish from what Zuma was cooking. A one-time journalist from the Party underground, Tony Holiday, who had mentored Jeremy Cronin and other students and had served prison time before becoming a university lecturer, was one of the first to break the silence about his preference for Mbeki over Zuma and had very recently posted a warning in the media about the disaster facing South Africa if Zuma became the next president.[2]

'Look, I'm almost finished,' I continued. 'Just let me sound a warning about JZ and "security".' I referred to the question of the security of the revolution, which Zuma had been conveniently raising in his personal defence. We had to be vigilant and on guard against real counter-revolutionary threats, not the imagined ones of the opportunists, not to be tricked into chasing tokoloshes and crying wolf at shadows, I argued. That brand of conspiracy was let loose when it was deemed necessary, and the whispers multiplied: 'a hidden force working against him; out to destroy his career; out to prevent him becoming president; counter-revolutionary agents here and abroad ultimately hell-bent on splitting our movement and destroying us all'. Zuma would manipulate the security and intelligence system in his own interests, I insisted. I did not say it but the elephant in the room was Thabo Mbeki. With all the talk of 'conspiracy', Mbeki in fact was Zuma's enemy and target.

'Comrades, I may be intelligence minister, but I am no tool of anybody and no mastermind of conspiratorial plots, and I refuse to raise spectres to divert the people from the real enemy. I serve the president of the country and there is no abuse of power.' I had to tread carefully, for I was one of Mbeki's ministerial appointees and a minister of intelligence at that. A tricky portfolio as the entire country, not to mention one's movement, imagined you were by definition full of guile and subterfuge, an expert at the cloak-and-dagger game, a man who supposedly knew everybody's deepest secrets, and thus was potentially dangerous.

The comrades heard me out, politely and without a show of hostility. It was clear, however, that they did not agree, their minds set on a different narrative, the Zuma narrative, which was already gaining traction. It was like looking at 'The Last Supper' and striving to interpret what each and every disciple was really thinking about the leader.

An articulate and persuasive man, Blade took time to underline the faults of Mbeki. His starting point was how the incumbent president, like Mandela before him, had sidelined and insulted the Party, at two previous congresses they had addressed, for public criticism the Party had levelled against the ANC. 'How can you air your criticism in public?' Mandela had glowered. 'The tradition has always been to keep any complaints within the fold.' Mbeki in his turn had been testy, one of the rare occasions I had seen him displaying anger – and I recalled how dismayed I'd been by the way both he and Mandela had shown their intolerance at the time. Discontent was mainly focused on Mbeki, however, for all in the entire movement were wise enough

– or cowardly enough – to silently endure the old man's scolding. The Party view, however, along with that of the media and many analysts, was that Mbeki had been the theoretical architect of most of Mandela's policy decisions. When Mandela had effectively rejected the more radical clauses of the Freedom Charter, nationalisation of the mines, banks and monopoly industries, this was believed to be the result of Mbeki's influence too. With land restitution proceeding at a snail's pace, the Charter's vision of land distribution and agrarian reform was being realised painfully slowly, and this again was seen as Mbeki's handiwork.

The biggest attack on Mbeki was over the sudden replacement in 1996 of the government's Reconstruction and Development Programme (RDP), with its emphasis on addressing the needs of the poor, with the Gear strategy. This had appeared out of nowhere, since, unlike the RDP, no consultations had taken place, and it carried with it all the signs of technocrats tying the government into the new neo-liberal global order. While Mbeki was mocked by the left for 'changing gear', to allege – as his critics did – that he had led Mandela by the nose was, to my mind, not only an insult to the iconic leader of the country but clearly wrong. Mandela may not have been a theoretician like Mbeki, but he was no fool and clearly had a mind of his own. It was Mandela who, on returning from the World Economic Forum in Davos in 1992, bluntly informed the ANC's National Executive Committee (NEC) that he had been informed by the captains of industry and world leaders that if we implemented socialist policies, there would be no foreign investment and we would become an isolated state like Cuba.

It was one thing to take on Mbeki. It was quite another to take on Mandela. And even Joe Slovo and Chris Hani, the foremost communists, had been prepared to swallow the Davos narrative out of deference to the man. After all, we were assured of achieving political power in quick time, after which we could attend to the economic challenges. Let us take things one step at a time. Looking back with the advantage of hindsight, I believe we were virtually sleepwalking into an economic order that was being created under our noses. The focus on the life-and-death political imperatives, amid the violence, uncertainties and dangers of the early to mid-1990s, blinded most of us to the economic pitfalls that we were walking into. The country would pay for this in the future.

Blade complained that Mbeki no longer bothered to consult the Party or Cosatu, and favoured a coterie from American business schools. Trevor Manuel, his finance minister, had notoriously announced that Gear was non-negotiable. According to Blade, Mbeki also allegedly gave favours to an emergent black business faction led by Saki Macozoma, referred to as the Xhosa Nostra, owing to their background. Associated with this grouping was the head of the National Prosecuting Authority (NPA), Bulelani Ngcuka, husband of Phumzile Mlambo-Ngcuka. She had been appointed by Mbeki as the new deputy president after Zuma's dismissal from that post. Mbeki's talk of the need to advance female leadership – and his appointment of Phumzile in particular – was seen as a ploy to keep Zuma from succeeding him as president.

Then, as Blade itemised, there was the oft-stated Party position that the government was becoming too centralised. By that he implied that Mbeki was concentrating power under his control. Linked to this was an allegation that he was abusing power and acting against his rivals and those he did not trust or favour. Jeremy had faced criticism from the ANC for an interview he gave about the alleged 'Zanufication of the ANC' – implying that under Mbeki the movement was going the way of Robert Mugabe's ruling party in Zimbabwe. He had been ordered to withdraw that remark by the NEC and to apologise. The Party also characterised South Africa as a Bonapartist state, implying a move to dictatorship. I had countered this by pointing out that our democracy did not rest on army bayonets.

Jeremy's embarrassment over the Zanufication issue was minor compared to the concerns of a growing number of comrades who were being investigated for corruption and similar irregularities. The National Prosecuting Authority's investigative arm, the Directorate of Special Operations (DSO) or Scorpions, was made up of former apartheid regime officers and those from the liberation movement.

Apart from Schabir Shaik and Zuma, others, such as the the former transport minister and struggle veteran Mac Maharaj, and Ngoako Ramatlhodi, who had been a provincial premier, had been interviewed by the Scorpions with respect to transactions they were supposed to have benefitted from.

The investigation of comrades who had sacrificed enormously hurt deeply. Maharaj had spent years in prison and, like others, could have been approached for an explanation at a political level. It was known that bank accounts he had held abroad were utilised to bring in funds for Operation Vula, which he commanded. Ramatlhodi referred to such 'victims' as 'the walking wounded' amid a growing perception that Mbeki was motivating state agencies to 'settle old scores'. There was no evidence of this. It did appear, however, that the NPA was cherry-picking investigations into struggle comrades, and there was decidedly bad blood, for example, between Bulelani Ngcuka and Mac Maharaj, especially after Maharaj and Moe Shaik accused Ngcuka of being an apartheid-era spy.[3] But what such disgruntled comrades insisted on was that the president should have ordered such inquiries to be called off. In a constitutional democracy like South Africa, however, such executive interference was patently unacceptable, and Blade would well have understood that. But it was politics at play, and those who wanted Mbeki out of the way were sharpening their knives and seeking to justify their plans by any pretext. Not that this was spoken of to my face. And it was not so much the Party that took that personal approach, but others. It was enough for Blade to hint that Mbeki was abusing power.

'No evidence,' I insisted. 'Nothing of the sort I've seen in my work.' I inquired: 'Comrade Blade, would you, in the president's position, be prepared to order the state not to investigate misdemeanours by your officials? That would be an abuse of your oath of office.'

In retrospect, if the government had established a high-level, independent panel to decide on what cases the NPA should pursue, it would have avoided the kind of suspicion that arose about Mbeki's role. The doubts I was encountering were by no means frivolous or without foundation.

There might have been further discussion, but I distinctly heard the polite voice of Blade as we ended the discourse that eventful day: 'We understand you, comrade Khumalo, but I would say that a Zuma presidency represents the best opening for the left in the country.'

'You think you can manage him, comrade Blade?' I replied. 'You will discover he is a law unto himself.' I added: 'Mark my words, the Party one day will deeply regret this support for Jacob Zuma.' I should have had the insight to add: 'And the country as well.'

I never thought I would win the battle. The politics of the movement had reached the stage where those on both the left and the right within the ANC Alliance who wanted to replace Mbeki with Zuma at all costs believed what they wanted to believe. It had eaten into their ranks like a new religion. As for the harm to the country, it would not take long for further scandals in the Jacob Zuma saga to shock us all.

PART TWO

A Tangled Web

2004–2007

Oh, what a tangled web we weave when first we practise to deceive.
— WALTER SCOTT, MARMION

Wolf Boys

Johannesburg–Pretoria,
August–September 2005

LIFE HAS ITS STRANGE TWISTS, and I seem to have had more than my fair share. I happened to be in the Cornish fishing village of St Ives, at the beginning of September 2005, with my then wife, Eleanor. We were on a short break in the UK, having been invited to a friend's wedding near Land's End. Then after spending an incredible day with the writer David Cornwell, better known to the world as John Le Carré, we decided to spend the night in nearby St Ives. While we were wandering about the village, in an eerily quiet dusk, with mist rolling in off the sea, I regaled Eleanor with the old rhyme, 'As I was going to St Ives I met a man with seven wives ...'

I paused for effect: 'Jacob Zuma?' I joked as my mobile phone rang.

It was Saki Macozoma, a fellow ANC national executive member who had become a director of Standard Bank. I did not know him socially and we were not close, but simply exchanged courtesies at political meetings. He complained to me that the National Intelligence Agency (NIA) had been keeping him under surveillance and he wanted to know why. I knew nothing about this and asked him to explain further. He told me that over the previous days both he and his wife, and associates at work, noticed that he was being watched – at home and work. He had ascertained that his car was being followed and he had photographs to prove it. He informed me that he had complained to a top NIA officer, Gibson Njenje, a fellow ANC member known to him. Gibson had come clean, apologised, said it was a mistake and had called off the surveillance team. I assured him I would immediately look into this when I got back home within a few days. He thanked me but said he would be submitting a formal complaint through his attorneys.

The fog was thickening as we made our way back to our hotel along cobblestone alleyways – a perfect setting for a Le Carré novel. While his stories are replete with sinister goings-on in the corridors of power in London and Moscow, I was taken aback by this strange turn of events at home.

I returned to Pretoria post-haste and, before gathering with the NIA leadership, had a meeting with Saki Macozoma. His story made me wince.

The previous week he had walked from his home in a quiet, upmarket Johannesburg suburb to buy the newspapers. He encountered a couple of men driving around the suburb, apparently lost. Their vehicle had out-of-town registration plates so they were easily spotted. He asked whether he could assist and they produced a piece of paper with an address. It was the same street he lived in, but whereas his house number was, let us say, 14, the number on the piece of paper was 41. He pointed them in that direction. He soon noticed another car with two men driving around. Like the first, it had out-of-town registration plates, which was unusual. This raised his suspicions. On returning home he found his wife in an agitated state, saying that men in a car had been taking photographs of their home. Together they noted several vehicles that afternoon all with unusual number plates. Next day, driving to work, he observed one such vehicle on his tail. Watching from his office block, he spotted several similar vehicles. Apart from the issue of why Macozoma was being watched, the actual operation, akin to blundering Keystone Cops antics, was acutely embarrassing. I once again assured him that I knew nothing about this and would be immediately meeting with Njenje and the head of NIA, Billy Masetlha, to find out what was going on.

Sitting in my office, I faced Masetlha, the head of NIA, Gibson Njenje, his deputy, and Bob Mhlanga, manager of counter-intelligence, and younger than the other two, who were both 1976 Soweto-generation activists. I had known them through my years of service in Lusaka, where they were based after initial training in Eastern Europe.

When I was appointed minister of intelligence in May 2004, the director general's post was about to become vacant. Masetlha was in office by the year's end. He had considerable experience as an intelligence officer in exile and had held a variety of posts within SASS, home affairs and the President's Office. He had been serving there as security adviser to the president before he was released for the NIA post. On my part I agreed with Mbeki, whose responsibility it was to appoint DGs, that Masetlha should be given the opportunity to prove himself. I was a bit wary of all these changes, and interviewed Masetlha several times before agreeing to give him the job.

Gibson Njenje was a more settled character, who always appeared to me serious about getting on with his work. Whether in exile or back home, he avoided any sensationalism and had kept out of controversy. He had moved in and out of intelligence work in government for stints in the private sector.

I had known Bob Mhlanga when he was a keen 20-year-old in Lusaka working for the head of the ANC's security department, Mzwai Piliso. He had advanced speedily up the ranks, but swift promotion, so detrimental to thorough grounding, had given him boots, in my view, that were too big for him. All the same, I recalled pleasant conversations with the young man whenever I visited Piliso, and he had displayed commitment and discipline in those days.

Sitting before me, the trio were tense and silent, and I had the sense, through years of experience in similar situations, they would all be singing from the same hymn sheet. Bob kept playing nervously with his car keys.

They watched intently, waiting for me to make the first move. I thought of my lunch just a week previously with John Le Carré. He had used the phrase 'wolf boys' in discussing a visit we discovered we had both made to a German security minister and his silent 'wolf boy' protectors. They did not take their eyes off visitors for a second. Whether it was American, Arab, French, Russian, Chinese or African, all security services had their complement of 'wolf boys', as did South Africa.

I had the trio's written report before me, which I had read, and asked them to give me a full oral explanation. NIA had learnt that an agent from a foreign service was landing at Johannesburg's international airport, and their surveillance teams were deployed to watch for him. They had missed him, however, but were aware that one of the people he intended to meet was Saki Macozoma. They stressed that Macozoma was not suspected of being an informant and did not know that the man was an agent. That was the gist of their story. As for the inefficiency of the surveillance teams, the trio tried to pin the blame exclusively on the field officer in command of the operatives; he had been placed under suspension.

I told them I thought their story was implausible. Since Macozoma was not the target, and since he was a senior ANC member, why not seek his assistance about the identity of the agent once he was approached by him? I was insistent about this, as I had emphasised since becoming their minister the need to utilise ANC sources, with their extensive contacts, to secure sought-after information.

I pointed out that a sensitive political issue such as the surveillance of an ANC leader should have been raised with me in the first place. I did not say so, but if Masetlha did not trust me he was duty-bound to have informed the president, which I knew he had not. The president was as surprised as I was that Macozoma had been placed under surveillance.

I turned to the utter incompetence of their surveillance operation. Where such methods were needed, these had to be well planned and effectively carried out. They had failed to brief the surveillance teams; they had failed to provide them with adequately registered vehicles;

they had not even supplied the correct address; and the target and his associates had easily detected what was going on. They were grossly inefficient; failed to oversee the operation at a high level; left their foot soldiers groping around and directionless; and brought the agency into disrepute. The bungled operation was their responsibility, not the fault of the field officers. It was their dereliction of duty that required a serious disciplinary inquiry.

I certainly believed they were trying to pull the wool over my eyes. Something serious was amiss, which they were concealing from me. I consequently requested the inspector general of intelligence, Zola Ngcakani, to conduct an investigation into the legitimacy of the operation.[1] Ngcakani was a tried and tested veteran of the ANC, an elderly man of sober habits and views, elegant and upright with the gravitas of a judge and the demeanour of a retired diplomat. I felt he was a safe pair of hands. But would he be able to outwit the wolves?

CHAPTER 8

A Long Night

Government residence, Pretoria, October 2005, Week one

THERE WERE MANY TASKS and I was seized by another matter. I stared at the file. It was very thick and uninviting, and I was dog tired. It was undated and purported to represent the joint findings of the National Intelligence Agency (NIA), the National Intelligence Coordinating Committee (NICOC) and the South African Police Service (SAPS) regarding the leaking of sensitive information from the elite crime-busting Directorate of Special Operations (the Scorpions) to the media. I stared at the logos on the cover – NICOC, NIA, SAPS – and felt my bed calling. I yawned again and stretched. Not the kind of bed-time reading I cared to wade through in the dead of night. But I had been impatiently waiting for it well before the Macozoma incident and instead of leaving perusal to the following day I began to page slowly through the weighty tome.

I had arrived home late after a very long day seemingly chasing shadows. Eleanor had an appetising meal ready for me in our ministerial home on the government's Bryntirion estate in Pretoria, close to the Union Buildings. It was a splendid parkland setting, offset by intimidating security fencing and police-manned access gates. It boasted a presidential residence, a palatial Herbert Baker guesthouse decidedly creaking in places, and a score of double-storey residences for government ministers spread out across the tree-lined grounds with their extensive lawns and flower beds. Compared with the great Herbert Baker, the architects of the ministerial residences were not up to designing even an outhouse. Most of the homes, like the one I resided in, were box-like, gloomy and shabby with uneven floorboards – much the worse for wear – dating back to the 1940s. Just a few were uninspired post-1970s erections. Eleanor, who had done much with her decorative talent to brighten the abode, waited for me to finish my meal.

'Your man Billy was here delivering a hefty file,' she puckered her nose. 'I put it on your desk,' adding, 'Rather ill at ease I would say – didn't care to wait for you – out of here like a shot.'

At last he's delivered the long-standing report, I muttered to myself. I had been pressing for it for weeks, sensing it might be linked to Masetlha's strange behaviour. My suspicions had been aroused by the Macozoma scandal and the elusive phantoms that had invaded my life. I assumed Masetlha was at last rushing the report to me, given the inspector general's investigation hanging over his head. I banished all thought of bed and sat down at a battered desk eyeing the document as though it was a jack-in-the-box. I was getting attuned to Masetlha's ways. He would have known I was working late at the ministry, where he could easily have handed it to me. But that gave him the opportunity to leave it at the house, where he knew we wouldn't come face to face. What was more, only he as head of NIA had signed off on the report. There were no corresponding signatures from the heads of the other two agencies whose logos adorned the cover. Yet it was supposed to be a joint investigation. In checking up with them later, I discovered they had not seen it at all, which rendered it a non-report. In fact, the police commissioner, Jackie Selebi, his one-time close associate from Soweto days, was indignant that the report had not passed by him, and made it clear to me that he was losing patience with his old chum. Although the two had issued a joint statement denying media reports about an angry dispute between them, I sensed this was a public relations spin and that there must indeed have been a basis for that account.

With relief I noticed that the actual report was under a hundred pages. The rest of the file, the bulk of it, consisted of attachments and inserts, hundreds of pages, of sections and subsections from this Act and that Act, letters between department heads, analyses of media reports, with dubious guesswork and nothing really substantive about where the media leaks were emanating from. The DSO/Scorpions and certain of its officials were prime suspects. But much was subjectivity dressed up in an ostensibly objective guise.

This was the world of 'link charts' in diagram form featuring a prime suspect at the centre with lines linking him or her to others. These links were made by dint of phone intercepts, mobile phone billing records, or occasions when the individual was observed having coffee in a cafe with someone else who, once identified, would end up as yet another link in the chain of contacts spiralling out from the centre of the chart. The chart itself was like a spider's web with a photograph of every contact in his or her specific place. I once had enquired about a suspect linked to a foreign embassy. The allegation was simply based on a phone call. What, I asked, if the call was innocent, an enquiry about obtaining a visa, for instance? Did that merit the opening of a file; the development of a link chart; the wasting of precious time and resources; the addition of one more name as part of a fishing expedition? There had been a tentative explanation from a shifty case officer. Sorry, I said, something like that needs to be substantiated and not simply based on a phone call. But I received no response apart from an unblinking dinosaur-eyed gaze. I have no doubt that it was this kind of stubborn insistence that led some to assume I was shielding foreign agents.

I had to read and re-read the report to be sure I understood what it was getting at. It was well past 2 a.m. The ministerial estate was dark and silent — almost eerie. Only Mbeki, an inveterate night owl, would be wide awake, busy surfing the internet — the thought spurred me on in my endeavours. Better read every damn annexure. I pored over page upon page of bureaucratic documentation. It was just the type of paperwork with which disgruntled bureaucrats relish taxing their minister. And then as I was nodding off I sat up with a start. Nestling between a few substantial annexures I came across a dozen pages of emails.[1] I could easily have missed them had I been idly flicking through the attachments — as most ministers were inclined to do. The names Saki Macozoma and Bulelani Ngcuka jumped out at me, and an email message between them with the provocative title 'Death knell' and the sentence 'we are making sure the Zulu bastard is nailed to the cross' almost jolted my eyes out of their sockets.

I scanned further emails, one containing the promise by Macozoma to see to 'the promotion of Phumzile Mlambo-Ngcuka' to the deputy presidency. As previously explained she was the wife of Bulelani Ngcuka, former National Director of Public Prosecutions (NDPP), under which the Scorpions resided. As I have related, Phumzile had been promoted by Mbeki to replace Zuma as his deputy in June 2005. The mail was dated February, well before Zuma's June dismissal. How on earth could Saki possibly have guessed that Schabir Shaik would be found guilty the following June and that the judgment would sink Zuma, consequently forcing Mbeki's hand? That was impossible unless Macozoma was a brilliant clairvoyant. There was no way he could have been forewarned unless the judge was in his pocket. And, anyway, a good four months away from the judgment the judge could not have already made up his mind. This alone pointed to a concocted email that had been backdated in a crude attempt to provide credibility to Macozoma's promise — and ensnare the gullible. Those manufacturing or manipulating such emails would pepper the text, made up of truths and half-truths, with such 'predictions' and backdate the correspondence to prove credibility — a simple conjuror's trick.

But the most obvious pointer to the fact the emails were fake was that they were not encrypted. The supposed plotters would certainly have taken the trouble to use a coded programme to ensure the security of their dangerous exchanges. They would be courting disaster, including imprisonment, by taking such an absurd risk. None of them were fools. They were all highly educated and aware of the need for secure communication. I shook my head in disbelief. There was reference to 'nailing' Masetlha, and isolating him from the 'Chief' and the 'reigning [*sic*] in of Motlantle [*sic*]' and need to 'seek Bulelani's assistance in uncovering where Motlantle [*sic*] got his [recently purchased] house from'. That was a reference to the ANC secretary-general, the highly respected Kgalema Motlanthe. The idea that comrades who had been involved in the struggle would be so blasé about their security as to plot in such a reckless and naïve manner was absurd. Further, these were people who were often in each other's company, living in close proximity, encountering one another in their daily activities. Why on earth would they run the risk of mailing one another when they could easily converse in person? The observation 'Oh, what a tangled web we weave when first we practise to deceive'[2] repeatedly came to mind as I contemplated such utterly crude attempts to mislead, misdirect and sow confusion. The tragedy is that it often works. Those who manufacture the mischief are clearly encouraged by the ease with which the politically naïve fall for their ruses. Those with common interests jump at the chance to raise a commotion.

A few pages on I was even more startled to come across the names of Tony Leon, the Democratic Alliance leader, and Anton Harber, the editor of the *Mail & Guardian*, elaborating on the 'Whiteman's Struggle'. This was in a 'chat room' conversation with unlikely bedfellows from the old white regime serving the new: policemen and prosecutors such as Johan and Izak du Plooy, Gerrie Nel and General Roos involved in the work of the National Directorate of Prosecutions and the DSO/ Scorpions. Without any regard for their security they had blithely conspired to foment splits within the ANC and supposedly planned how to plant dubious stories in the media. The idea that such clued-up individuals would be communicating nefarious plots in such a manner, which could open them up to charges of treason, was unbelievable. And Harber and Leon would certainly not align themselves with such reactionary twaddle as the 'Whiteman's Struggle'. This was bizarre.

In fact, the most jarring of reputed statements was that of the state prosecutor Gerrie Nel, saying of Judge Sisi Khampepe, who was then presiding over the Scorpions' future in a judicial commission: 'This woman has our future in her hands. It's either she sides with us or she goes the Kebble way.' Crooked business tycoon Brett Kebble, benefactor of ANC Youth League leaders among others, had died under mysterious circumstances, and here was a state prosecutor being prepared to 'openly' advocate the elimination of a judge. This was sheer fantasy. And as for motive, it was not as though Nel's whole career as a much sought-after jurist would go down the drain if the Scorpions were to be dissolved. He could get a job anywhere. It hardly followed that he would be prepared to kill to save his career. It seemed to me that the nonsense was primarily aimed at those who wanted to believe that a conspiracy aimed against Zuma actually existed. The mails purportedly stemmed from two groups of plotters not necessarily in league but both aiming at preventing Jacob Zuma from becoming president of the country. The one was an ANC faction around Macozoma and Ngcuka, and the other a white supremacist group around Tony Leon.

All thought of sleep banished, I read the emails with total concentration, studying and considering every line, fullstop and comma. Although not an expert in electronic communications, I had enough knowledge of emails to understand that computer-generated mail had a fixed consistency following automatic machine-defined protocols, conventions and formats over which the sender had no control. These had nothing whatsoever to do with a person's compilation of his or her message. This applied to the setting of sender's name, address, date and time sent, with commas, fullstops and symbols automatically generated by the computer in the send and receive field, which follows a strict pattern, spacing and order. If the sequence of such automated punctuation is inconsistent, which was the case with the mails I was studying, then the protocols were not computer-generated but manufactured by hand, as in laboriously typing out the format on a keyboard. And I could see the sequences between various emails were inconsistent. They could not therefore be genuine. Someone had gone to extraordinary lengths to make them look as though they were.

In due course, the inspector general would employ IT experts to forensically examine the emails. Much more knowledge relevant to electronic mail and computer coding was beyond a novice like me. All the technicalities aside, the actual 'political' subject matter of the emails was unsophisticated and extremely crude. That alone should have raised doubt about their authenticity since people like Macozoma, Mlambo-Ngcuka, Tony Leon and Anton Harber just did not talk and write like that.

My initial reaction as the first light of day was seeping through the curtains of my study, with the sound of early birds stirring, was a chilling sensation. The house was dark and silent. I paced up and down in the study, the old floorboards creaking, as I collected my thoughts. I visualised an uproar in the country. If these fake emails were leaked to the media, an occurrence which had become only too common, the opposition, not to mention the likes of the waspish Tony Leon, would be apoplectic. It would put the government on the back foot, desperately fighting against the perception it was up to no good. There was not a moment to lose. I drafted a letter to Masetlha raising my concerns about the emails and enquiring about their origin. With that letter on the record, I began to feel at ease, since by that action I had at least covered the government against any allegation of dirty tricks, which in my view the emails were designed to provoke. But it was not only damage limitation that had to be attended to. It was trying to figure out who was behind the mischief and what was Masetlha's role. One had to avoid being bogged down by the disinformation but instead look for its source. The air had become thick with conspiracy. I needed some fresh air and paced up and down on my lawn with the dew-laced grass squelching underfoot. Two inelegant hadedas, with their long decurved bills, were stalking about looking for worms as dawn arrived. Extremely nervous creatures, they took flight at my appearance, emitting their shrill *haaah-dah-dah* cries as though from some place in purgatory — a mocking chorus to the spectres I was hunting.

Wide awake, almost disbelieving what I had read, I decided to re-read the twenty or so emails. In so doing I realised how even the most obvious errors could be easily missed.

A short mail from Bulelani Ngcuka to Saki Macozoma, subject

'The death knell', on 6 February 2005, in response to Saki, indicating that he would provide him with some financial security, ran: 'I'll appreciate that Bulelani. I'm in dire straits man, I really am. I'll wait for your call – Bulelani.' I sniggered in disbelief. That was Bulelani addressing himself, instead of Saki. Who were these guys making such blatant errors?

As if that was poor workmanship, just a few mails later, Saki wrote to Phumzile, Bulelani's wife, on 26 April, indicating that he would be helping Bulelani to the tune of R5 million 'as a token of our gratitude.' In her letter of thanks Phumzile expresses her appreciation. But her reply was dated 20 April – six days before he had sent her the letter. Surely once such blatant errors were pointed out, no person in their right mind would believe the trash – or so I thought.

It was going to be a perfect spring day, with the jacarandas starting to bloom in their stately mauve colours. I decided to take my early morning run around the estate, which kept me fit and focused in my advancing years. No point in trying to sleep for an hour or two at the most. The exercise would help to order my thoughts: nothing like the loneliness of the long-distance runner in moments like these. There were stirrings on the estate at the police post, and a civil servant was already washing a vehicle outside his bungalow in the early morning sunlight.

A feature of Bryntirion is the nine-hole golf course on which I sometimes chanced my arm. I jogged past Trevor Manuel and Alec Erwin, two early birds, teeing off at the first hole, taking advantage of the early morning light. They would be over and done before 7 a.m. and soon afterwards begin their day at the finance and public enterprise ministries respectively. When it came to the economic policy of the country, they were part of Mbeki's inner circle and consequently objects of the growing ire of the left. Inveterate wits, they hurled advice at me: 'Pick up the pace. The spooks are on your heels.' If only they knew. It was nesting time for the resident plovers. The so-called blacksmith variety makes the distinctive '*ping ping*' sound of metal striking metal. Whether golfer or jogger, you had to be on the lookout for their nests, for if you got too close, the male would swoop down on you like a Battle of Britain Spitfire and peck at your head. The nests were camouflaged in the rough terrain beside the fairways and the dive-bomber sorties were designed to divert one away from coming across them in spring when eggs had been laid. Now why did that remind me of plans being hatched?

I lost no time in briefing Mbeki in person. He had been dismayed about Saki Macozoma's surveillance and keenly awaited the inspector general's findings. More adept at computer technology than any of his ministers, he could easily see the fault lines of the emails. Like me, he was most perturbed. I lost no time either in bringing things out into the open. Call it the Dracula treatment — expose that which is sinister to the light of day. I issued a media statement warning the public of 'hoax' emails doing the rounds.

That evening I met Anton Harber to brief him; and the following day I briefed Tony Leon and his chief whip, Douglas Gibson. It was hard to say what they actually thought. They were certainly grateful that I had alerted them, Anton Harber included. I could not help thinking, however, they might be in two minds: that the emails, as fabricated as they were, might either be from Mbeki supporters out to damage Zuma or from Zuma supporters out to harm Mbeki. A classic example of spy versus spy. Paranoia was playing out in the political and media sphere. The ANC's opponents would be only too pleased to hear about yet another example of brutish factional infighting within the ANC. To my mind, even a scant reading of the emails showed they were obviously fake and that the aim was to reinforce Zuma's claims of a conspiracy against him. With my inner knowledge I deduced that a secondary aim was to get Masetlha off the hook on the ground that the correspondence justified the surveillance of Macozoma. But unless someone was as informed as I was, how could they possibly see that?

I was intrigued too by the references to Motlanthe. I believed he was an honest man and do to this day, and felt that he might have been caught up by doubts about conspiracy and his responsibilities as ANC secretary-general. The implication that he had somehow benefitted from ill-gotten gains inclined me to the view that whoever was responsible for formulating the emails might be seeking to win him to their side. I knew of no such indiscretion on his part and dismissed the references to his newly acquired home, which was by no means a luxurious mansion.

A recent fire at Luthuli House came to mind. It had occurred on the weekend when the surveillance operation against Macozoma began. Why had Billy Masetlha, according to eyewitnesses and a media report, been so determined to get inside the burning building? It was said he had donned fireman's gear and had made a beeline for Motlanthe's vacant office on the seventh floor where the fire had broken out. I had a hunch that there was a compelling motive behind this, for I had got wind of the fact that copies of the emails were being left anonymously at his door. The pieces of a complex jigsaw puzzle were beginning to fall into place. I met the inspector general, Zola Ngcakani, and it was agreed without fuss that he would extend his investigation to cover the emails, their veracity and source.

The appearance of those fake emails made me increase my usual vigilance. In wishing to contact Anton Harber to brief him that evening, I found myself resorting to the tradecraft of the clandestine days of struggle. I did not wish to contact him directly, given that he was obviously a target of forces which might include elements within my own services. I consequently decided to use a mutual friend as go-between. I got my driver to take me to David Beresford, the writer and journalist, who resided in Parkview, Johannesburg. He had been a reliable source of information when I was chief of MK military intelligence in exile. Back in South Africa I sometimes dropped by for a chat and a drink. There were two entrances to his house. My driver usually parked at the front entrance, as we did that evening. I explained to David that I needed to speak to Anton Harber, who lived close by, and that he should not mention my presence, but simply ask him to come over. I instructed David to ensure that Anton use the rear entrance which was out of sight of my driver. Though I had forged a good relationship with my driver, he was after all provided by the NIA and could conceivably be reporting my every move to the likes of Masetlha. David, who had written a bestseller about the IRA,[3] was amused by the intrigue. With a twinkle in his eye, and without any question, he did exactly as I requested. Anton Harber arrived within ten minutes and the two of us had a private discussion in which I briefed him of his supposed involvement in high treason. Anton is an unflappable, softly spoken man and he took in what I was explaining without any sign of agitation.

Driving back to Pretoria that night, I mused about the surreal situation that had come to pass in the country. There I was, a chief of the intelligence services who dared not trust my own driver, a man I had grown fond of and who I believed had become loyal to me. I mused about Anton Harber, a patriotic South African with impeccable anti-apartheid credentials, who had done much by establishing his newspaper, the *Mail & Guardian*, during the apartheid years as a crusading mouthpiece for justice and truth. He had been targeted by the NIA, was being smeared by the emails, and the minister was indulging in clandestine methods of engagement with him. The irony was that journalists like Beresford and Harber had once been under the watchful eye of the apartheid spooks, and were now targets of bumblers in the NIA. When I got back to Bryntirion, those ubiquitous hadedas were hunting insects. One sight of me and off they flew in their ungainly way, emitting their hideous shrieks, which sounded like infants in distress.

CHAPTER 9

On Billy's Trail

Pretoria, October 2005, Week two

Soon after I became minister of intelligence services, a senior member who had served in the apartheid regime suddenly died in office. I was key speaker at his memorial service in Pretoria, where the old and new order spooks mingled to pay their respects. Among the assembled I spotted Billy Masetlha. He had worked with the man in the early days of the amalgamation of the liberation and apartheid institutions, and had risen to head our foreign service, the SASS. Billy had been redeployed several times, which I came to believe pointed to work tensions he had likely generated, and was then directly serving President Mbeki as his security adviser. We had a friendly chat, after which I addressed the gathering, paying respects to the widow and the deceased's family and colleagues. Billy followed suit, expressing much the same sentiment concerning the transition under Mandela and the importance of building trust in the security and intelligence sectors. When he was on form, Billy Masetlha could be impressive. However, he could also come across as a mix of over-ambition and that particular disease of spooks whose power to manipulate people and facts leads to an unhealthy arrogance.

How had our relationship changed in a year? I had come to think of Billy as someone with a hidden agenda. He had a calculated charm, or so I felt, was one of the foremost of the June 1976 student group who had joined the ANC, was intelligent and did not lack charisma. His area of work and his locality in the exile years and beyond had barely connected with mine.[1] Once in exile, the intellectually bright and ambitious like Billy soon caught the eye of ANC leaders and experienced rapid promotion. An articulate group drawn into the exile leadership stratum formed around Thabo Mbeki, who needed bright cadres in the publicity section he ran out of Lusaka — the Department of Information and Publicity — and in the international solidarity arena. Others joined the ANC National Intelligence and Security Department, known as NAT, which was headed by Mzwai Piliso, who needed socially smooth characters for information gathering. By the late 1980s Billy had been recruited. Mzwai's interest in Billy appears to have resulted from important information Billy provided concerning a testy veteran leader, one John Motsabe, who had been scheming with a Tswana-speaking group (Billy's ethnic origin) bent on secretly advancing their leadership fortunes in the tense build-up to the ANC's 1985 national consultative conference in Kabwe, Zambia. Within a few years, following changes in NAT with the removal of Piliso, Billy became very close to the new head of its intelligence structure, Jacob Zuma.

As fate would have it, Billy became director general of the National Intelligence Agency (NIA) under my executive leadership. Billy was recommended by the Presidency and by several ministers with whom he had worked over the years. Close colleagues of his in his initial years in the government secret service were later to express the view that he was overly ambitious and believed he had his own secret agenda. This, they explained, was the reason he had fallen out badly with the former intelligence minister, Joe Nhlanhla, who had him transferred out of his department. Although this history was news to me, I could not be totally sure of what I was hearing since there was a great deal of backbiting among former comrades, who tended to fall out for a number of reasons — particularly because of rivalry over top positions. As for Joe Nhlanhla, he had suffered a debilitating stroke some years previously and there was no possibility of obtaining his point of view. Even so, although he was highly principled and absolutely incorruptible, he was one of the most inarticulate, irascible and emotional of people, and at the best of times I would have been cautious about his judgement. After he was recommended to me, I grilled Billy for over a week, interviewing him many times, before indicating to President Mbeki that I would be prepared to give it a go with him as head of the domestic NIA and its counter-intelligence arm. Billy had in fact done a stint of service as director general of home affairs under Mangosuthu Buthelezi. That had not worked out, and Buthelezi had managed to get agreement from Mbeki to replace Billy – which is how Billy landed up working in the Presidency. Billy claimed the reason for disagreement was political differences, but I came to believe, and heard from Buthelezi, that he had failed to follow the minister's directives. In agreeing to Billy's appointment I cautioned him that falling out with me would be an unfortunate hat-trick given the experience of Nhlanhla and Buthelezi. I hoped this might deter him from possible future failings.

Billy commenced work in December 2004, a bare six months after I had become minister. At first things started well, as he was busy getting to grips with his department and had his hands full. It was into the new year, however, that I began to notice what I perceived as a hint of disrespect reflected in his attitude to me.

This started in February 2005 on a trip to Cuba. I believed we had a great deal to learn from the Cubans and regarded them as close allies. I consequently put together a delegation of top officials including Billy Masetlha, and Tim Dennis, the director general of SASS. Boarding the flight at Johannesburg's international airport (now O.R. Tambo), Billy noticeably failed to greet me and isolated himself on the long haul to Havana while the other officials were as sociable as could be. He appeared attentive enough on arrival and during meetings with our hosts, but on a recreation day, when we took to the sea in a motor launch to fish and swim, he chose once again to isolate himself and get drunk in front of our hosts. I later came to think this had been a sign of the inner tension he was experiencing.

Back home he began arriving late at the regular executive committee meetings I held in my boardroom. These were attended by a dozen of the leadership, heading the various intelligence sectors. All the men were in formal suits and ties, the women in power dress, all keen to impress with their attentiveness and the value they could add to proceedings. Billy was invariably late, offering mumbled excuses about having been caught up at NIA headquarters across town. After the third such occurrence I told him in no uncertain terms that his lack of punctuality was unacceptable. He was visibly nervous and apologised profusely.

One of his fellow officers happened to confide in me shortly afterwards, explaining that Billy's behaviour was cause for concern. He had spent Christmas [2004] at Nkandla, Zuma's rural homestead, where Zuma had an *indaba* with his confidants. Billy has not been the same since. The officer had asked Billy what he had been smoking at Nkandla?

Although Billy never came late to my meetings thereafter, my concern about his behaviour was only to increase. Of particular note was a fallout involving a judicial commission of inquiry into the workings of the investigative branch of the National Prosecuting Authority (NPA), the Scorpions or, more formally, the Directorate of Special Operations. Judge Sisi Khampepe (mentioned in the emails) had been tasked by President Mbeki to consider the location and mandate of the elite crime-busting unit, which had become controversial: should it remain with the NPA as its investigative arm or be redeployed to the police? A hot turf war had erupted, linked to perceptions that the Scorpions were inclined to investigate liberation movement figures suspected of corrupt deals and that these were in fact selective prosecutions linked to political agendas. While there was genuine unease on the part of a number of ministers and officials, the Scorpions had undoubtedly proved their mettle, and their sting, through numerous successes in their fight against high-level crime. The surface issue was that they had no intelligence-gathering mandate such as the NIA and police intelligence; that they were not members of the National Intelligence Coordinating Committee (NICOC);

and that they were not under the parliamentary oversight of the Joint
Standing Committee on Intelligence. I believed that the Scorpions'
success merited support, and that through simple administrative
steps they could be incorporated under NICOC, brought under
parliamentary oversight, and be given a mandate to collect intelligence.
I had seen far too many successful structures rendered ineffectual,
including during the struggle days, to agree to drastic changes. There
was a perception that the NPA was cherry-picking cases to investigate
for political reasons, and I shared the disquiet about that. What
was required was to appoint an independent board with the task of
deciding on prosecutions.

I had permitted Masetlha to submit a separate NIA submission
arguing for the transfer of the Scorpions to the South African Police
Service, but had ordered him to make a number of changes about
issues that I deemed contentious and unnecessary. One such referred
to the Scorpions as having been trained by the FBI. Not that I liked
or wished to protect that rather infamous agency, but I pointed out to
him that the training had been set up by ANC ministers and that his
own intelligence service members had initially received some training
from the British. It was therefore inconsistent to point fingers at the
Scorpions. He also had identified two members of the Scorpions, a
South African and a British citizen living in South Africa, intimating
they were suspect agents. Such suspicions were normally never made
public, and I required him to delete the identities in order to avoid
unnecessary controversy and possible law suits being filed against
us. No doubt that this later led some people to attempt to smear me
as protecting 'enemies' of the state. While he undertook to make
the changes, I soon discovered he had only done so in copies sent
to me but not to Judge Khampepe. The media quickly spotted the
differences between his submission and mine, and contradictions
between us then certainly came out in the open. In answer to a reporter
I expressed my disquiet. The newspaper headline ran: 'Kasrils lashes
out at NIA boss'. The subheading explained: 'The minister is at odds
with intelligence head Billy Masetlha over the future of the Scorpions
as an independent unit.'[2]

As a result of all this, Billy Masetlha was looking decidedly nervous. He had been avoiding me since the inspector general's investigation had got under way and various members of the NIA were interviewed by the inquiry. He was at my side looking contrite as part of a NIA event where I was to deliver a speech.

The entire intelligence community, domestic and foreign, was abuzz with talk of the botched surveillance job on the publicly respected Macozoma and the ongoing investigation. There is nothing like the gossip and indiscretion among some ANC spooks when discussing on street corners, at Sunday barbecues and in dark corridors whatever is remotely controversial – and, further, sharing their views with journalists of choice. I suspected that Masetlha was leaving no stone unturned to give his version of events, including my alleged counter-revolutionary behaviour, to his select confidants in the ANC susceptible to any spin-doctoring. I did not care to play games with him. There were rumours that were spread that I was working with Israel's Mossad. As much as that might irritate me, and the whiff of anti-Semitism which accompanied such an outrageous assertion, I could shrug the claim off, knowing that my solidarity with the Palestinian cause was not only sufficient rebuttal but strengthened me within my own skin. My concern and focus was primarily on countering the confusion which would be rife within the intelligence community and beyond. I needed to hammer home the necessary warning to my staff not to abuse the burden of trust that had been granted to them by the Constitution and the people of the country.

It had long been planned that I open a new NIA archive building on the vast intelligence services estate situated on the outskirts of Pretoria – a place referred to as 'the Farm' – where NIA and SASS had their imposing buildings, reception areas, residences and huge satellite dishes for the interception of communications. The site was a well-known landmark to motorists driving by on the Delmas Road, who were left no doubt in awe of the location.

The hard-working woman who was curator of the archive welcomed me, Masetlha and senior management according to protocol. Her smile and tone were natural. Whatever scandals might be rocking the establishment, she was proud of the new premises and the function of the archive. Masetlha meekly ran through a few words of welcome to his minister, with thanks for my making the time to be present. He attempted to put on a brave face but was uncharacteristically subdued. I welcomed the opening of the new archive and thanked the staff for their dedicated work. It gave me the opportunity to emphasise how vital the keeping of records is. I stressed the importance of preserving documentation to maintain a record of work, for intellectual memory and for future research purposes. That was all regular stuff and pretty low key. Then I upped the ante. 'But there are other reasons too,' I added, causing some attentive heads, including Billy's, to lift a trifle. 'The archive represents a paper trail, a record, of everything we do. It holds us accountable to our regulations, to the Constitution and the rule of law.' At that you could have heard a pin drop. I talked about the imperative of those in the security services, of necessity working in secret, to abide by rules and regulations and not abuse the power vested in them. I could not have had a more attentive audience and I thought my message was sinking in. I spoke of the need for professionalism and identified the principles the services should abide by. There were five and I spelt them out:

One: We were not above the law.

Two: We were accountable to the elected and duly appointed civilian authority.

Three: We accepted the principle of political non-partisanship.

Four: We owed our loyalty to the Constitution, the citizens of our country and the state.

Five: We strove to maintain high standards of proficiency in the performance of our functions.

I emphasised that any deviation would not be tolerated. At the conclusion copies of my speech and posters announcing the five principles were distributed. These were handed out with instructions to display the posters prominently throughout the services. I announced that civic education lectures and discussions would soon start as part of training programmes and everyday work.

Becoming accustomed to Masetlha's ways disinclined me from

being complacent even though I felt I had him on the back foot. I believed he was a doughty opponent who would not simply give in. Clearly, what must have been worrying him most was the relentlessness of the inspector general's investigation. I pondered the growing issues hanging above both Masetlha's and my head. What was the connection between the Macozoma surveillance, the surfacing of the emails, and the Khampepe inquiry into the Scorpions? What about the strange incident of the fire at Luthuli House and Masetlha's appearance there?

One night I tossed and turned in my sleep and dreamt of Masetlha smoking a magic substance with Zuma and his cronies at the Nkandla residence, with sangomas casting spells to oust Mbeki from office. They were guarded by Mossad agents in black masks, and above their heads the hideous hadedas shrieked and groaned like banshees. Do not believe that spy chiefs sleep peacefully.

CHAPTER 10

The Plot Thickens

Pretoria, October 2005, Week three

By the middle of October 2005, around the time I had opened the new NIA archive building, the inspector general (IG), Zola Ngcakani, completed what was to be the first phase of his investigation. The venerable veteran delicately placed a number of hefty files on my desk.

'Minister,' he began, in his quietly spoken manner, 'there can be no doubt that Masetlha and his two subordinates have been up to some serious misdemeanours.' He gave no hint of any weariness of heart. He was a kindly, gentle fellow, and I sensed his type would wish no pain or suffering on youngsters, particularly those such as Bob Mhlanga, who could so easily have been misled.

The IG painstakingly explained his method of investigation, his team's interviews with the principal officials and those involved in the surveillance, including interaction with the complainant, Sakumzi Macozoma himself, and their studying of all relevant reports and documentation. He dealt at length with the NIA trio's story that the surveillance operation was motivated by Macozoma's links with a visiting foreign agent.

He turned to his findings and recommendations.[1]

He found that the surveillance operation against Macozoma was unauthorised and unprocedural. The reasons for the operation were without substance and merit. Attempts had been made to mislead the minister and the investigation team as to the true nature of events. The surveillance operation was unlawful.

Based on the findings, it was recommended that I consider disciplinary steps. The report identified the need for a policy review that included the rules governing the way in which surveillance targets were decided upon. During his investigation, the IG was informed about a NIA project known as Project Avani, which entailed the monitoring of service delivery protests and the political climate in the country. On the information at hand, he believed that it was necessary to ascertain whether this project was in any way linked to the unlawful surveillance operation.

In studying the report over the next couple of days, I found it disturbing to read how the three senior officials had stubbornly stuck to the account they had presented to me of seeking to track and uncover the identity of a visiting foreign services agent whose mission was to determine the likely successor to President Mbeki. The story was full of holes and contradictions, the timeline did not make sense, their 'legend' or 'story' just did not add up. Besides the question of truth, the botched nature of the surveillance operation alone had brought NIA's reputation into question. Interviews with members of the surveillance team showed that they had been hastily assembled and poorly briefed and prepared.

It was shameful that senior officials had made the field commanders of the operation on the ground responsible for their own failures and had promptly suspended them – a clear case of making scapegoats of the foot soldiers. If I had any pity for the young Mhlanga and the invariably courteous Njenje, whom I had always liked, this was dissipated by the way they had sought to shift blame onto the shoulders of their subordinates, quite possibly at the behest of their boss, Masetlha, in an apparent effort to assuage ministerial concern. Such thoughts aside, what we really wanted was a truthful account of what had been going on, and I was prepared to give them every opportunity to come clean.

On the basis of the IG's report, the trio were suspended on full pay until such time as they truthfully accounted for the operation. I commenced with Mhlanga and Njenje, receiving them separately in my office. The IG, seated beside me, politely read out his findings. I gave each, in turn, the opportunity to reconsider their accounts and assist us in getting to the truth or face suspension while further investigations were conducted. But both Njenje and Mhlanga remained po-faced and obdurate.

It was Masetlha's turn to face the music a few days later in the presence of President Mbeki at his residential office. I had informed him that he needed to see the president to discuss the outcome of the IG's report as it related to him. Masetlha was visibly shaken as I read out his notice of suspension, on full pay, following on the heels of the IG delivering the findings of his report. He too was obliged to cooperate with the IG's further investigation and, like the other two, under strict order not to visit his workplace. Masetlha had been banking on the president to protect him.

I knew from Mbeki that Masetlha had rushed to present his own report to him the previous day. I presumed this would have depicted me as a sinister actor in a foreign conspiracy. Whatever Masetlha's story, I simply learnt from Mbeki that he had rejected Masetlha's tale out of hand.

Any allegations about my connections with foreign intelligence agencies would have been discarded since that was part of my job. I had thoroughly briefed Mbeki about every interaction I had with foreign services from East to West. The only time I had met with senior Mossad officials was in his company when a sinister Israeli government duo had attempted to convince him that Iran was on the eve of producing a nuclear weapon. We quite correctly dismissed their facile claims. (To date no such weapons have materialised.)

The NIA's Project Avani, to which the IG had drawn my attention, came to the fore. This was linked to the report Masetlha had delivered to my home and was meant to be an investigation into the public unrest directed against local authorities and its causes. It would be important for the IG to ascertain the origin of the emails that had surfaced in that report. What was disturbing was that it appeared that Masetlha had extended the terms of reference of Avani in early July 2005, without informing me or seeking my approval. This involved the physical surveillance and intercepts (voice and mail) of political, media and state officials, utilising NIA's satellite facilities. That kind of operation was a regression to apartheid-era practices, which had no place in a democracy and which I had sought to ensure should not creep into the security services under my watch.[2]

CHAPTER 11

Services Day

Pretoria, November 2005

IT WAS NECESSARY TO KEEP the intelligence agencies and services fully briefed on the extraordinary events taking place and the key lessons that should be learnt. I needed to clarify issues and counter speculation rife among staff and the media. Of particular concern was the appearance of the clearly fake emails, reinforcing the allegations of a conspiracy to prevent Jacob Zuma from becoming president.

I consequently issued a public statement, warning against 'sinister emails' doing the rounds, labelling them 'clearly fraudulent' and 'reminiscent of Stratcom[1] operations during the apartheid era'. This was widely reported in the media.[2] I urgently needed to appoint an acting director general in Masetlha's place, and had little choice about the candidates. The appointee was Manala Manzini, who was held in esteem by the ANC and, most importantly given the uneasy situation, commanded a high degree of authority. It was that quality that I believed was most needed if we were to limit the damage to the morale of the intelligence community.

I introduced him to the top management at a special briefing the day after Masetlha's suspension. The inspector general reported on his investigation, findings and recommendations. I took the opportunity to once again elaborate on the five principles of intelligence.[3]

Turning to the oath of allegiance, I continued: 'Like you I have sworn an oath of allegiance ... [to] serve the Constitution and the laws of the country ... the President ... and the people of our country. I cannot ... turn a blind eye to any infringements ... We cannot ... bend the rules ... we cannot put our own interests above that of the national interest. Once we do so we set ourselves on a slippery path where the rot will set in and spread.

'We [had] concrete experience of this during the dark days of apartheid,' I continued. 'We cannot allow abuses to occur under our democracy ... We have seen recent intelligence failures in the United Kingdom and the United States, where the product presented was not objective or credible but was tailored ... to particular political perceptions. [I was referring to the fabricated "justifications" about weapons of mass destruction offered by the British and United States governments for the invasion of Iraq.]

'We have seen this just across our borders, where the product presented tells the politicians what they want to hear and not what they ought to know. We have seen this in many of the communist countries.' I appealed to the managers 'to show your professionalism, to keep your focus on the tasks at hand, to ensure that those members under you understand with clarity what is required ... If any of you think that the intelligence service has got a role in deciding who should be the next president, then you are in the wrong place. You should leave and join a political party ... However, if you are a professional intelligence officer then you will know that you cannot use your power or the state's resources for some other agenda.'

I could only batter away and hope I was making sense.

The annual Intelligence Services Day on the tenth anniversary of the institutions established in 1995, at their vast out-of-town headquarters, provided the most appropriate occasion to address matters as an eventful year was drawing to a close. As special guest, President Mbeki delivered the keynote address to upward of a thousand attentive personnel. This was an impressive event with the inauguration of a wall of remembrance to those in the services who had passed away, with an attendant opening of a memorial garden for their families, and the awarding of medals to personnel for distinguished service. In his speech, which paid tribute to the service's development, loyalty and achievements over the years, the thrust of Mbeki's message was concerned with duties and responsibilities, and the mechanisms of institutionalised checks and balances against abuse of power.

'It is of the upmost importance', he stated, 'that our intelligence services should perform their tasks in an impartial and professional manner, in accordance with the Constitutional prescripts and the laws of our country, always respecting the privacy, dignity and human rights of all our citizens.'

Fully understanding underlying problems within the intelligence services and beyond, Mbeki pronounced: 'I would like to make it clear to all of us that any actions taken by the intelligence services designed deliberately to interfere with the normal political processes of parties or organisations that are engaged in lawful activities are expressly forbidden.

'Similarly no member of the intelligence services is allowed to pass on information to any unauthorised person, be they friends or relatives, or to use their position to gather and disseminate information to help settle personal, business or political disputes ... No officer is allowed to owe loyalty to networks outside the intelligence organisations in which they are employed.'[4]

In earlier days of our democracy, this admonition might have passed as a warning to former apartheid-era employees. There was no doubt in my mind that the current problem lay with some of the former ANC officers who had been sucked into troubled waters.

With that, service medals were awarded and the community sat down to a convivial luncheon. As I saw off the departing president, I noticed a pair of ring-necked doves at play in the memorial garden. A happier omen than those inelegant hadedas.

CHAPTER 12

Knocked Down by a Feather

ANC National Executive Committee meeting, Esselen Park, 18–20 November 2005

A FEW DAYS BEFORE PRESIDENT MBEKI warned members of the intelligence services that no member was permitted to pass on information to any unauthorised person, quite an extraordinary development had taken place at a tense meeting of the ANC's sixty-strong National Executive Committee (NEC).[1] The secretary general, Kgalema Motlanthe, announced that he would be handing out a dossier of emails that he had received from an anonymous source.

The document of more than 150 emails purported to reveal a conspiracy to prevent Jacob Zuma from succeeding Mbeki as the next president of the ANC. There could have been objections to Motlanthe's intervention on the grounds of the non-procedural approach, but it was a period when everyone was on tenterhooks and at pains to avoid confrontation: placid on the surface but like ducks paddling furiously below. Indeed, as pointed out by the *Mail & Guardian*: 'By handing the emails to the NEC, Motlanthe was openly flouting the official line. Already on October 23, Intelligence Minister Ronnie Kasrils had issued a public statement, warning against "sinister emails" doing the rounds, labelling them "clearly fraudulent" and "reminiscent of Stratcom operations during the apartheid era".'[2]

I had high regard for Motlanthe and did not doubt his integrity. It occurred to me then that my hunch about who might have been anonymously depositing copies of the emails on his doorstep was possibly correct.

Like others, heads down and in silence, I focused on the document before me, and to my surprise encountered scores and scores of poorly cyclostyled copies of emails. I scanned the pages from the initial emails, already familiar to me, commencing in February 2005, to a profusion of many more, climaxing in occurrence during the period July through to September, and petering out in October at the time of Masetlha's suspension that year.[3]

The gist of the collection was the existence of a sinister conspiracy against the ANC deputy president, Jacob Zuma, together with the secretary general of the ANC, Kgalema Motlanthe, and Billy Masetlha. This was the so-called conspiracy to prevent Zuma from becoming the next ANC president, about which Zuma had been alluding for several years without ever producing a shred of evidence. As previously mentioned, it appeared that there were two groups of plotters. The one group, allegedly a Xhosa faction, was led by Saki Macozoma, a fellow NEC member in our very midst. The group included prominent figures in the ANC, government, the political opposition, state prosecutors, Scorpions members and business. Their objective was the political and economic control of the country. Their primary targets were Zuma, Motlanthe and Masetlha.

The second group, acting independently of the first, was headed by Tony Leon, leader of the parliamentary opposition, supported by apparent white racists in the Scorpions and by leading journalists. By sheer coincidence this group similarly targeted Zuma, Motlanthe and Masetlha in order to provoke the alleged division within the ANC, lead to its breaking apart, and allowing the 'white man' to again assume control of the country, led by their 'champion', Tony Leon.

Examples of the proof that the fake emails were manually generated

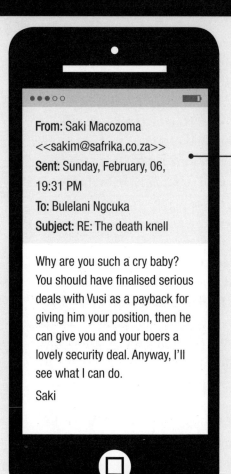

From: Saki Macozoma
<<sakim@safrika.co.za>>
Sent: Sunday, February, 06, 19:31 PM
To: Bulelani Ngcuka
Subject: RE: The death knell

Why are you such a cry baby? You should have finalised serious deals with Vusi as a payback for giving him your position, then he can give you and your boers a lovely security deal. Anyway, I'll see what I can do.

Saki

- In printouts of both received and sent Yahoo emails the first line of the addresses is **Subject**, the second **From**, the third **To** and the fourth **Date**. There is no **Sent** line.
- In printouts of both received and sent Yahoo emails automatically generated, the Yahoo email programme places the day before the month, not the month before the day. They thus automatically generate a full date **as Sunday, 06 February 2005, 19:31**. Note the additional comma in the fake email.
- All emails dated 6 February 2005 (and only those dated 6 February 2005) place the date before the month.
- Similarly, all emails dated 6 February 2005 (and only those dated 6 February 2005) contain no year in the automatically generated datelines.
- Yahoo users have the option of 12-hour or 24-hour clocks. But the time '19:31' does not require 'PM' to specify the evening. The time either appears as 19:31 or 07:31 PM, never as 19:31 PM.

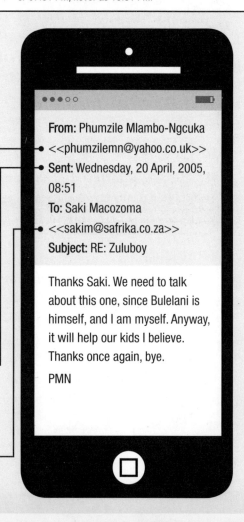

From: Phumzile Mlambo-Ngcuka
<<phumzilemn@yahoo.co.uk>>
Sent: Wednesday, 20 April, 2005, 08:51
To: Saki Macozoma
<<sakim@safrika.co.za>>
Subject: RE: Zuluboy

Thanks Saki. We need to talk about this one, since Bulelani is himself, and I am myself. Anyway, it will help our kids I believe. Thanks once again, bye.

PMN

PMN replies to emails sent to an email address that does not exist – and does so six days before receiving the emails to which she responds.

Printouts of Yahoo emails automatically generate dates in a format containing only two commas, **Wednesday, 20 April 2005, 08:51 (Wednesday, 20/04/2005, 08:51)**. There is no commas after the month.

Double pointed brackets: All email programmes, including Yahoo, automatically reproduce saved email addresses with a single bracket (<), not the double bracket contained in the faked emails (<<).

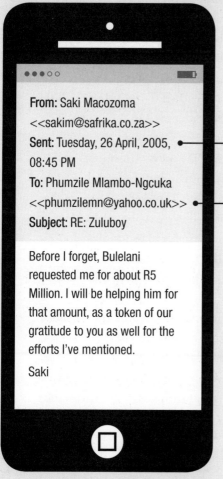

From: Saki Macozoma
<<sakim@safrika.co.za>>
Sent: Tuesday, 26 April, 2005, 08:45 PM
To: Phumzile Mlambo-Ngcuka
<<phumzilemn@yahoo.co.uk>>
Subject: RE: Zuluboy

Before I forget, Bulelani requested me for about R5 Million. I will be helping him for that amount, as a token of our gratitude to you as well for the efforts I've mentioned.

Saki

Printouts of Yahoo emails include a comma after the day (Tuesday) and the year (2005) but not after the month (April).

Double pointed brackets: All email programmes, including Yahoo, automatically reproduce saved email addresses with a single bracket (<), not the double bracket contained in the faked emails (<<).

- 14 minutes later, SM sends precisely the same to the same non-existent address.
- It contains precisely the same automatically generated 'errors' – errors, which are also apparent in other emails included in the fake emails package provided to NIA and to the ANC commission. Some of the emails have double brackets at one side of the automatically generated addressed and single brackets on the other.

From: Saki Macozoma
<<sakim@safrika.co.za>>
Sent: Tuesday, 26 April, 2005, 08:59 PM
To: Phumzile Mlambo-Ngcuka
<<phumzilemn@yahoo.co.uk>>
Subject: RE: Zuluboy

Before I forget, Bulelani requested me for about R5 Million. I will be helping him for that amount, as a token of our gratitude to you as well for the efforts I've mentioned.

Saki

All the errors I had noted in the emails I had already seen were rife throughout the Kgalema dossier. I hoped that my NEC colleagues would be up to the challenge of at least spotting the most obvious mistakes in language usage and the unbelievably foolish nature of the 'conspiracy' scenario. The concern, as I well knew, was that virtually all, save for a handful of computer and email literates, would be befuddled by the technical aspects. Most colleagues had staff attending to their correspondence and would never have sent an email in their lives. The conjuror's trick was to blind the ignorant and naïve who knew next to nothing of IT, so that mail between A and B would be unquestionably believed. After all, the 'proof' was manifest in print before their very eyes. Everyone had heard of the 'hacking' or interception of emails, and here appeared visible proof of that. The question of how these came into the secretary general's hands could be a moot point. I knew that most people would not question the technical aspects of the IT, but I hoped that the bizarre contents of the emails would be seen as ludicrous.

The collection of correspondence commenced with the emails I had seen dating from early February 2005, between Saki Macozoma, Bulelani Ngcuka and his wife, Phumzile Mlambo-Ngcuka. The trio, with others, appeared to conspire against Zuma. Phumzile would be rewarded with her appointment to Zuma's position of deputy president of the country (which did in fact come to pass in June of that year) and her husband Bulelani would be amply rewarded with funds to 'catapult' him into the business world. The subject heading used for these emails was 'death knell of Zuluboy', alluding to the conspirators' aim of 'making sure' that the 'Zulu bastard is nailed to the cross'.

By 20 April, Macozoma, the ringleader of the 'Xhosa' conspirators, in an email to a senior government official, identified Kgalema Motlanthe – misspelt as Motlantle throughout the document, whether by an Afrikaner or African author – as an impediment to their aims: 'By the time the NGC [ANC's National General Council, due to meet at the end of June 2005] arrives we should have got him [Zuma] out of office. The NGC should be used to make sure that he is dead buried and that he has no constituency ... If we fail to do this how are we going to contain Motlantle [*sic*], Cyril [Ramaphosa] and other hopefuls?'

On the same day Macozoma reminded Phumzile of his promise to make her the country's deputy president: 'I can you tell [*sic*] right now that Zuluboy's position is yours ... You can be assured of the position because the Chief [Thabo Mbeki] believes in you. Another thing that guarantees you thies [*sic*] positions is the fact that ... you are of Zulu descent, that makes it impossible to accuse us of tribalism.'

On 16 August Tony Leon featured in a so-called chat room with his group of conspirators: the journalist Matthew Buckland and the prosecutors and Scorpions investigators Gerrie Nel, Izak du Plooy and Johan du Plooy, carefree of any danger from their treasonable discourse:

IdP: We are about to raid Zuma's premises ... We are going for all his houses as well as his attorney and [Zweli] Mkhize, the MEC for KZN. It will be a spectacle.

TL: Do you have enough manpower to do that?

JdP: We'll use the 'A Team' from the old days and few darkies to sprinkle on ...

TL: What about Motlantle? [*sic*]

IdP: His time is coming, [Vusi] Pikoli [headed NPA after Bulelani Ngcuka] has given us the green light to 'keep him in the news' until we have enough time of effect a raid on him and his comrade [Manne] Dipico.[4]

MB: We are running a story about [Motlanthe] this weekend about his house in the golf course. We need to nail him to the same cross with his financial advisor Majali.[5]

The emails of 27 August again featured the same 'chat room' personalities:

TL: I hear you are being victimised by NIA, what's going on?

JdP: We have had meetings with them and they are very hostile

IdP: They are very angry about the raids as you know ...

TL: Do you think they have a leg to stand on?

GN: Netshitenze[6] [*sic*] has assured us that nothing will happen to us since Mbeki believes in what we do. However I think we need to sort out the NIA bastards.

JdP: We need to find something on Billy Masetla [*sic*], and get him out of NIA because he is the thorn in our sides.

B: I'll check the archives for the time when he was still at home affairs, maybe there's something we can get from there. Anything, his personal life, his weaknesses, his bank accounts, etc.

GN: We will get our friends ... to check on that, see if we can't start harassing him on things he hasn't paid yet ... We need something substantial eventually, that would justify a raid. Pikoli would be delighted to go get something and raid and destroy Masetla [*sic*], he hates him with a vengeance.

On 12 September, there is email communication between Macozoma and Vusi Pikoli, who succeeded Bulelani Ngcuka as head of the National Prosecuting Authority:

SM: I had a chat with Bulelani regarding the issues at hand. I think we need to up the tempo on Masetla [*sic*]... What are your boys finding on this guy? He needs to be replaced ASAP!!

VP: You guys need to help me out ... [Bulelani Ngcuka] is offering me some shares ... For now my guys don't have anything on Masetla. However one of my guys, Nel, has a potential good friend in NIA, in the technology section ... he may be able to assist. I agree that Masetla is becoming a problem.

SM: I'm glad you have a potential ally on the inside. Let's use the Boers where we can.

On 9 October, Phumzile Mlambo-Ngcuka writes to Macozoma:

PMN: Hi Saki. What is your view regarding the Khampepe Commission. Don't you think we need to reign [*sic*] in that woman. Zuluboy's trial is commencing, Masetla [*sic*] is attacking Vusi's team, the commission is on, we have the youth league and communists giving us trouble, it looks like we are losing the battle to the populists.

SM: As discussed I have requested Vusi to invite Billy Downer[7] [for our meeting] sometime next week for the briefing regarding Zuluboy's case. As for Masetla [*sic*], you need to inform me on how things have gone with Ronnie [Kasrils]. You have nothing to worry regarding Sisi [Khampepe], she is fully aware that her career depends on the findings ... We cannot allow [Jackie] Selebi [the national police commissioner] to control this team.

On 15 October, Pumzile Mlambo-Ngcuka writes to Ronnie Kasrils:

PMN: Hi Ronnie ... There is not much accept [*sic*] to congratulate you on handling Billy who is fast becoming an uncontrollable bullterrier. You did very well to inform the media and lambaste him in public. How is Leonard [McCarthy, head of the Scorpions] doing?

RK: He [Masetlha] is becoming a real nuisance now ... He does not even honour some of the meetings I call. I hope you guys won't mind me using the M&G newspaper, I have some good contacts there. I've also sent a statement to Anton Harber, he says he has good contacts within the Sunday Times. Leonard is okay ... [but] bothered by the fact that Billy knows too much about the issue of our overseas friends and our co-operation with them. What is wrong with me organizing meetings with Mossad, since it's known that I am a Jew. I'm contacting the best to assist our country with counter-terrorism ... then I'm judged. It's hard to be of Jewish descent.'

I was aware that there had been intimations that I was a Mossad connection, which was a cheap smear. I never played at 'Jewish victimhood' or spoke in that manner, but knew from Barry Gilder, who had been transferred from home affairs to head the National Intelligence Coordinating Committee, that some people were harping on our Jewish connection in an effort to place me in an ethnic bracket.

I believe that what those manufacturing the emails were doing was cloning a real timeline of events so that the emails appeared authentic, seemingly introducing new topics and characters as they actually transpired in real life. This was easily effected by following events, mixing truths with half-truths for the sake of authenticity, fabricating communiqués and then backdating them. An example in point occurred on 19 October, in a chat room exchange with Leonard McCarthy, in which I say: 'I'd like to inform you that I will be meeting with Gerry Adams the IRA leader today before noon ... I'd like you to be present ... to prove that you do not only talk to British, US and Mossad people.'

Gerry Adams had indeed been in South Africa and I had co-hosted a party for him that evening, so the date was correct. But I would not ordinarily refer to Adams as an IRA leader. He had become president of the political party Sinn Fein, and whatever his past IRA connections, new circumstances required meticulous political correctness in reference to him, to which I strictly adhered.

I also noted with some amusement that I first made an appearance in the email script as soon as I began tangling with Billy Masetlha. So in an email that Mlambo-Ngcuka wrote to Saki Macozoma (on 9 October) she states that 'we need to get Ronnie to deal with Masetla'. The unsuspecting reader accepting the email date stamps as genuine would regard this as proof of an impending entanglement with Billy. By sleight of hand a concocted email, handcrafted but made to look genuine, and backdated prior to any action against him, could be made to look authentic since such an imbroglio did take place.

However, so amateurish and prone to error was the sequence of the emails that on close examination I believed any objective reader without a political bias would recognise they were fake. (The problem was, however, twofold: IT could fool the naïve; and those with a partisan political agenda needing or wishing to think anything bad about their rivals would suspend objectivity and reasonable belief.)

By way of example, in an email from me to Phumzile on 20 October at 21.30, I write: 'As you are aware I have now managed to suspend the two Masetla [*sic*] allies[8] ... Billy is going to be a difficult one. And I will really need you to come to my rescue by assisting me.'[9]

Phumzile replies: 'I don't think that you need to worry ... Billy will have to go.'

Yet Masetlha had already been suspended several hours before Phumzile was supposed to have written this. If the emails had been genuine, I would have known and, as I was responsible for Masetlha's suspension, would have referred to it, rather than asking for someone to 'come to my rescue' in dealing with him. An authentic email from me would have referred to that piece of salient news.

This was followed by an email from Phumzile to Saki on 21 October 2005, at 6.30 a.m., in which she laments: 'It's time we nailed Billy to the cross. We cannot have one man seeking to disturb our plans.' Saki replies at 6.39 a.m.: 'Relax on that one Phumzile, we'll nail him.'

Genuine, real-time emails would have had both these exchanges refer to Masetlha's actual suspension nearly twenty-four hours earlier, during the day of 20 October. In real life I would have been informing Phumzile on the night of 20 October that we had suspended Masetlha and his two subordinates.

I had the advantage of familiarity with the subject matter, so was able to read through the dossier well ahead of my colleagues. I decided to leave the conference room and seek an early cup of coffee. I bumped into Kgalema, and could not resist beseeching him with the words: 'Comrade Kgalema, surely you can't believe these emails are genuine?'

I was shocked to discover he did, for it confirmed my worst fears that such potent emails, which I considered fake, could apparently take in someone like him. I felt weak at the knees. I could have been knocked down with a feather.

CHAPTER 13

Connecting the Dots

ANC National Executive Committee meeting, Esselen Park, 18–20 November 2005, continued

FEATHER-DUSTED, BUT NONETHELESS as determined as ever, I returned to my seat feeling depressed. Once all had completed the reading of the emails, I concentrated on nothing but the discussion.

It was Kader Asmal, as usual, who spoke out first, and he was damning of the emails, which he termed clearly fake and an effrontery to any rational-minded individual's cerebral capacity. He later chided me for having coined the term 'hoax emails' as 'hoax' was not as explicit as 'fake'. Kader Asmal, focused as a reader and quick to spot errors, referred to the absurdity of the chat room welcome to Anton Harber which had enquired: how were things at Caxton's? Kader guffawed in that exacting way of his, as though talking down to his students in a lecture hall, explaining that Caxton's was not a place but part of Harber's title in his new post at Wits, as Caxton Professor of Journalism.[1] Of course, Kader Asmal, like others, also demolished the idea that liberal democrats like Harber, Buckland and Tony Leon could be involved in a crusade for a return to a white racist South Africa.

It was Saki Macozoma, clearly burning with rage, who spoke next and, in a most aggrieved manner, expressed his anger at the surveillance operation that he and his family had endured, and the libellous nature of the emails, which he decried as clearly fabricated and malicious. He denied ever having sent any of the mails, and explained that he had never utilised the email address that appeared as his.

I told the meeting that the emails were a clear attempt to reinforce the claim of a conspiracy at play against Jacob Zuma and was a blatant attempt to pull the wool over our eyes. By way of example of how fake things were, I provided the simple example of how different people, from entirely different backgrounds, consistently misspelt names such as Motlanthe (as 'Motlantle') and Masetlha (as 'Masetla') in the exact same way. This was highly unlikely.

I pointed out some other easily detectable technical faults and errors, such as the errors in timeline in the correspondence between Mlambo-Ngcuka and me at the time of Masetlha's suspension. But I decided to keep the technical aspects to a minimum. As my main thrust, I decided instead to focus on the apparent disregard of security, by both the Macozoma group and the Tony Leon group, as comrades could well understand the dangers involved in risking sedition and treason. Most present had some experience of clandestine work in the struggle days, of the use of codes or jargon to preserve secrecy, and would be on more comfortable ground debating this. I clearly recall saying to Jacob Zuma on one particular occasion in the NEC: 'Msholozi [his clan name], remember the three little letters MCW [Military Combat Work] which we studied with *amaRussia* [the Russians]?' He could not resist a smile and I continued: 'You know how strict we were to preserve secrecy. Can you imagine these conspirators, all well aware of the painful consequences they could face if exposed, stupidly committing their seditious thoughts to emails, when we have all heard in these times how prone such communications are to interception?'[2]

I continued, that since Phumzile and I lived on the presidential estate, and my front door and her back door were a mere hundred metres distant, if we wished to discuss something sensitive and potentially dangerous to us both, why would we resort to emails? I could simply walk over to her back door by night, knock for her attention, and chat to her in the garden under a tree, where we could not be bugged.

I enquired of Motlanthe how he had come into possession of the emails. His reply was that the bundle had been left outside his Luthuli House office door. I almost asked whether there was any relation between that and the day of the fire when Masetlha had engaged in firefighting theatrics.

There was some general discussion about a conspiracy that was clearly afoot, but by whom it was difficult to be sure, even conceivably by a third force wishing to create confusion and set comrades at one another's throats. This was a possibility that could not be immediately disproved. Although the overwhelming majority of NEC members clearly regarded the emails as indeed fake, Kgalema requested that he be given a mandate to establish an independent ANC task team to investigate their veracity. Five or six hands immediately shot up in support, and at a glance we could see the minority who sided with him: Ngoako Ramatlhodi, Tony Yengeni and Fikile Mbalula, the Youth League leader, being the most prominent. Mbalula had glanced at me sitting quite coincidentally next to Macozoma when he entered the meeting. He had waved a dismissive hand at us with the words 'just to be expected' – as if sitting together was proof of a conspiratorial link.

Yengeni and Ramatlhodi were different propositions. Tony Yengeni, known to me from underground times, was a courageous MK commander. Once he received his military training abroad, he had no interest in hanging around near the leadership waiting for a plum job in exile, which could have been his for the taking. He was fixated on returning home and had the political understanding to realise the need to focus on building underground cells, linked to the people, in order to launch armed operations. When he was captured in Cape Town and brutally tortured, he did not break. I worked with him after 1990, organising mass action, and again admired his dedication and flare. As an ANC MP in the new parliament, and as ANC chief whip, he was similarly dedicated, but a weakness for luxury cars and fashionable clothing got him into trouble. Disciplined by parliament for evading the truth about a R150,000 concession he had received for a Mercedes

Benz, he was criminally charged and spent a year in prison, where I visited him and discovered how anti-Mbeki he had become. I felt his antipathy to Mbeki stemmed from a resentment that the president had failed to prevent the criminal proceedings against him.

As for Ramatlhodi, I had worked with him in Zimbabwe in building the political underground in South Africa and was impressed with his skill and dedication. I was fond of him too and had made a speech in his honour at a family celebration when he graduated as a lawyer. He had been a young member of Mbeki's Lusaka group and he clearly admired the future president. Back home he became premier of Limpopo province, when it was still called the Northern Province, and as water and forestry minister I worked well with him and his officials. At some point the Scorpions began to investigate him for possible corruption, which never was proved, but it appeared to me that he, like Yengeni, believed Mbeki should have interceded to quash any investigation from the outset. Like Yengeni, too, he had a good political head, and so it was possible that both personal and political grievances were the reason, from what I picked up, why he was running with the Zumaites. All the same, it was disturbing that comrades like them were becoming so disaffected with Mbeki and his leadership style for it was perceived that he operated within a narrow circle of confidants – in exile and back home.

I was among the first who supported Kgalema's request for the establishment of an independent ANC inquiry into the emails. While the majority could have insisted this was unnecessary, and that it reflected a lack of trust in a state process, it was probably the right way to go if we were to have a chance of settling differences – or so some of us hoped.

What we gained in return was an agreement that comrade Motlanthe would provide President Mbeki with the set of emails so they could be handed to the inspector general for his investigation. This would be more arrows to the IG's bow, and I knew he would be delighted. All the other copies had to be handed back to Motlanthe.

The meeting gave me a renewed opportunity to connect the dots in the puzzle which had been unfolding during 2005. On returning home from the NEC meeting, I sat down at my desk, and began jotting down a timeline under the heading 'Who Dunnit?'

· Xmas 2004: Billy visits Nkandla
· His changed attitude
· July: Khampepe Commission
· ANC NGC: Zuma's comeback!
· Surveillance on Saki M
· August: fire Luthuli House?
· Sept.: IG investigates
· Oct.: emails target Billy!
· 20th: Suspension (no more emails!!)
· 23/11: Kgalema dossier?
· Billy>Kgalema>Zuma?

Connect them dots!!

What the IG had cleared up, to my relief, was that the admirable Kgalema Motlanthe was no more than an unwitting recipient of the email packages deposited on his doorstep. The summary of Zola Ngcakani's report released to the media made that clear.[3]

I slept well that night, looking forward to meeting the inspector general the following day, and handing him the new batch of emails. Ngcakani would have them professionally analysed and his investigators would seek to track down the source.

CHAPTER 14

Emails Unlocked

Pretoria, November 2005 to March 2006

THE MOST SPECTACULAR BREAKTHROUGH in the inspector general's investigation came with a raid on a Gauteng home on 1 December 2005. Following investigations of NIA records, including payments for services rendered, an individual whom the IG believed could assist in inquiries was tracked to the address. Accompanied by police with a search and seizure warrant, Zola Ngcakani's key investigator, Imtiaz Fazel, found the person they sought at home. His name was Muzi Kunene, an IT specialist and company director with a chequered history. A shaken Kunene refused to answer any questions. Computer equipment, documents and his mobile phone were seized for testing. A laptop computer that Kunene had sought to conceal by hiding it in a laundry basket was a prize discovery.

What was surprising among the finds was the photographs on display in his house of Kunene proudly posing with Zuma at a formal event. This was when a partnership had been formed between Kunene's IT firm and a leading IT company in the States. He had become the CEO in 2002 and the deputy president, Jacob Zuma, had clearly been a guest of honour at the occasion held to celebrate his new role.[1]

Muziwendoda (Muzi) Kunene, originally from KwaZulu-Natal, had been an IFP member, with links to a German religious and educational mission in the province that was considered by ANC members to be particularly right-wing.[2] He had received IT training courtesy of the institution and benefitted by being sent to Germany for further training. He visited Namibia in 1989 in the company of a self-confessed SADF military intelligence agent, Koos Greeff, to sow anti-Swapo[3] propaganda in the run-up to that country's first democratic elections.[4] Kunene's notes revealed contact with an NIA assistant of Masetlha's, Funi Madlala, who was an IT cyber specialist. There was also reference to a meeting with Masetlha.

The identification of Kunene was a spectacular breakthrough in the IG's investigation – the smoking gun that was needed. The IG's report featured forensic evidence acquired from Kunene's computer. An eye-opening discovery in his computer revealed work on the email collection in the Kgalema dossier.

The analysis of the emails by experts was to prove vital to the IG's investigation. These included a foremost forensic criminologist, Irma Labuschagne, the head of the Cyber Unit of the South African Police Service, and a top IT expert.[5] The forensic criminologist's analysis was extremely detailed. In the first place she concluded that the style and language used in the emails and accompanying chat room material could not be authentic. Emails of a confidential nature would at least be in a cryptic style employing shorthand, acronyms and initials. Where subject matter was of a treasonable nature, involving educated people, an actual coding programme would have been utilised. As evidenced by the extensive number of identifiable errors in text – in terms of expression, grammar, syntax, spelling and so on – the alleged author(s) conveyed messages in a naïve way, strangely repeated the full names of the so-called conspirators and continually included unnecessary detail, unusual in genuine correspondence. The author(s) had little education and a poor command of English and Afrikaans. One such example related to the prosecutor Gerrie Nel, a fluent Afrikaans speaker, who in the emails wrote in bad Afrikaans.[6] Among other highly questionable peculiarities was the almost total use of English in the texts where people familiar with one another would more commonly prefer to use their common language.

Then there was consistency in the misuse of the same phrase by different persons, for example:

Ngcuka: 'to make sure that the Zulu bastard is nailed to the cross' (page 2);

Macozoma: 'to nail this coffin' (page 8);

Buckland: 'we need to nail them to the same cross' (page 15);

Mlambo-Ngcuka: 'It's time we nailed Billy to the cross' (page 74).

Different individuals who knew Motlanthe well all spelled his name incorrectly in the exact same way, i.e. Motlantle. These included Vusi Pikoli, Peter Vundla, Saki Macozoma, Trevor Manuel and Phumzile Mlambo-Ngcuka. So did people more distant from him, such as Tony Leon and Johan du Plooy. Notwithstanding that the two alleged conspiratorial groups were distinct from one another, they continually made the same mistakes in the way in which they spelt the names of the main participants. Billy Masetlha was referred to as 'Masetla'; Kgalema Motlanthe as 'Motlantle'; Joel Netshitenzhe as 'Netshetendze'; and Khampepe as 'Kamphepe'.

The criminologist found it highly unlikely that any of the individuals who purportedly sent the emails were in fact the author(s). On a conceptual level the 'storyline' appeared infantile and naïve. The criminologist believed there were probably two writers involved and probably another person who fed the writers with information. The documentation reminded her of the way in which a 'soapie' was written for television whereby the head writer provides the daily 'storyline' to various scriptwriters.

While it might be argued that the criminologist's opinion was based on human judgement and experience, the IG turned to computer science for proof based on forensic evidence. A reputable computer scientist was employed to examine the printed emails and chat sessions to assess whether or not the information represented authentic intercepted data communications.[7] He was absolutely clear: the allegedly intercepted emails were fabricated and could not have been transmitted via the internet. Technical errors abounded with innumerable inconsistencies relating to such features as angled brackets, headers, timestamps and what is called spurious data. All these should ordinarily appear in standardised formation as automatically produced by a computer with machine-generated protocols and repetitive formats. The inconsistencies and errors showed beyond doubt that the emails were manufactured and not intercepted. In short, they were fake.

Moreover, messages sent by the Cyber Unit of the SAPS to the mail addresses showed they did not exist. A forensic investigation of computers belonging to the alleged participants was undertaken to establish whether the emails had been sent from those machines. This found that no email communication took place between them on the respective dates and times referred to in the emails.

There was much more evidence. The inquiry revealed that Masetlha had contracted an agent to 'intercept' the emails, for which service he received payment from NIA. His identity was established as Muzi Kunene.[8] Information found in his possession provided evidence that it was he (with or without others) who fabricated the emails.

The investigation also brought to light the fact that the involvement of Kunene was known only to Masetlha and Funi Madlala, NIA's manager of cyber operations and IT, whose identity became public when criminal charges were laid against him. It was apparent that the Project Avani team, in particular its most senior members,[9] had not readily accepted the authenticity of the 'intercepted' emails, which remained in the exclusive custody of Masetlha (with minor exceptions) and Madlala. Attempts to verify the authenticity of the emails were reportedly met with the obstructionist tactics of the director general, who wanted the team to believe they were true.

As a result, I exonerated Gibson Njenje and Bob Mhlanga from involvement in the email fraud. However, they were found complicit in the illegal surveillance operation against Saki Macozoma and in the fabrication of the story about what had led to that botched operation as well as guilty of deliberately attempting to mislead the minister and the IG.[10]

The IG's investigation had occupied some six months of dedicated work by his team, from September 2005, when I set his terms of reference, through three phases of inquiry, to March 2006, when he submitted his final report. This consisted of numerous volumes amounting to thousands of pages with relevant annexures. The investigation involved dedicated and painstaking effort, hours of interviews with numerous persons and witnesses, extensive cooperation with the police, hundreds of hours' worth of analyses by experts, and complex forensic studies of various computers and electronic equipment, not to mention the demanding effort of writing meticulous reports. Anyone doubting the integrity of the investigation and the objectivity of the findings would be hard put to prove otherwise.

For me as the minister it could not have been more satisfactory to interact with the IG, Zola Ngcakani, and his most capable chief assistants, the chief operating officer, Imtiaz Fazel, and his legal adviser, Advocate Jay Govender.

Apart from the fact that the investigation was so definitively able to conclude that the emails were fake and had been concocted to present a supposed conspiracy to prevent Jacob Zuma from becoming president of the country, the most significant achievement was to identify to some degree those behind the falsification of the material.

Based on his findings, the IG recommended that I consider bringing disciplinary hearings against the NIA director general, Billy Masetlha; the general manager: counter-intelligence, Bob Mhlanga; and the operational support manager, Funi Madlala; and criminal charges against Masetlha, Madlala and the source of the fabricated emails, Muzi Kunene.[11] Action against Gibson Njenje was dropped as he had resigned from NIA in early November.

The IG presented his report to cabinet, which fully endorsed it. Masetlha's long-time peers and comrades-in-arms during the liberation struggle, the police commissioner, the chief of the defence force, the head of the National Intelligence Coordinating Committee, and the directors general of defence, justice and the intelligence services, also publicly endorsed the IG's report and condemned Masetlha's conduct. The police commissioner, Jackie Selebi, announced that the law enforcement agencies would have to consider issues of criminal liability arising from the report and carry out their own investigations.[12]

President Mbeki dismissed Masetlha from office on 22 March, citing a 'breakdown of trust' between them, which was the conventional formula for terminating the service of senior executives and was well within his powers. The IG and I were on hand as Masetlha received the news at Mbeki's residence on a sunny afternoon. I recall the chimes of several period clocks in the spacious residence as the meeting got under way. There was certainly no joy or crowing on our part although Masetlha looked quietly defiant and shook his head in disagreement as Mbeki informed him of the parting of the ways. It was a shame Billy Masetlha had brought upon himself. We were relieved to see his back, but not happy about the turn of events. None of us wanted to see him facing criminal charges, though this would depend on police investigations beyond the control of even the president. I am certain none of us thought this was the end of Masetlha, a man with political ambition who never gave up. We were not out to ruin his political career. That would depend on how the ANC membership regarded him. I well knew there were many who sided with him, including powerful forces angling to ensure that Jacob Zuma was elected as the next president after Mbeki. We would also have to hear from Motlanthe's task team looking into the emails, independently of the IG's investigation.

As I ambled back to my residence on the presidential estate, I realised that there had been no emails since Masetlha's suspension in October 2005. Lost in thought, I was not even bothered by those ubiquitous shrieking hadedas. Arriving home, thinking of that long night in October when I had trawled through the report Masetlha had dropped off, and had my first glimpse of the fake emails, I thought of the dots I had been connecting — from Macozoma's surveillance through the emails to Kunene and the Luthuli House fire and their arrival on the doorstep of the unwitting Kgalema Motlanthe. I had a strong sense of foreboding that, given the conspiratorial murk in the country, the saga had not ended.

CHAPTER 15

Hook, Line and Sinker

Pretoria, March 2006 to March 2007

THE VOICE AT THE END of the line was indistinct and aggressive: 'Balula here, I want the same treatment as Macozoma!'

I didn't know a Balula and told the man so.

'Balula! Balula!' He grew irate and continued yapping. We remonstrated and I put the phone down.

When I checked with my secretary, she too had thought the caller, who first came through her, was a Balula, but added 'from the ANC Youth League'.

I called back to apologise to Fikile Mbalula, who snapped at me, saying I had pretended not to recognise him. I reined in my temper and asked what he wanted.

In an aggressive tone he told me he believed he was under surveillance by NIA, and demanded the same treatment I had afforded Macozoma.

I told him that as with Macozoma's complaint we needed information. If he wished I was ready to meet him and have the acting director general, Manala Manzini, present, but we needed facts.

He said he would be at my office within an hour. In the event he kept Manzini and me waiting for three hours.

He arrived in a sullen mood, swaggering in as though in a school yard, not bothering to apologise for being late. He provided a flimsy story with no facts, simply a suspicion that a stranger in the street outside Luthuli House appeared to have taken an interest in him. He could provide no identification of the man whatsoever. Hardly the stuff we could go on and certainly nowhere akin to Saki Macozoma's complaint, which provided vehicle registration numbers, photographs and witnesses. He kept yawning during the meeting, eyes puffed and watery.

I explained that of course we would look into the matter. I arranged for him to have a further discussion with Manzini, and requested he put his complaint in writing. Manzini later reported that there was nothing of substance forthcoming, and we never received anything in written form nor did we hear from Mbalula again on the matter — except in the media.

The ANC Youth League, spoiling for a scrap, was among the first to issue a statement decrying the treatment that Billy Masetlha had received. 'We reject the report by Ngcakani … as nothing else but a cover-up … on the basis that Kasrils and Ngcakani were implicated.'[1] Implicated because we were referred to as conspirators in the fake emails? That was a laugh.

The Youth League's stance reflected deepening division within the ANC, which could not be laughed off. In the prevailing climate — perceptions of spy versus spy, accusations of abuse of state power and resources, and fierce contestation between support for Mbeki and for Zuma — analysts were bound to see issues through such a prism.

Even investigative journalists like Sam Sole and Nic Dawes, who only had minor insight into Muzi Kunene's role, saw things that way: 'the situation may not be as clear-cut as a surface reading of the emails suggests. Firstly, mixing fiction with fact for a particular impact is a well-known intelligence technique … Whether this is the case … is not clear. But either way, the emails are evidence of a high-level conspiracy: either against Zuma if they are even partially true, or against Mbeki if they are false.'[2]

The two journalists from the *Mail & Guardian* were not the only ones to deal with the saga in a so-called even-handed manner, seeing no virtue in the incumbent President Mbeki, who must also, in their perception, be as culpable as Zuma. Time has since revealed how adept Zuma was in posing as the innocent victim of an odious conspiracy.

Journalist Paul Vecchiatto took a different approach, dealing with the facts before him, and avoiding any presumptions. He homed in on the smoking gun of the IG's report – the technical inconsistencies of the emails. He quoted one of the country's top national IT specialists: 'The controversial email spoofing by members of the National Intelligence Agency (NIA) has been described as "the work of amateurs with little or no understanding of technology" by Mervin Pearce, a member of the board of directors of the International Information Systems Security Certification Consortium.'[3]

Vecchiatto continued: 'Pearce says the fact that spoof emails could have been generated through technology such as "anonymisers" – websites that help mask the original identity of the sender – or through an "email impersonator" indicates the sender [more accurately, the manufacturer] in this case had very little real knowledge about the internet or IT in general.'

The next step in the email saga was the proposed investigation by the independent ANC task team set up by Kgalema Motlanthe. It was the political commentator Moshoeshoe Monare who commented that 'the hoax emails issue has ensnared Motlanthe' in a conflictual situation with Mbeki, explaining, 'When Motlanthe and a handful of the party's executives resolutely refused to accept a government report dismissing contentious emails as fake, it was a reaffirmation of an extra-parliamentary ANC that did not trust … its own president and state organs.'[4]

The task team was headed by the ANC veteran Hermanus Loots (alias James Stuart). Other members of the team were the veterans Sophie Williams de-Bruyn and Joe Jele and the retired military generals Gilbert Romano and Jackie Sedibe.[5] They were reinforced by the advocate Patric Mtshaulana. He had joined MK in the 1976 generation. I had enjoyed a good relationship with him in the Angolan camps, where he had been harassed for expressing critical views and I had defended his right to express himself.

That all was not well within the task team was evident when we learnt that General Sedibe resigned at the outset and later so did Joe Jele. It took well over a year for the task team's report to be ready for presentation to the NEC. We patiently sat and listened as Hermanus Loots presented the findings, accompanied by Sophie Williams de-Bruyn, General Romano and Advocate Mtshaulana. Joe Jele's absence was notable but not explained.

The gist of the findings, as explained by Loots, was that the emails were genuine and that the inspector general's report was flawed. In particular, Billy Masetlha was vigorously defended. It was argued that the IG was wrong in finding that Masetlha was the author of the emails. 'In our view,' Loots explained, 'this was unfounded,' and the inquiry absolved Masetlha of guilt. If Masetlha was the author, the team argued, why would he want to discredit Judge Khampepe, as he was himself involved in her commission? That was an odd deduction. For me the logic was faulty. Copies of the report were handed out, and I jotted down some notes as Loots held the floor.[6]

Loots rejected the contention that Masetlha was the author of the emails. Yet the IG had never said he was. What the IG discovered was that Masetlha had paid Muzi Kunene for that task. The IG's specialists, the criminologist, police and the IT experts were conclusive in the view that the emails and chat room documentation were bogus. The IG's position was that the criminal proceedings he had recommended would hopefully reveal further evidence, including who was responsible for creating the emails.

What was surprising about the Loots report was that it showed no interest whatsoever in Muzi Kunene, despite his chequered past, his connections with the IFP and SADF intelligence, and his link with Masetlha and with Zuma, even if that was cursory.

While NEC members such as Alec Erwin and Frank Chikane observed at the meeting that the Loots report found no NEC members party to manufacturing the emails, and argued with others for its rejection on the grounds they were not authentic, as proved by the

IG, I was skimming through the attachments to the documentation before us. It appeared that the task team needed to understand how easy it was to 'hack' or intercept computer traffic and discussion groups. One annexure described a very strange night-time odyssey. The team had been taken to the offices of a computer specialist who was adept in the art of 'hacking'. In what read like a hammed-up version of a bad play, Mr X, the hacker, proceeded with his demonstration to the group. I well remember the lines, which went something like: 'Okay, so the equipment is prepared and we will now seek to intercept [pause] ... this is the tense part [pause] ... look how my hands are trembling [pause] ... I must take a drink of water ...' Then eureka! The hacker strikes it lucky. Out of the blue, by sheer fluke, he and the team are party to communication intercepts of Tony Leon engaged in chat room discussion at that very moment in time. How impressive. Like children at a magic party, the observing team appeared — according to their report — to have fallen hook, line and sinker for one of the oldest tricks in the world. No doubts were raised about the coincidence of the chat room being in operation just at the right time for the demonstration. No thought that Mr X might have conceivably concocted the chat room mail and simply had this handy on a prerecorded tape ready to switch on for a naïve audience. Loots and his colleagues had swallowed the bait.

I enquired who had taken the team to Mr X's office and who had conveyed them there. Loots replied that Billy Masetlha had done so. This caused consternation and anger in the NEC. The report was dismissed then and there on the technical grounds that the engagement of the hacker was illegal and the involvement of Masetlha was unprocedural. Unfortunately, it meant that the NEC did not reject the entire Loots report for the utter nonsense it was. The NEC could easily have done so, for virtually all but a small minority were of that view. Pallo Jordan and Baleka Mbete requested that the minutes of the meeting reflect the view that there had been an intelligence project to destroy the ANC; that lessons from the saga needed to be learnt; and that further investigation as recommended by the inspector general was required.

In the end, the NEC resolved that there was no conspiracy against Zuma originating from within the ANC, though he might have been subject to what it called 'hostile action by forces opposed to the National Democratic Revolution'. In this regard, it shifted the suspicion about the origin of the emails to 'reactionary forces' which, the ANC noted, had historically used whispering campaigns as devices 'to disrupt and destroy progressive movements worldwide'.[7] It was not only Zuma who had such suspicions. Revolutionaries all over the world had cause to be vigilant. There were countless CIA-type machinations that had unseated people's leaders and governments through assassinations and coups. Charlatans and demagogues, however, played on such fears and twisted suspicions to their advantage when need arose.

I was not happy with the outcome of the meeting, but at least the NEC had not been deceived and hooked like so many others. The problem was that this type of walking on eggshells to maintain the peace boded ill for the future. All manner of problems could be dealt with by invoking counter-revolutionary foreign forces bent on destroying the ANC.

CHAPTER 16

In Cold Blood

Pretoria High Court, 2011

THE FIRST TIME I SAW Muzi Kunene in the flesh was when he entered a Pretoria court under heavy police guard, in chains. He had been brought directly from prison, where he was serving two years of a life sentence for kidnapping, murder and robbery, which had taken place subsequent to the email saga. He joined Billy Masetlha and Funi Madlala,[1] the NIA cyber unit manager, on a charge of defrauding the National Intelligence Agency of R150,000 in an illegal payment. The charge had been brought by the NIA director general, Manala Manzini.

A well-built, middle-aged man, with a dark shiny dome, Kunene was dressed in a blue tailored suit without tie, complemented by a black silk shirt. Next to him, Masetlha and Madlala looked distinctly shabby as they embraced him. I could see Kunene in his past role as company director and man about town. His appearance was impressive and, without the manacles, one would have thought he was a well-to-do businessman.

As the former minister I had been called to give evidence about the email saga. This was a mere formality and, after a couple of hours of my answering to the prosecution, the defence barely directed questions at me.

While it was interesting to observe Masetlha and Madlala, who were not in custody, I was engrossed by Kunene, and my mind ran back to the gruesome press accounts of the abduction and cold-blooded murder of a luckless estate agent, Lynne Hume, at his hands, which had landed him in prison. By those accounts the man was a merciless killer who had shown no pity whatsoever for a young woman whom he had tricked and robbed and whom he was prepared to murder in order to wipe out his culpability. The kidnapping had taken place in 2007 at Kunene's rented home in Ballito, KwaZulu-Natal, where Lynne Hume had been lured for the purpose of robbing her. She had then been spirited elsewhere to be executed in cold blood. Kunene had attempted to cover his tracks and had returned to his Gauteng home, which was the scene of the IG's raid in 2005. With the investigators of Hume's murder closing in on him, the media had speculated on his bizarre behaviour. Kunene had created a smokescreen, claiming that ANC members were out to eliminate him. The allegation emerged from wild cloak-and-dagger tales he recounted during a radio interview. On his way home, bleeding from a flesh wound to his hand, he claimed he had been followed by two men who had fired shots at him.

There was speculation at the time that he was unhinged and that the wound was self-inflicted. Investigations soon revealed that he had shot himself.

That shooting incident was followed within a week by an armed attack on his son Msebenzi. Kunene Junior was rushed to hospital bleeding from a gunshot wound to the head.[2] Msebenzi Kunene subsequently gave evidence that his father had attempted to silence him because of what he knew about Lynne Hume's murder.

Under the heading 'Kunene gets life in jail', newspapers subsequently reported: 'IT consultant Muzi Kunene was sentenced in the Bloemfontein High Court to life imprisonment for the murder of Ballito estate agent Lynne Hume.'[3] The court found that the accused had driven Hume from Ballito to a remote spot and shot her in the passenger seat of her white Volvo. The car was then set alight. Her body was burned beyond recognition.

In the course of the trial Kunene sought to defend himself by claiming, 'I am a Zuma supporter. That's why I'm being framed.'[5]

Kunene's son, who was party to the murder, was granted indemnity in return for turning state witness against his father.

Referring to the conspiracy theory forwarded by Kunene, the court found that there was no truth in the allegations. Kunene tried to explain away images of himself escorting Lynne Hume from his home which were recorded on CCTV cameras. His story was that an impersonator disguised to look like him had carried out the crime, and that the police had created his double by having a former Koevoet[4] soldier undergo plastic surgery to impersonate him. Kunene also forged an affidavit by a deceased police officer that described an elaborate conspiracy plan by police to frame him. The presiding judge rejected Kunene's defence as a fabrication — the IT work on the policeman's affidavit showed it to be full of clumsy errors.

Observing Kunene in the Pretoria court, two years into his life sentence, I mused over his relationship with Masetlha and his connection with Kgalema Motlanthe, on which the media had speculated. In fairness to Motlanthe, I draw attention to the following report from the *Mail & Guardian* of 25 November 2005. 'A source within the Inspector General's office told the *Mail & Guardian* this week that neither the office nor the police was investigating Motlanthe. "He is not part of our investigation and we do not think it is worthwhile questioning him about the e-mails," the source said.

'According to the source, the only link between Kunene and Motlanthe is the fact that they both hold shares in Pamodzi.[5] "But this is not good enough to link Motlanthe to our investigations."

'It is believed that after he was arrested (on 1 December 2005), Kunene called Motlanthe, among other people, to arrange a lawyer for him. Motlanthe would neither confirm nor deny this when contacted ... this week.

'However, he acknowledged that he knew Kunene. Asked about his business ties with Kunene, Motlanthe said: "I am not a businessman. I do invest a little money that I saved in various companies. I just invest my savings. If I invest money in Standard Bank, I am not in business with whoever invests their money there."'[6]

I believe Motlanthe was genuine in his fixation about the fake emails and must have been tricked. I do not believe in the corruption allegations floated about him in the media, which in time dissipated. I thought of him, then as now, as a principled, dignified and honest man. While he may have been misled, like so many at the time, into believing that Mbeki and people like me were working against him, I am of the view that he was genuine in his belief about the emails. In this respect it is important to highlight a point made in the inspector general's report that Masetlha knowingly used the fabricated material to confuse the secretary general of the ANC, 'whom he conceivably was also seeking to mislead'.[7]

I would accept that Motlanthe believed he was acting in defence of the ANC against a possible group of plotters. One might defend him by arguing that it was morally right to expose one's own government when it resorted to fomenting plots against 'the people'. In that case one has to be extremely careful of one's facts. He bravely contested the post of president against Zuma at the ANC's Mangaung national conference, and he has spoken out powerfully as a voice of principle and sanity against corruption in government. After the disclosures about Kunene, I asked him what he thought of the man, and he told me: 'That man requires help.'

PART THREE

Ordeal

2005–2006

*If you can control your body and your sexual urges,
then you are a man, my son.*
— JUDGE WILLEM VAN DER MERWE
ADDRESSING JACOB ZUMA, MAY 2006

CHAPTER 17

Call from Fezeka

Johannesburg, 4 November 2005

'UNCLE RONNIE, JACOB ZUMA has raped me,' was the call I received on my mobile phone. The woman added, 'This is Fezeka.' My body geared to the shock as though someone was pointing a gun at me: blood ran cold, neck hairs prickled, throat turned dry, mind stuttered.

While the young woman simply used the name 'Jacob Zuma' – 'Jacob Zuma has raped me' – she maintained the formal 'Uncle Ronnie' in addressing me. But the respectful title 'uncle' did not grace Jacob Zuma's name, then nor ever again. This spoke volumes from a cultural point of view. Without that title, Zuma's name, in the mouth of a younger woman, sounded strange, shocking, almost naked, stripped of his clothing, his dignity. Although the voice was steady and strong, almost flat and unemotional, the unadorned terminology pointed to someone who had thrown respectful convention to the winds and was extremely angry and deadly serious.

'Uncle Ronnie, Jacob Zuma has raped me' reverberated in my brain. Was this for real? Was I being set up? Was my phone tapped? Sinister spooks listening in, waiting to catch me out about who knew what? My humanity overcame feelings of fright and flight, and concern for the young woman overrode my fears.

'Fezeka,' I heard myself enquiring hoarsely, 'are you OK?'

'I'm going to charge him.'

'What do you mean "raped"?'

'Jacob Zuma raped me last night.'

'Where?'

'At his house in Forest Town. I visited for dinner and he invited me to stay the night. And he raped me.'

'But did anyone see that? Do you have a witness?' I almost blurted, and immediately felt stupid, for I was struggling to comprehend.

'No,' she said, still keeping remarkably calm. 'The others were all asleep, including his daughter. We all had dinner together. He invited me to see him after that in his room, for a chat. And he raped me.'

'Have you seen a doctor? Are you OK, eh, like any injuries?'

'No physical harm to speak of, but he forced himself on me.'

'The doctor gave you a full examination and you're OK?'

'Am OK. But I am angry.'

I was getting a hold on the story, but could not be sure it was rape. She said he forced himself on her: was she confused, mistaken? I cursed myself: don't think like the conventional male! Like everyone else, I knew Zuma's liking for female flesh, but rape? That accusation as far as I knew had never been flung at him. He certainly could get by on his natural charm, or so I thought.

I was relieved she was not physically harmed. She was over thirty years old, an adult; she had been medically examined, so there was already a doctor involved. That was reassuring.

'What next, Fezeka?'

It appeared she was on her way to lay a rape charge at a police station in Johannesburg, and that she was being accompanied by some women from what sounded like a rape crisis organisation.

That was serious but a relief, for it let me off the hook, I must admit. I asked her why she had called me and she simply explained that she wanted me to be aware of what had happened. I was still in an ambivalent state, feeling torn between human concern for her and my political position. I sensed I should keep her at arm's length for her own good.

For her own good? Was I honest or just minding my own interest? There was an icy hand at my heart. Buck up, I thought. Was I doing the right thing or was I taking the coward's way out?

I asked her what she wanted me to do; and she replied 'nothing'. She just wanted me to be aware.

Maybe I was a bit too studied in my reply, which was something like: 'Well, Fezeka, you're an adult and certainly must decide what's in your interests. I would like to be of help, but if I got involved it would politicise the issue, given the rift that has developed between Zuma and me.' I almost visualised the flapping ears of those possibly bugging the call.

She said she understood and left me to agonise over the situation as I was being driven to a function. 'Did you get the time that call came through?' I asked my protector sitting next to my driver. He confirmed my own observation. The call was made on Friday, 4 November 2005, at exactly 10.40 a.m. I sensed I should make a note of that.

Fezekile Ntsukela Kuzwayo, who soon came to be known at large as Khwezi, was the daughter of a struggle comrade with whom Zuma and I had worked in Swaziland back in the 1980s. His name was Judson Kuzwayo and in those days he went by his MK name of Mthethwa. It was he who was supposed to have picked Zuma and me up near the border with Mozambique on that night I sprained my ankle.

Baba and Homeboy stole into Swaziland on operational missions and often called at the Kuzwayo home, always at night, to avoid the eyes of prying neighbours. Invariably exhausted, they would enjoy home-cooked meals prepared by Fezeka's mother, Beauty Sibongile Kuzwayo. Judson Kuzwayo was a skinny man with a narrow face and high cheekbones who spoke in a staccato manner, business-like and to the point. He and Homeboy enjoyed knocking back a good few rounds of Klipdrift brandy and Coke while relaxing in the sitting room, talking politics and assessing the latest security situation. After serving a ten-year sentence on Robben Island with Zuma, with whom he had been arrested in 1963, he got a job as a researcher at Natal University in Durban and so he was erudite, well read and thoughtful. He commanded a clandestine committee based in Swaziland, with another ex-Durban couple, Ivan and Ray Pillay, as his closest confidants. They had excellent contact with that city and indeed the Natal province, which included an internal machinery, codenamed Providence, of which Pravin Gordhan was a most innovative and reliable head. They had worked closely with Zuma and Judson Kuzwayo in Durban in the mid-1970s after Zuma's and Kuzwayo's release, until they were redeployed outside the country.

Baba and Homeboy would often engage young Fezeka, during her early school years, in light conversation. They were both uncles to her, and she looked forward to seeing them whenever they visited. Fezeka would run errands for them, find newspapers and whatever else they needed, candy for Baba who had a sweet tooth, ice cream for Homeboy. They showered her with both these treats. Homeboy was on hand to assist her with her school work. Both parents were invariably at work during the day, and so, whether Homeboy and Baba were together or on their own, it was Fezeka who was their minder. They would be in and out of the household for just a few days, observing the rule of never staying in the same place for long. They were family, and the young girl was attached to them as her own true uncles, although she was under strict instructions not to tell any of her friends about their visits. When they were staying in the house she was forbidden to bring friends home. She showed a remarkable understanding in this regard and never let out the secret. People in Swaziland well knew of the undercover war being fought from their tiny kingdom and of the killings and shootouts that often took place. The young girl was faithful to her uncles whom she swore to protect. She once saw a bullet-ridden corpse in a township garden nearby and heard the man had been an ANC freedom fighter, like her father and uncles. Nothing would lead her to betray them. When she had not seen them for some months, she would begin nagging her dad: 'Pappa, please Pappa, when are my uncles coming to visit?'

Around 1985, after a series of brutal assassinations by apartheid hit squads, Swaziland became too hot for the Kuzwayos. The ANC deployed Judson and his family to Zimbabwe. He was to die tragically in a car crash later that year and his death left both mother and daughter bereft.

Sometime in February 2005 a young media assistant in my ministry, Kimmy Msibi, informed me that Fezeka Kuzwayo was around and would very much like to see me. I was delighted. Kimmy was of the same age and background as Fezeka. She had always been close to Fezeka, had similarly grown up in exile, and her parents, like the Kuzwayos, had worked with Zuma and me.

Kimmy explained that Fezeka was working in Pretoria in the social welfare sector. She was bright, outgoing and openly lesbian. She had publicly declared herself HIV positive, and actively campaigned on both issues. I arranged for the two of them to come and have tea.

Fezeka strode in with a confident air. Unlike Kimmy, who retained her child-like petiteness, she had emerged as a well-built young adult, strong-boned and athletic, with a jauntiness about her and a fine smile. She was simply dressed in a white blouse and black slacks. As we drank tea, we chatted about the old days and joked about Zuma's and my visits. When we spoke about her father and mother, a note of sadness crept in. She clearly pined for her father while Mama was not very well. She lived in KwaMashu in Durban and Fezeka helped her as best she could. Inquiring about her own life, I was impressed at how open she was about her sexual choice and HIV status. I asked if she was on antiretrovirals, and thought about President Mbeki's beliefs about the causes of HIV when she criticised the medication, holding up her palms and saying they had turned black; she had greater faith, she said, in homeopathic remedies. This brought her to the topic for which it appeared she mainly wished to see me.

She was seeking to study alternative medicine in Australia and was looking for a grant and seeking to raise funds. I promised to discuss possibilities and obtain an estimate of living costs from the Australian High Commission. I would also investigate the possibilities of raising funds through her late father's former colleagues, many of whom were in government. I consequently wrote to half a dozen of them, including Tokyo Sexwale, who had become a well-off businessman. He responded positively. I informed Fezeka sometime during the year but did not hear from her until the telephone call that fateful morning in November 2005.

When I took Fezeka's call I was being driven to a departmental function. Arriving there, I was met by a tense-faced Lorna Daniels, my media officer and Kimmy's chief. She asked if I was aware of the rape allegation as she had already heard of the incident through Kimmy. It was obvious that the story would soon hit the headlines. I hurried over to the president's office to inform Mbeki. I distinctly recall saying to him: 'Mr President, there is a monster walking the land and his name is Jacob Zuma.' It was not that I accepted that Zuma had raped Fezekile Kuzwayo, but just to have taken advantage of her was shocking. Mbeki was as shaken as I was when he heard about the call I had received. For us there was absolutely nothing we could do but let the law take its course. It was assumed Zuma knew about the development.

In the week after that dramatic phone call, two police officers came to see me at my office. Ascertaining that I had received a call from the young woman about her rape allegation, which they were investigating, they asked if I would make a statement. I was surprised and queried the need since I was not a witness to the event. They explained that in rape charges, owing to the fact that there were seldom witnesses to the act, statements from individuals in whom the complainant had confided were acceptable and needed. I realised then why Fezeka had phoned me since she would have been informed of that requirement by those assisting her in laying the charge. I immediately complied and provided a short statement of no more than two pages simply dealing with the phone call. It was a relief when the officers said they did not think they would need to call me to give evidence in the event of a trial.

Rumours of consternation in the Zuma camp abounded. The media began digging around and the gossip was that ANC members close to Zuma, including government ministers, were intervening to pressure Fezeka and her mother to withdraw the complaint and accept some form of compensation. I thought they might succeed as the family was clearly in need of financial assistance. The ANC had strong influence over Beauty Kuzwayo, who was a loyal veteran, and the prospect for any but the most courageous of women going through a rape trial, and such a sensational one as this, was daunting not just for Fezeka but for her mother. For all the hope for a fair trial and justice in a democratic South Africa, a bias in favour of males was the cross that the country's women were forced to go on bearing when it came to sexual violence and abuse.

Fezeka was not the kind of person to be bought off by money or stopped by intimidation. Zuma's allies failed in their endeavours, including enormous and wilful pressure from 'aunties' to whom she had once been extremely close. This demonstrated how determined she was and that her vulnerable mother, despite pressure from the ANC, stood by her daughter. Undoubtedly Zuma's intermediaries made handsome offers. The fact that Fezekile and her mother turned them down spoke volumes about her courage and dignity, and the shamelessness of those seeking to shut her up.

CHAPTER 18

Kanga Man

Johannesburg, November 2005 to May 2006

THEN THE WRATH BEGAN to turn on me. In the conspiratorial mood of the country, there had to be a culprit to exculpate the accused. Zuma had long shown he was adroit at the blame game and at playing the victim. The ANC closed ranks if it was under siege, understandably during the struggle against apartheid, but unforgivably to protect leaders under fire in the new democratic era, regardless of what they had done.

The story going the rounds was that I had sprung a 'honey trap' on the unfortunate Zuma, knowing his notorious incapacity to control his libido. The idea was laughable. If I was a devious mastermind, I certainly would not have banked on Zuma being enticed into bed by an HIV-positive lesbian, and the child of a much respected struggle colleague at that. I would have thought he would have had some respect for his former comrade, particularly in view of his tendency to play on his Zulu culture.

The narrative circulated by the rumour mill went this way: since I had received a phone call from Fezeka before she charged Zuma, I must have directed her to do so. The very fact that I knew her, that she called me Uncle, that her friend Kimmy worked for me, all combined to prove my complicity. The fact that I was Mbeki's minister pointed to him as the source of all Zuma's misfortunes. The story certainly took hold for some time. Even the media and opposition parties bought into it, to some extent. In my view those who had were befuddled by the belief that Mbeki, the black intellectual, the remote leader, to them a Machiavellian figure, must somehow be implicated in a conspiracy against Zuma. This was the prism through which some looked at the whole issue. Certain commentators thought that being even-handed, six of one and half a dozen of the other, made them objective. But it only turned them into suckers for Zuma's conspiracy theory. Mbeki's hand had to be involved and he had to bear responsibility as well.

Much has been written about Zuma's rape trial, which commenced in the Johannesburg High Court in March 2006. Judge Willem van der Merwe, a middle-aged, conservative white male presided. By all accounts he was very much steeped in the prevailing male-orientated ethos. Zuma had the luck of the draw.

There is nothing new I can shed on that hugely reported trial, but I want to highlight some absurdities both inside and outside the court, where the unfortunate Fezeka, referred to at that time as 'Khwezi' for the sake of anonymity, was metaphorically hanged, drawn and quartered.

What was commonly accepted by both sides was that the 61-year-old accused was a family friend of the 31-year-old complainant. She visited him at his residence in Forest Town, Johannesburg, on 2 November 2005 and after dinner stayed the night. Later that evening a sexual encounter occurred.

The crux of the state's case was that Zuma had a sexual act with Fezeka against her will, after inviting her to stay the night. The defence's case was that sexual intercourse between the two had taken place, though it was consensual, after Fezeka had behaved in a sexually provocative manner. At no stage had Zuma believed the sexual encounter was against her will. Zuma's daughter Duduzile (child of his late wife Kate) was in the house and a policeman was outside on duty. Neither was made aware of any protest by Fezeka, who had a mobile phone and who could have left at any time. Zuma's lawyers were controversially permitted to lead evidence that she had a record of making similar allegations of rape against a number of males over the years.[1]

The mob that gathered outside the court as proceedings commenced has cast abiding shame on Zuma and on the ANC and its allies. Their antics were akin to a medieval witch-hunting frenzy. 'Burn the bitch!' the mob screeched while burning photographs of Fezeka. Her real name and address, not known at that time outside ANC circles, was distributed in a sinister act of intimidation. Who can ever forget Zuma egging on his supporters, with his bellicose rendition of the MK song 'Bring me my machine gun' at the end of every day's proceedings. In all the years of exile, in all my years in the military camps, I had never before witnessed him singing that song. That stirring warrior song, which had inspired so many in the struggle against apartheid, was debased by Zuma for all time. The conductor-in-chief of the lynch mob was the ANC Youth League leader, Fikile Mbalula. In 2009 he was rewarded by President Zuma with the post of deputy minister of police, later minister of sport, and then of police. Co-leader of the bloodhounds was none other than the YCL chief, Buti Manamela. He did his best to ingratiate himself with the abuser. If Zuma did not rape young Fezeka, he certainly abused her, first at his home and, ruthlessly, again and again in court and in the public arena. Manamela was duly rewarded with a post as deputy minister in the Presidency itself.

There was nobody more frenetic than a woman from Zuma's home province dressed in traditional regalia who gyrated obscenely, impersonating Fezeka's 'enjoyment' of the sex act to the delight of the throng who encouraged her as though at a Roman orgy. At the first opportunity the ANC made her a member of parliament in recognition of her antics. Not to be outdone, the ANC Youth League called on people to attack those who supported Fezeka. Senior ANC, Cosatu and SACP leaders were invariably in attendance, with nary a sober word of rebuke against this disgraceful spectacle of gender intimidation and misogyny. They brought the whole country into disrepute. I could not believe these were leaders I had once found impressive.

Certain aspects of Zuma's evidence, and the way in which his defence was conducted, have stuck in the public domain, by no means to his credit. Even more than Italy's one-time premier, Silvio Berlusconi, with his corrupt practices and 'bunga bunga'[2] escapades, Zuma must be the most ridiculed head of state of modern times.

What was unusual was Zuma's decision to give his evidence in Zulu, although he was fluent in English, the language of the court. The choice reinforced his portrayal of himself as the embodiment of the traditional Zulu male — a simple man from Nkandla — who, as the *New York Times* correspondent observed, claimed 'all the privileges that patriarchal Zulu tradition bestows on men'.[3]

In explaining Fezeka's alleged provocative behaviour, Zuma recounted how she had visited him wearing a skirt: an ordinary knee-length skirt, not a miniskirt. 'She used to come to my place dressed in pants but on this occasion she came dressed in a skirt. And the way she was sitting in the lounge was not the usual way I know her to be sitting … [She] had not kept her legs crossed together but they were open.' It appears the courageous freedom fighter was subverted by the mere sight of a woman's thighs. Later that evening, before going to bed, Fezeka had 'changed into a kanga',[4] which Zuma said 'was a sexually provocative outfit', although it is worn daily by millions of African women throughout the continent.

Then there was the choice of baby oil with which he gave the young woman a massage. Claiming this had sexually aroused her, he explained, under cross-examination, why he had proceeded with penetrative sex when he did not have a condom: 'In the Zulu culture you do not just leave a woman in that situation because she may even have you arrested and say you are a rapist.'

He agreed that the government-sponsored Moral Regeneration Movement, which he chaired, 'was about bringing back the morals, the values, the traditions' of society with an emphasis on HIV/Aids and condom use, and that he 'many times said that leaders must take responsibility in that regard'. He would later apologise to the nation for aspects of his behaviour that were so remiss in respect of the responsibilities he shouldered. But he never apologised to Fezeka or to Beauty Kuzwayo, his one-time close friend.

The most talked-about evidence was the reason Zuma gave for taking a hot shower immediately after his sexual bout with the young woman. 'Because it is one of the reasons that would minimise the risk of contracting the [AIDS] disease,' he explained to the court. The whole country was agog.

Fezeka said in court that she 'had frozen' when the rape began, and for its duration, and therefore did not cry out for help. This explanation was dismissed by the judge. He accepted Zuma's argument of consensual sex, stressing that she had cooperated and did not cry out for help. He rejected the opinion of a clinical psychologist who said that Fezeka's lack of resistance to Zuma was probably due to the disproportionate power relationship between the two.

The judge took little account of expert opinion that could have helped him understand Fezeka's version, or ensured that he recognised the challenge that victims invariably face in rape trials of making themselves heard. He largely ignored, or did not appear to understand, evidence that helped clarify the extremely complex and multi-layered interactions that might lock a young victim into silence. As the Congolese historian and activist Jacques Depelchin explains: 'The silence of the rape victim does not mean that rape did not take place ... The silences or repressed silences are the result of power relations.'[5]

Judge Van der Merwe did not address at all the many contesting impulses evident in Fezeka's evidence. He flatly dismissed her contention that Zuma was her '*malume*' and that she deferred to him — arguably the key to why she 'froze' and why she had difficulty making a scene in his house.

In his evidence Zuma had discounted a familial relationship with Fezeka on the grounds that all children used such terminology as '*malume*' in Zulu and African custom, and that he consequently was not inhibited or duty-bound to observe the relationship of a real uncle in his interaction with her.

Beauty Kuzwayo gave evidence in support of her daughter, but Judge Van der Merwe dismissed it as 'incoherent'. Beauty was not only elderly, and under enormous pressure from the ANC, the organisation for which her husband had given his life, but she was a nervous woman, easily flustered, who would have been feeling extremely uncomfortable in Jacob Zuma's presence in court and with the baying mob outside. Perhaps the most surprising evidence allowed by the court was the sensitive revelations from Fezeka's private papers which the defence produced. The manner by which the document, a draft memoir in her hand, had been acquired was sinister and took the young woman by surprise. In it she wrote about her sexual experiences and abuse suffered as a child, which she referred to as rape. It was common knowledge within the ANC's exile community that there had been instances where she had been sexually abused by young males, and probably raped, after her father's death. This had led at the time to an ANC investigation which was not successfully concluded. Many observers believe that the court should not have accepted her sexual history as admissible evidence. This was compounded by the court allowing the defence to parade witnesses who claimed to have had consensual sex with her, after which, they alleged, she said they had raped her.

Former Constitutional Court judge Zak Yacoob has commented on the way that Fezeka Kuzwayo was treated during the trial.[6] He was making a point at a workshop about the way that the sexual histories of women victims are used as mitigating factors in rape cases. Yacoob said the sexual histories of rape accusers such as Fezeka were 'irrelevant' in his view, and so he would not have factored them into his judgment if he were hearing the case. He did not comment about the strength of the evidence against Zuma but about the treatment of the young woman by the court.

Yacoob said that in court cases there were always two narratives. Fezeka's was rejected because she was painted as someone who had previously demanded sex and who did not report the rape quickly enough. He said he would have disregarded this objection if he was hearing the case. 'On the basis of how the witness was treated, I may have found differently. But I would not have criticised the witness for not having reported the incident early. I would not have taken into account that she had demanded sex from people before, because as far as I was concerned that is irrelevant; even a prostitute has the right to say "no".'

Concluding his remarks, Yacoob observed: 'Judgments are not black and white. They are nuanced and very complicated. And it is quite impossible to say that a judge was right or wrong, although it is possible to say that judges may have differences of opinion.'

In the evidence he gave to the court, Zuma told the tale of a conspiratorial web that had been woven around him. When he referred to people out to destroy his career, the judge asked who they were. I was watching on television as Zuma answered without a pause: 'Bulelani Ngcuka and Ronnie Kasrils.'

I recalled the number of times in meetings of the ANC's NEC when I had challenged him to substantiate his vague claims that there was a conspiracy against him. Sitting next to the ever polite and far too diplomatically silent Mbeki, he would decline and say the time was not ripe. Every time he behaved in that enigmatic way, throwing out unsubstantiated allegations, I could not but think of the fate of Thami Zulu – the not 100 per cent Zulu. I noted that the respected Judge Willem van der Merwe failed to ask him if he could substantiate the allegation he made against me and Bulelani. It went unchallenged. How I wished I had been called to appear for Fezeka as a witness.

Judge Van der Merwe accordingly found Zuma not guilty of raping Fezekile Kuzwayo. He concluded, however, that Rudyard Kipling might well have added to his well-known poem 'If' the following line appropriate to Zuma: 'If you can control your body and your sexual urges, then you are a man, my son.'

Zuma was a greatly relieved man but, having played the culture card so manifestly, what a humiliating slap that quasi-Kipling line from a white Afrikaner judge should have been. But if you have no sense of shame, then such a remark must be inconsequential.

Jacob Zuma certainly did not follow the judge's advice. Following the rape trial, the ANC leadership compelled Zuma to pledge that he would no longer engage in extramarital sex, which he soon flouted. It is obvious that for them and their truant leader pledges are meaningless.

Zuma had been found not guilty of rape. As far as the ANC was concerned, he was therefore eligible to become its leader and the country's future president. That certainly meant Gwede Mantashe's vulgar argument against 'morality' was now the accepted norm. But it was a norm that refused to acknowledge that Zuma's behaviour, during the sexual encounter, afterwards and throughout his trial, was abusive and exploitative. It should have been inappropriate for any citizen, but inconceivable, I would have assumed, for a man aspiring to become president of a once proud movement and country.

Even before the trial Zwelinzima Vavi, the charismatic Cosatu leader, had expressed support for a future Zuma presidency. He declared in 2005 that the pressure building up for a Zuma presidency, which would sweep Mbeki away, was an 'unstoppable tsunami'. For Vavi the manner in which the Shaik trial had been run was a 'systematic campaign' to assassinate Zuma's character. In time he would confess to having been profoundly misled. He forgot that a tsunami sweeps away all before it. Another fervent Zuma supporter of the time, the beguiling ANC youth leader Julius Malema, followed in Vavi's footsteps. Having drummed up support for Zuma's defence, he remarked then: 'No one who gets raped stays for breakfast.' He was young and unpolished, and had been wooed by Zuma, who effusively declared that he had the makings of a future president. But he was to grow into manhood and become the bane of Zuma's life. To his credit Julius Malema later expressed a profound apology to Fezeka as he did to others he had insulted, such as Thabo Mbeki and Helen Zille, the DA leader.

A courageous criticism of Zuma came from an ANC stalwart, Joyce Sikhakhane-Rankin. She knew the Kuzwayo family from their time in Zimbabwe. Fezeka had stayed with her for a while after her father's death, and Joyce was acquainted with her psychological condition and the sexual abuse she had suffered after losing the protection of her deceased father.

Phoning in to a radio talk show, she said that if the young woman had indeed wanted sex with Zuma, as the judge had found, then Zuma should have rejected any notion of sharing his bed with her, and called a taxi to take her home.

In the court of public opinion there were no doubts. Zuma had escaped a guilty verdict on the charge of rape, but the callous manner in which he had taken advantage of the young woman was undoubtedly abusive and a stain on his character. Zapiro captured the outrage best in a cartoon which will certainly characterise for all time the Zuma legacy: the showerhead protruding from his elongated skull.

PART FOUR

Cry 'Havoc!'

2006–2008

.

Cry 'Havoc!', and let slip the dogs of war.
— William Shakespeare, *Julius Caesar*

CHAPTER 19

The Dogs of War
National Executive Committee meeting,
Esselen Park, 2006

FOLLOWING ZUMA'S ACQUITTAL on the rape charge, the NEC met to take
stock of the implications of this outcome, including his assertion that
there was a conspiracy against him. I took careful notes of some parts
of what was a lively and revealing discussion. I am consequently able
to give an accurate account, certainly of my own contribution, which
follows in the form I noted it:

1. A most critical point in our history – a turning point? How we
   answer the questions posed by Thoko [Didiza], Frene [Ginwala][1]
   and others will determine whether we seize defeat from the jaws of
   victory of 1994. Forces watch, as Geraldine [Fraser-Moleketi] said,
   who want to see us destroy ourselves. Turning point? Issues of our
   morality/integrity particularly and bound up with all our hallowed
   principles – issue of women's emancipation most particularly/ and
   that impacts on every facet of our society and its development/
   particularly national psyche/ issues fundamental to the progressive
   development of our society and its impact in Africa and the world.
   Either go forward or in danger of sliding backwards. All thrown
   into question because of nature of defence in JZ [rape] trial.

2. Not JZ bashing. As Sankie [Mthembi-Mahanyele, deputy secretary of the ANC] had pointed out, our debate stems from NEC decision to consider many issues arising out of the court case.

3. Some rejoice at acquittal, but need to/forced to interrogate the issues. Judge: 'JZ has only himself to blame.' Trial challenges our principles on sexual relations — not an issue of adultery.

4. JZ supporters cry Foul! He is not to blame. She was a Jezebel, entrapped him/ Honey trap set by those plotting to bring him down — regardless of her HIV status. Such conspiracy relieves him of culpability. An Alice in Wonderland subversion of facts. A pitiful excuse to hide one's own errors — and blame one's misdemeanours — whether corruption etc. — on others. Rest of world has conspired — President, Cabinet, state officials, law enforcement agencies, judiciary, media, Western agents, etc.

5. I congratulated JZ. Asked [him] why he said in court I'm against him? [He] said 'let's talk later'.[2] [I was] not concerned just about myself but fate of all. Agree with Frene [Ginwala]: 'We must ask for evidence of this conspiracy!'

6. Conspiracy: Throughout history practitioners of Machiavelli not Marx ... — Revolutionaries follow progressive morality and ethics in Politics and Life. ANC tradition — to work things out through democratic process. Yet, at this time, we do face a conspiracy. Facts — skulduggery at NIA — up to necks in email plot aim of which to give credibility to anti-Zuma plot. Emails — traitor-made — clumsy: 'Oh, what a [tangled] web we weave when first we practise to deceive.' A pale imitation of apartheid-era Stratcom dirty tricks — Meiring Report 1998. There is a hand behind the plotters. Who? Guess?[3]

7. Naledi [Pandor]: Octavius [Caesar] to M.A. [Mark Antony] 'let loose dogs of war'.[4] The consequence of unchecked plot. Linked to cries of 'burn the witches' — Stalin purges! We dare not go down that road to hell. Plot getting so thick with intrigue it's near point [of] no return. Some boast: 'Die is cast for 2007 [Polokwane] and it's going to be a slaughter.'

8. What needs to be said: 'For God's sake, cool it.' Suppress one's own ambitions for sake of movement. Find credible candidate who can unite us all behind progressive ANC policies and Alliance platform. That is the imperative. The fundamental need. That is required to ensure a Turning Point that is the correct one – not one that leads to ruin. Ten years' time let our country bless us not condemn us. Ho Chi Minh: 'Greater the unity, greater the victory. More unity – more victories.'

9. Funny thing about Julius Caesar: Cassius, Brutus think Caesar wants more power. Kill him. Mark Antony incites the crowd – burn Rome. True motives revealed: Hit list [drawn up] with Octavius and [the oaf] Lepidus [a stooge whom they use]. Finally Octavius vs M.A. [the latter is defeated and killed with his lover and ally Cleopatra, and Octavius becomes emperor of Rome].

I had neatly jotted the points down while others were speaking. This was uncommon since I normally scribbled out short notes, but the meeting was of such import that I wanted to be sure of my contribution. In the event I summarised it in the delivery. When I got to the end about drawing up lists and bumping off rivals, I remember Cyril Ramaphosa in particular laughing his head off.

Communist Party comrades remarked afterwards that it was an interesting speech. One of them, it might have been Blade Nzimande, who always treated me with respect and a touch of warmth, said, 'The problem is, Khumalo [my *nom de guerre*], your Man wants a third term.' The reference was to Mbeki, and this desire on his part had arguably become one of the biggest bones of contention uniting those who turned to Zuma, and cast Mbeki into the mould of an ambitious Caesar.

CHAPTER 20

Polokwane Tsunami

Polokwane, Limpopo province,
16–20 December 2007

No AMOUNT OF SCANDAL appeared to deflect Zuma's fanatical following. They might well take solace in the fact that the judge in the rape trial had found cause to declare him not guilty, but his degenerate behaviour and lack of moral integrity, which pointed to a grossly flawed character, would have penalised him from membership – never mind leadership – in any half-decent organisation. Despite obvious shortcomings, his adherents turned a blind eye to his shameless faults and touted him as a credible leader. At the expense of the ANC and the country, many in this broad grouping, with no ideological axes to grind, were prepared to ignore his follies, for they saw in him the man who could topple the despised Mbeki. The SACP and Cosatu, with their decidedly ideological concerns, might have regarded Zuma as the best prospect for opening up space for the left, but in my view this rendered them as complicit as the emergent crony capitalists and rent-seeking opportunists who protected him. Zuma was adept at playing the part of the simple country man, the innocent victim. Time and again, this proved the winning card in appealing to the sympathy of sections of the masses – the wretched of the earth on the receiving end of misfortune. Some were conned by guile and deceit into identifying with their folksy hero as the answer to their fervent prayers; none more so than the political leadership behind the tsunami call.

Zuma's opportunity would come at the ANC's 52nd national conference in the northern town of Polokwane from 16 to 20 December 2007. One of the obstacles in the way was the Scorpions, the anti-corruption and anti-fraud investigation unit, whose ardent prosecutors believed they had a solid case to have Zuma charged after their success in the Schabir Shaik trial. Time was running out, however, for at that national conference an unprecedented number of delegates would vote to either retain Mbeki or, in all probability, replace him with Zuma, who was the clear favourite. They would also elect a new National Executive Committee.

The Scorpions were established with much fanfare in 2000 as an arm of the National Prosecuting Authority (NPA). The minister of police at the time, the ANC stalwart Steve Tshwete, had provided the Directorate of Special Operations with what became its popular name. The Scorpions' function was to gather information about crime, fraud, racketeering and corruption at the highest levels, and arm the state with intelligence-driven prosecutions. Scorpions investigators were expected to operate without fear or favour, whether the culprits were senior public figures or not, and combat the alarming level of crime and corruption in the country. This meant their likely targets were Mafia-style crime bosses, corporate executives in the business world, corrupt politicians, and state officials including police chiefs. The key objective had to be to acquire evidence as damning as possible to get the culprits in the dock. As Nelson Mandela had previously urged the NPA: 'In upholding the rule of law, the emphasis must be on court No. 1, No. 2 and No. 3.'[1]

It is hardly surprising that with such a remit the unit would find itself in a turf war with the police and the National Intelligence Agency (NIA) and come up against extremely powerful opponents. These allegedly included former liberation struggle personalities within the state, who took entitlement to the extreme levels of 'it's our turn to eat' or 'payback time' for the sacrifices they and their families had endured during the struggle. They believed, or so it was perceived, that they were above the law and that Mbeki was duty-bound to protect them from unwelcome investigation by apartheid-era sleuths. Since he had not met such expectations, the already flawed Zuma was their star.

The tasks of Tshwete's Scorpions could be dangerous work. There could be an ugly backlash particularly when a network of patronage was involved. Not surprisingly, therefore, the next hate figures in the firing line for the Zuma faction was the head of the Scorpions, Leonard McCarthy, and his former boss, Bulelani Ngcuka. I had once met McCarthy at a social function prior to taking over the intelligence portfolio. I again encountered him in his official capacity early in 2005 when he briefed a group of ministers, including Charles Nqakula, the safety and security minister, Brigitte Mabandla, the minister of justice, me and others in the cabinet's security cluster.[2] This meeting concerned outstanding Truth and Reconciliation Commission (TRC) matters pertaining to the list of ANC members, Mbeki among them, that were potentially subject to prosecution, owing to the fact that they had not applied for individual indemnity. I had been impressed then by what I considered McCarthy's professional manner, his commitment to his duties, his ability and practical approach to resolving the problems at hand – which he did, in this case, without much fuss or rancour.

When I emerged as the solitary minister supporting the retention of the Scorpions at the time of the Khampepe Commission in July 2005, McCarthy sought my counsel. He was seeking advice as to how the Scorpions could resolve the objections they faced, as expressed, for example, in Billy Masetlha's submission, urging that they fall under the police service. By 2005 the director of the NPA, Bulelani Ngcuka, under whom the Scorpions resided, had resigned his position to go into business, and McCarthy had lost a confidant and friend. He made no bones about not having the struggle background to fully assess the political chemistry of the ruling power and government, and now and again he sought my insight. He prided himself on coming from a solid family background, with religious parents and a father who had been a dedicated school inspector. He often quoted the down-to-earth words of wisdom of his father. He had studied law and became a public prosecutor in the latter years of the apartheid era. As a man of mixed race he had to be dedicated to make his mark. He had not been involved in the struggle at all, which put him at a decided disadvantage with ANC colleagues, who looked down on him. But he was a tall, imposing figure and not intimidated. Notwithstanding his disadvantages, his devotion to duty and professionalism were not overlooked, and were much in demand, and he was soon placed in important posts, leading to his senior appointment as deputy head of the NPA and director of the Scorpions. There were those in the ANC who had come under suspicion of corruption that perceived that McCarthy and his boss, Ngcuka, had deliberately sought to carry out probes into their lives. I have mentioned my opinion that it would have been preferable had an independent committee been established to decide for the Scorpions which cases to take on, thus distancing them from unpopular decisions and the inevitable allegations of selectivity.

Perhaps the single most significant event that dogged McCarthy's career, and arguably South Africa's fate, occurred in 2001. This was when Bulelani Ngcuka, as head of the NPA, sensationally announced to a select group of newspaper editors that in the wake of Schabir Shaik's arraignment on corruption charges, Jacob Zuma was not being charged. This, despite the fact that Ngcuka declared there was prima facie evidence against Zuma. If anyone was left to handle the hot potatoes, it was Leonard McCarthy and also Advocate Vusi Pikoli, Ngcuka's successor in the NPA hot seat and a former ANC activist.[3]

During 2007 the NPA's case against Zuma was coming to a head. Pikoli, who would have been a strong and reliable leader of the NPA, ran into controversy and was suspended by Mbeki, ostensibly for 'granting amnesty for criminals' who were prepared to implicate the police commissioner, Jackie Selebi, in corrupt deals. Pikoli's explanation for what some perceived as Mbeki's action in protecting Selebi from prosecution was that in the ANC there was a culture he had bucked: that of 'covering up for comrades'.[4] Mbeki's actions did not assist perceptions that while he protected Selebi, he was unwilling to lift a finger for others, Zuma chief among them. Pikoli was subject to a commission of inquiry and dismissed from the post by Kgalema Motlanthe, who served a nine-month interregnum as president between Mbeki and Zuma.[5] With the new director of the NPA, Mokotedi Mpshe, out of his depth and lacking confidence, McCarthy was searching for some political insight when he came to see me.

He sought my counsel as he was being pressed by his team of prosecutors to charge Zuma before the year's end. The problem was the fast-approaching ANC national conference, and the question was whether to serve the indictment on Zuma before or after the event. In meeting him, I made it clear that I would have nothing to say on whether Zuma should be prosecuted or not. Doing so would be a case of violating the law and interfering with the course of justice. This was an independent question for the NPA and Scorpions, and I respected the separation of powers between the executive (my role as minister) and the judiciary (represented by McCarthy). I was prepared, however, to provide insight into the political processes then under way of which he claimed ignorance – or at least an area where he felt out of his depth. While he may not have been as naïve as he sounded, I did not mind if he was interested in comparing opinions. That was fair enough. My responsibility as intelligence minister was obviously enhanced by interacting with the likes of the head of the Scorpions. From time to time, tea with McCarthy was mutually useful and gave me a clearer view of what was happening within the prosecutorial arena.

The ANC's organisational structures held their provincial nomination conferences in October and November 2007. At these gatherings Zuma emerged as a clear favourite for the post of ANC president and, by implication, the future president of South Africa come the 2009 national elections. The rivalry between the Mbeki and Zuma groupings was heating up and became more intense than anything else experienced in the ANC's long history. There had never been so much at stake. The Scorpions feared that if Zuma defeated Mbeki and became ANC president, thereby virtually being guaranteed the national presidency, it would prove highly controversial, and almost impossible, to even consider charging him thereafter. The dilemma McCarthy faced was whether the prosecuting authority should charge Zuma on the eve of the conference or after – in both instances courting hostility. A real dilemma of damned if they did and damned if they did not. What it boiled down to, since they were on course to charge him, was a question of timing. I was not the only minister or government official to view the charging of Zuma on the eve of the conference as playing with fire. And I told McCarthy that the fire would see blood at Polokwane and throughout the country. Would it make any difference, if they waited until after the conference, whether Zuma won or not?

The prosecutors to a person were firmly of the view that the decision should ignore political considerations, and that they should act immediately. If they did not strike then and there, and Zuma won the electoral stand-off with Mbeki, the chance of ever charging Zuma, it was argued, would be irretrievably lost. It was a strong argument, but I felt that charging Zuma beforehand would be unnecessarily provocative and would quite probably unleash violence beyond imagination, so pent up with anger and hostility were the Zuma forces, and they were in the ascendancy. I know that I was not alone in that view and that McCarthy was bound to have consulted others. I expressed my opinion in good faith, nothing more and nothing less. As it transpired, Zuma was charged on 28 December, just over a week after the Polokwane outcome.

I did not have a good feeling on the road to Polokwane, a three-hour drive north of Pretoria on the national highway to Zimbabwe. I found myself reflecting on what Bob Hughes, British Labour Party MP and leader of the Anti-Apartheid Movement, had said to me in 1993 on a visit to his country's parliament. Pointing out where the ruling Labour Party front benchers sat, he remarked in jest that opposite was the Tory opposition and behind his party's leaders were 'the enemy' – the party's own back benchers, ever waiting the chance to supplant them. Little did I imagine that in our democratic South Africa those who had fought for freedom would have to watch their own backs as the inner-party struggle for position took hold with particular venom in the run-up to Polokwane. Truly, the revolution sometimes does devour its own children.[6]

The dramatic result of the conference is well known. It was the tsunami that Zwelinzima Vavi had predicted. He was referring to the ire and determination of the coalition of forces that had crystallised around Zuma and against Mbeki, incensed by more than anything that Mbeki's standing for a third term as ANC party leader was indicative of his ambition and an obvious vote of no confidence in Zuma.[7]

For those, like me, who had campaigned for Mbeki, it was a bitter blow and far more so than being knocked down with a feather, for although we had been hopeful, the slap-down had not come out of the blue. It was depressing for the losers. Not because we lost but because of the ugly, unprecedented and disturbing scenes of disrespect for the incumbent leadership. This had been televised throughout the country, and ANC veterans and supporters glued to the TV screens were numbed with shock and disbelief. Telephone lines were buzzing across the land as comrades contacted one another in sheer disbelief at that uncouth behaviour so alien to ANC culture.

I had attended all ANC national elective conferences since the movement's unbanning: Durban 1991, Bloemfontein 1994, Mafeking 1997 (when Mandela stepped down), and Stellenbosch 2002.[8] These had all been impressive and unifying events of high spirit and morale. Even the leading posts had been contested but in good grace. From the moment one arrived in Polokwane, an entirely alien spirit dominated. If you were an Mbeki supporter or, worse still, part of the NEC on the platform in front of almost four thousand delegates, it was like facing a lynch mob baying for blood. Our supporters were clearly in the minority. As the vote count turned out, the Mbeki share amounted to approximately 40 per cent of votes cast. And from day one they were drowned out by an ugly roaring tide that was frightening and vulgar. Mosiuoa 'Terror' Lekota did a valiant job as chairman, struggling to subdue the ribald jeering, as he strove to get the agenda adopted and business under way, but his was a lost cause. He was drowned out by the singing of Zuma's theme song 'Umshini wam'[9] in a sarcastic rejoinder to the criticism Lekota had made about its inappropriateness

Ronnie Kasrils in Angola, 1986, with fellow MK officers, Jabulani Jali (left) and Lulamile Dantile (right), who was assassinated in Lesotho later that year (Photo: *Armed & Dangerous*, Jacana Media, 2013)

Author's collection: Russian Makarov pistol with 9mm cartridges; Mozambican and Angolan identity documents; MK Luthuli Detachment Medal (Photo: David Nidree)

Ronnie Kasrils with Jacob Zuma, London, 1988 (Photo: Eleanor Kasrils, author's collection)

Joe Slovo, Ronnie Kasrils and Jacob Zuma, ANC NEC meeting, 1993 (Photo: Nigel Dennis)

Trevor Manuel, Jacob Zuma and Ronnie Kasrils, ANC NEC meeting, Hela Safari Ranch, Gauteng, 1992 (Photo: Khulu Mbatha Trust)

Author, appearing from the 'underground', being introduced at SACP Mass Rally, FNB Stadium, Soweto, July 1990 (Photo: Robert M Botha, *Business Day*)

From left: Minister of Defence Joe Modise, Linda Mti, Walile Nhlapo, Billy Masetlha, Abba Omar, Barry Gilder, Jackie Selebi and Deputy Minister of Defence Ronnie Kasrils, at the Umkhonto weSizwe medal awards, Defence ministry, Pretoria, 1996 (Photo: Ministry of Defence and author's collection)

Deputy Minister of Defence Ronnie Kasrils, with Minister of Defence Joe Modise, and Minister of Finance Trevor Manuel (foreground), during the defence budget debate, Parliament, Cape Town, 1998 (Photo: SA Parliament)

From left: Ronnie Kasrils, Thandi Modise, Fidel Castro, Blade Nzimande and Ahmed Kathrada, Robben Island, 1998 (Photo: Eleanor Kasrils, author's collection)

Deputy President Jacob Zuma, Zulu King Goodwill Zwelithini, Minister of Water Affairs and Forestry Ronnie Kasrils and Premier of KwaZulu-Natal S'bu Ndebele, at the renaming of the Chelmsford Dam after Zulu general Ntshingwayo, KwaZulu Natal, 2000.

From left: Ronnie Kasrils, Joe Modise, President Nelson Mandela, Admiral R. Simpson-Anderson, on board *The Protea* for a South African Naval Review, Table Bay, Cape Town, 1998 (Photo: Eleanor Kasrils, author's collection)

Thabo Mbeki and Ronnie Kasrils salute the ANCs 1999 election victory, which led to Mbeki becoming the country's president (Photo: AP/Peter de Jong)

President Thabo Mbeki presents veteran Joyce Sikhakhane-Rankin the Intelligence Services Woman of the Year Award, Intelligence Services Day, Pretoria, November 2005, while Kasrils looks on (Photo: Department of Intelligence Services and author's collection)

Kasrils laying wreath at the Wall of Remembrance, Intelligence Services Day, Pretoria, November 2005 (Photo: Department of Intelligence Services and author's collection)

Muzi Kunene (Photo: *Sunday Argus*, 31 May 2009)

Author with President Mbeki planting a tree, Garden of Rememberance, Intelligence Services Day, Pretoria, November 2005 (author's collection)

Author with President Mbeki, Intelligence Services Day, Pretoria, November 2005 (author's collection)

Mbeki peruses the Book of Rememberance, Intelligence Services Day, Pretoria, November 2005 (author's collection)

Kasrils receiving an award from President Zuma during MK Military Veterans Medal Parade, Airforce Base, Bloemfontein, August 2013 (Photo: GCIS)

Denis Goldberg, MK veteran and Rivonia Trialist, with Kasrils at the Umkhonto weSizwe medal awards, Bloemfontein, August 2013 (Photo: Amina Frense, author's collection)

Kasrils addressing a Right2Know protest rally, outside Parliament, against the Protection of State Information Bill, 2012 (Photo: Amina Frense, author's collection)

Nozizwe Madlala-Routledge with Kasrils at the launch of Sidikiwe! Vukani! National election campaign, Witwatersrand university, Johannesburg, April 2014 (Photo: Gallo Images)

From left: Former President Kgalema Motlanthe, Ronnie Kasrils and Aziz Pahad, at a exhibition, Liliesleaf Museum, Rivonia (Photo: *Sunday Times*, 8 March 2015)

Dali Mpofu, EFF chairman and Kasrils's advocate, at the People's Assembly, University of Johannesburg, Soweto campus, April 2016 (Photo: *Sunday Independent*, 17 April 2016)

Retired Constitutional Court Judge Zak Yacoob (right) speaking at a civil society protest gathering on the steps of the Constitutional Court, Johannesburg, calling for the removal from office of the state president, Jacob Zuma, April 2016. From left seated in red jacket: Zwelinzima Vavi, Bishop Jo Seoka, Mvuso Msimang and Ronnie Kasrils (Photo: *Daily Maverick*, 6 April 2016)

Sunday Times

MARCH 29, 2015

SPY TAPES: WE APOLOGISE TO KASRILS

The unprecedented *Sunday Times* street poster, 29 March 2015, apologising to Kasrils as result of the Press Council's findings in his 2014 complaint against the newspaper.

Ronnie Kasrils and Amina Frense at the launch of Redi Tlhabi's book *Khwezi* about Fezekile Kuzwayo at Exclusive Books, Hyde Park, Johannesburg, September 2017 (Photo: Madelene Cronje)

Deputy Minister of Defence Ronnie Kasrils and Eleanor Kasrils (1936–2009) at a ministry function, 1998 (Photo: Department of Defence and author's collection)

Fezekile Kuzwayo
and Zora, daughter
of Marc Wegerif and
Theresa Yates, Lushoto
Mountains, Tanzania,
2012 (Photo: Marc
Wegerif)

Fezekile Kuzwayo
and her mother
Beauty Kuzwayo,
Durban, 2016
(Photo: Theresa
Yates)

Fezekile Kuzwayo
with Zora, at a
friend's birthday,
Dar es Salaam,
Tanzania, 2012
(Photo: Marc
Wegerif)

Who Dunnit?

- Xmas 2004 – B visit Z • Nkandla.
- B changed attitude – Cuba trip
- July • Khampepe – we clash
- ANC NGC. Z come-back ↙
- Avani – Saki target!
- Media target KM
- End Aug – surveil Saki.
- Aug 28 – Fire! package for K?   /
- October emails target Billy!
- 23 Nov – K dossier
- 20 Oct. B suspensions (No More Emails!!)
- Q: Billy working for K? Z? Both??
    ___

Ronnie Kasrils's notes considering the mystery of the fake emails, 2005 in the new South Africa. Delegates showed scant respect for anyone associated with Mbeki and, using the football pitch signal of rotating forearms to indicate replacing a player, rudely mocked Lekota and the rest of us, who virtually sat frozen in our seats.

Proceedings finally got under way with a video address by Mandela on giant screens. I watched the crowd, intently trying to figure out who they were. At the front was the rowdiest delegation, from Zuma's home province of KwaZulu-Natal, where, we had heard, the ANC was now recruiting former IFP supporters. This was all well and good as long as they were receiving political education and not becoming instant delegates. I scanned their ranks, and what was evident was that many sat glassy-eyed, bored and unmoved during Mandela's recorded address, barely applauding when the old man's appeal for discipline and unity was over. The delegation from Mpumalanga had the same make-up. This bore out statistics which showed that most newly recruited members hailed from the rural areas.[10] I doubted whether many of those delegates would have passed muster had we the means to do a thorough audit of just when they had joined and how long they had been paying their subscriptions or even who was buying their membership for them.[11] They were examples of what is sometimes referred to disparagingly as 'voting cattle'. It was depressing, when one went into the voting station to cast one's vote, to note these newcomers were armed with checklists of those they had been instructed to vote for. There they were, squinting at names they could never have known anything about and slowly marking their crosses on the ballot papers as they had been instructed. Voting by remote control was what the ANC's inner democracy had degenerated into.

I had some hope that the 60 per cent camp might have sufficient deserters once they came to the secret ballot process. And that Mbeki might sway many of their number by his keynote address. That could arguably give him an advantage over Zuma if he played his cards right. It could possibly alter the 60–40 ratio to something more like a 50–50 chance. When you go into battle, you need to believe you can win. I knew how convincing Mbeki could be when he spoke without notes. But if he elected to read a two-hour-long speech, he would lose many in the audience. My advice to him was to rely on the oratory he possessed. However, when he came to the podium and began to read out his formal speech, which was an account of the implementation of the previous conference's resolutions, the ANC's and government's record over the past five years, and plans for the future, I lost all hope. It was heavy-going. This was not a crowd who cared to listen to such bookish facts. But Mbeki pressed on regardless. His mind, I believed, was fixed on his duty of being accountable to a historical legacy which, for him, trumped the transitory nature of the moment. It was more like being prepared to lose a battle but win the approval of history. The rational intellectual within the man always beat any vestige of populist emotion. That was Thabo Mbeki through and through. Many mistakenly assume he is a cold fish, but this misses the essence of the man's integrity – although many, even those close to him, would regard his decision to read a dry speech at the conference as a fatal error of judgement.

Perhaps the most pertinent aspect of Mbeki's political report was in asking the conference to 'honestly and frankly' consider three direct questions:

- Was the ANC capable of discharging its responsibilities to the masses of South Africa, the peoples of Africa and the rest of the world during this critical phase of the National Democratic Revolution [NDR]?
- Would our movement increase its popular support during the 2009 general elections, as had been the case in each general election since the first democratic elections of 1994?
- Did the ANC have the will and capacity to lead the country and people over the next five years in a manner that would enable the nation to celebrate the ANC's centenary in 2012 together, paying heartfelt tribute to the movement?

Undoubtedly Mbeki's second question was meant to prompt the conference into reflecting on the consequences of electing into the ANC's highest office a candidate so flawed that the outcome for the organisation could be and would be extremely grave, if not catastrophic. That was relying on an appeal to the intellect rather than the heart of the delegates.

Over the next days the ANC went through the rituals of discussing policy in the various commissions. It was during this time that groups were called to cast their votes. All minds were on the election results: policy issues, as vital as they were, came (except for the purists) a very poor second. By the time these were announced, tension had reached fever pitch. Zuma received 2,329 votes to Mbeki's 1,505 – a difference of 824 – and his supporters went ballistic. If we had managed to turn 413 voters, Mbeki would have pipped Zuma: by no means an impossibility. What hurt was not the frenzy of the crowd, the crowing at the losers, people gyrating in triumph or the general pandemonium, but the sight of Thabo Mbeki, which became etched in my mind. It has been said elsewhere, by Mosibudi Mangena, the Azapo leader and former cabinet minister, that Mbeki in adversity 'was a study in calmness, discipline and dignity ... dead calm in the eye of the storm'.[12] That was exactly how it struck me at Polokwane that fateful day. He walked over to congratulate Jacob Zuma, the ANC president-elect. It was a slow walk, he must have been hurting deeply, but the rational intellect of the man provided distance from the moment and I am sure that is how he was able to cope – then and later. Mbeki's entire bearing was honourable, dignified, stoic, brave, although the light had disappeared from his complexion and his face was ashen. He shook Zuma's hand and cordially embraced him. At last Zuma was at ease. He had reached the second top rung of the ladder. The country's presidency awaited him. That relaxed image of Jacob Zuma would be rarely seen again in the years ahead if one discounted his muscular but superficial joviality. I put on a brave face and, when interviewed, tried to be upbeat, explaining that the event showed the democratic process at work.[13]

Polokwane saw the beginning of possibly an irretrievable rot in the ANC. At Polokwane the faction that sought to unseat Mbeki did so at all costs. By hook or by crook they fanned the flames of anger and disunity; encouraged disrespect and thuggish behaviour; tampered with the nomination of delegates at branch level; flooded the conference with instant recruits whose political understanding was negligible; allegedly bought the votes of delegates with cash; and sought to settle old scores. The last thing on their minds was the open wounds inflicted on the ANC and the country. If some of the Mbeki supporters used some such methods, and I did pick up indications of the buying of votes on our side, it was not the wholesale machination and intimidatory tactics used by the Zumaites. The emergent leaders, victors at Polokwane, looked on silently as their storm troopers insulted Mbeki and his outgoing NEC. A new form of behaviour, alien to the ANC, swept through the organisation and stole its heart and soul without a thought of the consequences. The disease seeped through its intestines like maggot-infested meat. Some of those who led the onslaught would come to rue the day they did so, as their champion, Jacob Zuma, would stab them in the back while laughing in their faces. But it would prove too late. The emergence of a corrupt and vindictive strongman able to purchase loyalty on the basis of fleecing the state, crooked deals and a network of patronage, wrought irreparable damage and paved the way for the later so-called state capture by the Gupta family. This was the inevitable outcome of the turbulent and fetid backwash of the tsunami, which Zwelinzima Vavi and others had failed to take into account.

My friend Jeremy Cronin, judging Zuma would open up space for the left, was delighted with the Polokwane result. He introduced me to a journalist from *L'Humanité*, the French Communist Party newspaper, Pierre Barbancey. Seeking my views, Barbancey mentioned that Jeremy regarded Polokwane as a revolutionary advance. What was my opinion? The opposite, I replied; in fact, what had occurred was counter-revolutionary and the SACP would learn about Zuma the hard way – irrespective of how many communists he would initially appoint to his cabinet. In the event Barbancey wrote a glowing report influenced by Jeremy's view, but told me ten years later on the eve of a SACP's national congress, where we met again: 'I must confess that you were right when I met you in Polokwane.'[14]

A feature of ANC conferences is the hours and hours of time spent in commissions where policy is debated. As much as the ANC attempts to project policy as key, the fact is that, as at Polokwane, the election of leaders and the struggle between factions have become overwhelming. The final resolutions look impressive but tend to be a ritual where wordsmiths create a quasi-revolutionary spin, on the one hand, and a bland, all-encompassing rhetoric, on the other, under the rubric of the NDR – the National Democratic Revolution. Whatever the fine words, the proof of achievement must be in the implementation, and that is where the ANC has had woeful results. Mocking the optimistic claims of the 2007 conference were dire organisational shortcomings, growing unemployment, lack of economic growth, rising poverty, a widening gulf between rich and poor, deteriorating health and educational facilities, a rise in corruption and crime, police brutality and a relentless slide into a security state. 'National conference after national conference, NGC after NGC, the same burning issues have been raised. But there has been no viable success in really tackling them,' writes Khulu Mbatha, who served in the ANC from 1976 and later in government.[15]

Despite talk of a revolutionary shift at Polokwane, and no matter how much the SACP would try to shy away from acknowledging a dangerous personality cult surrounding Jacob Zuma, the legacy of the conference was bound to be the triumph of primitive factional methods of resolving rivalries and irreparable damage for the movement. And the country. The Polokwane Tsunami shipwrecked the ANC as we had known it.

CHAPTER 21

Exit Mbeki

Presidential Residence, Pretoria,
28 September 2008

A WEEK AFTER THE POLOKWANE conference, the Scorpions finally served their indictment on the newly elected ANC president, Jacob Zuma.[1] The charge sheet enumerated 783 counts of racketeering, money laundering, corruption and fraud.

There was outrage among Zuma's supporters, who predictably alleged the charges were a counter-revolutionary conspiracy to prevent him from standing for the country's presidency in the 2009 national elections. The claim was that the decision to prosecute had been deliberately delayed to see if he would win the ANC presidential elections at Polokwane. And, if so, then the Scorpions would strike. That was the irrational, self-serving logic Zuma and company revelled in. According to such reasoning, what if Zuma had lost? He most certainly would still have been charged. If the indictment had been served on him before Polokwane, his camp would have argued in the exact same vein.

The tsunami was, however, by no mean spent. After Polokwane the national government of President Thabo Mbeki should have lasted another sixteen months, until April 2009 when the next national elections were due. Whatever the fault lines between the two centres of power, Pretoria and Luthuli House, nothing was done to reconcile differences and effectively manage the transition. Mbeki appeared unconcerned. But the smell of the blood of the wounded Mbeki, and the vindictiveness of the victors intoxicated with power, proved overwhelming. While they rubbed their hands with glee at the prospect of the 2009 national elections, which would certainly elect Jacob Zuma as president of the country, the opportunity to rub salt into the wounds of their enemies arose from an unexpected quarter.

Zuma's legal team appealed against the corruption charges served on him after his election at Polokwane. Nine months later, on 12 September 2008, after considering the appeal papers and hearing argument, Judge Chris Nicholson in the Pietermaritzburg High Court held that Zuma's corruption charges were unlawful on procedural grounds. In his judgment Nicholson strayed from the issue at hand, and declared that he believed there was political interference in the timing of the charges brought against Zuma, criticised Mbeki's reasons for sacking him, and accused three consecutive national directors of public prosecution of wrongdoing.[2]

Zuma and his supporters were naturally ecstatic. They gyrated in jubilation outside the Pietermaritzburg court, with Blade Nzimande and Zweli Vavi at the fore, alongside numerous ANC National Executive Committee (NEC) members, as well as a more subdued Kgalema Motlanthe. At long last they had a judgment that concurred there was a conspiracy to prevent Zuma from becoming president of South Africa.

At least one aspect of the Nicholson judgment, that concerning political interference, was questionable in that no such issue was before the judge; and, moreover, he had come to that opinion without giving Mbeki the opportunity to be heard. Mbeki consequently immediately appealed against the decision with his cabinet's backing. The appeal was like a red rag to Zuma's supporters, who chose to interpret the move as yet another attempt by Mbeki to prevent their man from attaining the country's highest office. The tsunami had not abated and was still to reach its full extent. An angry NEC, composed mainly of

Zuma acolytes elected at Polokwane, promptly debated the issue for an entire day, the majority baying for Mbeki's blood. During the course of the day the issue of his immediate recall as the country's president arose but was not immediately agreed to since some equivocated while a few, such as Pallo Jordan and Joel Netshitenzhe, by no means Zuma supporters, counselled against it.

At the end of the day's deliberation a belligerent NEC concluded that Mbeki was no longer fit to govern South Africa and by the next morning served notice on him to resign forthwith from the position. Mbeki could have stood his ground and insisted that parliament – which had appointed him – should debate the issue and come to a decision. But as a disciplined member of the ANC, as he had consistently stated, he regarded the NEC's instruction as obligatory, tendering his resignation without demur on 20 September 2008. The ANC swiftly appointed the party's deputy president, Kgalema Motlanthe, in his place. This would be a stopgap measure until the May 2009 general election, which would give Zuma his opportunity. The likelihood was that Zuma would certainly become the country's fourth president in the democratic era. How different things might have been if in fact Motlanthe, an infinitely better candidate than Zuma, had remained president instead. Flushed with triumph, Zuma announced that he would be happy to serve one term as president. Famous last words. For me, when Zuma appears to accept a loss in power, be ready for the opposite outcome.

Mbeki's serving ministers were then summoned to meet Zuma and officials at the NEC venue. In jovial mood he asked a dozen of us who were no longer on the NEC whether we would stay on in our posts. Terror Lekota and I spoke up, disabusing him of the notion. I made the point in as convivial a manner as I could muster, that since we as cabinet ministers were party to Mbeki's decision to appeal against the Nicholson judgment, a decision for which Mbeki was being recalled, it was inappropriate that we should continue serving in office. Within the week twelve ministers tendered their resignations. Trevor Manuel was one of us, but not for long. He was soon back in office, the only one among us, as the country's minister of finance.

Mbeki presided over his last cabinet on 24 September in a sombre but brave mood. He was politically correct through and through. He effortlessly summed up the situation, stated that it had been an honour to lead us and the country, and invited cabinet ministers to speak if they wished. Almost everyone accepted his invitation, making eloquent, often lengthy and sentimental statements. Quite a few of the contributions were insincere, to say the least, as many present, one suspected, had already made arrangements with Zuma rather than Motlanthe, who would be sworn in as interim president without delay. Of these quite a few were women, who would never have had such opportunities without the gender empowerment methodically introduced by Mbeki over the years. I made a brief speech, thanking the president for having given me the opportunity to serve, and said that he would be vindicated by history.

Perhaps the most exceptional assessment of Mbeki as president came from a more neutral standpoint than that of his own party members. Mosibudi Mangena, who had been minister of science and technology in Mbeki's cabinet, and president of the Azanian People's Organisation (Azapo), declared in his measured way: 'When I entered the executive in 2001 ... I wondered what it would be like for a member of Azapo to work with ANC leaders in "their" government ... It was soon apparent that one had joined a hard-working team ... trying to do their best for the country ... Issues were discussed openly and transparently.

'Stories abound about former president Thabo Mbeki's dictatorial attributes. If he does have such features, he must have displayed them elsewhere. In government meetings he would allow everybody to have their say before summing up.'[3]

If Mangena had been in my shoes as intelligence minister, I believe he would have had the same opinion. In my four years in that powerful post I can attest to the fact that Mbeki never once displayed a dictatorial temperament. He listened to what I had to report or say and quietly discussed matters, not once asserting his decision over mine. And what Mangena had noted of his manner in cabinet was similar to Mbeki's handling of NEC meetings. If the collective ended up agreeing with him, it was after long discussions and then the invariable soundness of his summation.

Just prior to the speeches at the last cabinet meeting there had been a single item on the agenda. I had a report concerning reforms of the intelligence services. This was the culmination of over a year's sitting, research and deliberation of the Matthews Commission, which I had set up following the Masetlha saga.[4] The report, however, has been gathering dust ever since Zuma and the parliamentary Joint Standing Committee on Intelligence ignored it. The findings were of historic import and could have gone a long way in addressing the many abuses of power that have been manifest ever since. It was with relief that Mbeki had agreed that I could table the document at the cabinet meeting, which meant it was on the agenda for government and parliamentary attention.

In a supreme irony, and twist of history, the Nicholson judgment, which had led to Mbeki's recall, was subsequently thrown out by the Supreme Court of Appeal (SCA) in January 2009, thereby vindicating Mbeki. A unanimous SCA bench, led by deputy president Judge Louis Harms, ruled that Nicholson was wrong to declare the charges against Zuma unlawful.[5] As Adriaan Basson wrote, 'Harms erased all of that with one thick stroke, putting an abrupt end to the ANC's short-lived euphoria after Nicholson's judgment. It was, after all, a dream ruling for the ruling party, which now faces the real possibility of going into the 2009 elections with a fraud suspect at its helm.'[6]

Basically the deputy president of the SCA told Nicholson that he did not know what he was doing. Under the heading 'The judicial function', Harms lectured Nicholson on the functions of a judge. 'It is crucial to provide an exposition of the functions of a judicial officer because, for reasons that are impossible to fathom, the court below [Nicholson] failed to adhere to some basic tenets, in particular that in exercising the judicial function judges are themselves constrained by the law.' In particular, Nicholson failed to confine his judgment 'to the issues before the court by deciding matters that were not germane or relevant; by creating new factual issues; by making gratuitous findings against persons who were not called upon to defend themselves; by failing to distinguish between allegation, fact and suspicion; and by transgressing the proper boundaries between judicial, executive and legislative functions.'

The SCA found that Nicholson had let his personal opinion on matters cloud his judgement. 'Judges as members of civil society are entitled to hold views about issues of the day and they may express their views provided they do not compromise their judicial office. But they are not entitled to inject their personal views into judgments or express their political preferences.' This was specifically relevant to Nicholson's remarks about Mbeki's reasons for sacking Zuma and standing for a third term as ANC president.

All the same, shooting down Nicholson came too late to spare Mbeki the embarrassment of a premature recall from office by his own party. The tsunami had done its damage. Mbeki's adversaries paid no attention to the SCA judgment and did not even have the grace to apologise for the vindictiveness of their behaviour. But the SCA ruling did also spell out a big headache for Zuma, for it meant that the corruption charges, and hence further court hearings, still lay ahead for him.

I sat with Mbeki through his last night as South Africa's president on 28 September 2008. During the day a stream of comrades visited the official residence to pay their respects and display their solidarity. Ministers, state officials, all ANC to the core, who had admired the man through the years of struggle and into those of power, gathered about him. Mbeki was coolness personified. His staff served endless plates of snacks and poured the appropriate drinks. Most needed stiff shots of spirits. The mood was sombre and reflective. But at the back of everyone's mind was the unpredictable course on which the ANC was set. Commiserating with Mbeki was not on the cards. His stoicism and dignity said 'lay off'.

Guests began drifting away as the night wore on. Aziz Pahad and I remained until late since we lived nearby on the estate. We chatted and sipped whisky. We talked of the international situation. It was not forced. Mbeki enjoyed that subject, and it kept us away from the unpalatable subject: the imminent end of his term of office. Mbeki did not appear to be as preoccupied as Aziz and I were about the ticking of the clock. I do not know of Aziz's reflections, but every fifteen minutes the clock in Mbeki's office – to which the three of us had retreated – chimed asthmatically. Our conversation droned on, but I scarcely paid attention. Thirty minutes to go. Another whisky, please. 'Yes, comrade President, I think Russia will stand by Iran,' I was mouthing, though my thoughts were mesmerised by the swinging pendulum. The fifteen-minute chime. The clock needed oiling. A big gulp of the amber fluid. Aziz was rattling on. Mbeki was thoughtful. The man was oblivious to the passing of time ... nine interminable minutes more and his presidency would be over. Aziz was rattling on even more excitedly, which is the way he gets under pressure, so I realised he too was preoccupied with the passing of the time. Mbeki nodded sagely and, deep in thought, gave a response about the prospects for the African Renaissance. I have braced myself for the hour chime. It begins slowly and agonisingly. I count the beats, one ... two ... three ... Mbeki is speaking about the African Union ... nine more beats to go and his presidency is over ... Four ... five ... six ... I stand up, meaning to go over to shake his hand, but think better of it ... as he shakes his head over the problem of Gaddafi and the greater Africa 'messing up the entire concept of pan-Africanism, that man ... brother leader,' he guffaws in an understated way, his characteristic hallmark when scoffing about a rival. The point of midnight comes and goes. Mbeki holds forth for the next ten minutes about the African Renaissance. I am overwhelmed by the sense of history and by the sense of vision which marked his presidency, whatever errors one may number. I am overwhelmed by the fact that one second makes the difference between a man being president of a country and then not. I realise I am somewhat tipsy. What on earth had I imagined? That the man would turn into a pumpkin, and Aziz and I into dormice? We had simply reached a fleeting point in time. A chain of events, set in motion by contending forces and wills, often with unintended consequences, has culminated in this night. Perhaps Mbeki sees it as quite banal, which is why he is almost aloof from the drama and does not dwell on the moment at all. I think of Shakespeare's Macbeth:

Out, out, brief candle!
Life's but a walking shadow, a poor player
That struts and frets his hour upon the stage
And then is heard no more: it is a tale
Told by an idiot, full of sound and fury,
Signifying nothing.

I take my leave.

According to official regulations I had twenty-four hours to vacate my office and a month to get out of my residence. When your time of service expired, the state turned merciless and brushed you off in the quickest possible time. We were mere players after all. Our power was ephemeral and dissolved once the spotlights had dimmed.

As I sauntered home across the shadowy lawns in the milky moonlight, I mused about Mbeki's fate. Most would see in him a Julius Caesar, slain by his colleagues who feared he sought an emperor's crown. I saw an aspect of Hamlet, who procrastinated too long before accepting that his murderous relative bore him ill will, and hence his doubts prevented him from committing to a timeous course of action. Tossing and turning that night in bed, I was taunted by images of three sangomas, closely resembling ministers, who have stabbed Mbeki in the back. They cast their spells into the cooking pot and their incantation rings out in the forests of Nkandla:

Double, double toil and trouble;
Fire burn and cauldron bubble.

I wake with a start from my uneasy slumber. I realise I have been dwelling more on the character of Zuma than of Mbeki. I thought of pretenders and kings, of generals and presidents with whom I had been intimately involved. It is Shakespeare who so brilliantly reveals the lust and ambition of men and women: there are those who through service and sacrifice attain the throne; and then there are those who ditch their principles and values. Those are the ones of flawed character corrupted by power. As with a tsunami, none escape damage.

CHAPTER 22

Fake News

The Johannesburg *Star*,
12 August, 1963 and 2008

As the 2009 national elections approached, the prospect of Jacob Zuma becoming the next president of the country became more and more certain. People began to queue up to ingratiate themselves, and where possible to provide favourable publicity.

An edition of the Johannesburg *Star* in August 2008 carried a mock-up claiming to be a replica of the newspaper's edition forty-five years previously, in which it had supposedly reported on 12 August 1963 that the 21-year-old Jacob Zuma, 'one of the ANC's rising stars', had been sentenced to ten years' imprisonment.[1]

In Jeremy Gordin's biography of Zuma, he writes: 'He was apparently better known than either he or recent history has acknowledged. The headlines on page 6 of the City Late edition of *The Star* [12 August 1963] read: "JACOB ZUMA JAILED".

'Jacob Zuma, a prominent member of the banned African National Congress and activist in the ANC's military wing Umkhonto weSizwe, has been sentenced to an effective ten years' imprisonment for conspiring to overthrow the government. He was arrested with a group of 45 recruits near Zeerust in the Western Transvaal. The 21-year-old

Zuma, son of a policeman from Nkandla in Natal, became involved in politics at a very early age and joined the ANC in 1959 when he was a mere 17. Zuma was one of the ANC's rising stars when the political party was banned by the government.'²

The moment I saw *The Star* in 2008 I smelt a rat. As part of the MK Regional Command in Natal, I knew he was anonymous to the public and media when we sent him for training abroad in 1963. What was more, none of the many political trials at the time, other than when the big fish like Mandela or Billy Nair were in the dock, had warranted more than a couple of column centimetres to report that a group of Africans had been sentenced under security legislation. If Zuma was indeed regarded in Durban as 'one of the ANC's rising stars', *The Star* would have been hard pressed to uncover such a view, for the ANC was deep underground and there was no reference in the Natal press. Another error is the reference to the ANC as a 'political party', which it was not. Neither the ANC nor anybody else regarded the organisation as a party until the 1994 elections.

Amina Frense and David Niddrie, journalists of long standing, accompanied me on a search for *The Star* report at the Johannesburg Library, which keeps an archive of South African and international newspapers. The 12 August 1963 City Late edition has a dramatic front-page story featuring the escape from Marshall Square police headquarters of Abdulhay Jassat, Arthur Goldreich, Harold Wolpe and Mosie Moola. Page 6 has no mention of the Jacob Zuma story at all. We searched for any mention of Zuma in all editions from 1 June through to the end of August 1963, but nothing came to light. We also checked copies of the *Rand Daily Mail* and the *Natal Mercury*, Zuma's home town morning newspaper, which one would think would more likely than most carry news of the 'rising star,' but to no avail. We found nothing in our search for the entire month of August 2008.

The 14 June 1963 edition of *The Star* did have a story that simply mentioned forty-five Africans had been arrested near Zeerust on their way out of the country. They were being held under the 90-day detention law, allowing suspects to be detained in solitary confinement with no access to lawyers for up to ninety days at a time.

No names were provided, and no other information was given about the people's identities other than that two Indians and an African woman were among the group. Whoever unearthed that information from whatever the source must have thought that the story, given a good deal of spin, would make for good publicity for the forthcoming president. It was apparent that his image could well do with a facelift.

Both Lorna and I had without a shadow of a doubt seen the extract Jeremy Gordin featured in his book on Zuma, but that was in August 2008. A strange account indeed.

PART FIVE

Spy Tapes

2007–2008

Spying and novel writing are made for each other. Both call for a ready eye and the many routes to betrayal.
— John Le Carré, *The Pigeon Tunnel*

CHAPTER 23

Intercepts

Pretoria, 2007

AFTER THE SCORPIONS SERVED their indictment on the newly elected ANC president on 28 December 2007, Jacob Zuma's legal team used every trick in the book to prevent their man from facing the corruption charges. They employed the term 'Stalingrad defence', denoting that they would fight every inch of the way to keep him from facing trial, just as the Russians had fought street by street, house by house, in that city against the invading German forces during World War Two.

The delaying tactics began from the time of the conviction of Schabir Shaik on charges of fraud and corruption linked in part to Zuma. The drama then continued with the indictment served on Zuma in December 2007, his reprieve as a result of the Nicholson judgment, and then the overturning of that judgment by the Supreme Court of Appeal (SCA) in January 2009. At successive high points of the legal saga, boisterous crowds of Zuma supporters demonstrated in the streets in solidarity with him – foremost among them Zwelinzima Vavi and Blade Nzimande.

Then in early April 2009, a few months after the SCA's ruling, which opened the way for Zuma to be charged, he received a remarkable helping hand, just weeks prior to the general election.

151

The director of the National Prosecuting Authority (NPA), Mokotedi Mpshe, sensationally announced that all charges against Zuma were being dropped. The reason given was abuse of process, as revealed in intercepted phone conversations which had mysteriously come to light. These were electronic intercepts, not actual recorded tapes of a previous era, but they came to be referred to as the 'Spy Tapes'. Only a few select excerpts from them were released in April 2009 to coincide with the reprieve for Zuma.

It was claimed that political interference had been uncovered emanating from the activities of the previous head of the Scorpions, Leonard McCarthy (who had left the country for a post at the World Bank), in association with the former head of the NPA, Bulelani Ngcuka. This made it look as though Ngcuka was interfering unduly with the process – ruling from the grave, as it were. Proof was allegedly contained in intercepted mobile phone conversations between the two, and several other high-profile individuals, from November 2007 (preceding the ANC's Polokwane conference that December) to April 2008. The NPA under Mpshe had been handed the tapes by Zuma's legal representative and adviser, Michael Hulley. The question of how the intercepted conversations were obtained and how they came illegally into the hands of Zuma's legal team was overshadowed by the sensational nature of the conversations.

Initially only a portion of the intercepts were provided to the media to justify Mpshe's dramatic decision to drop charges against Zuma. The main opposition party, the Democratic Alliance (DA), approached the courts to obtain a full set of the transcribed copies of the intercepts. Given the Stalingrad defence of Zuma's legal team, it took the DA six years (until March 2015) to succeed. When their case was finally heard by the Supreme Court of Appeal, it ruled in their favour – although Zuma continued to use delaying tactics to avoid his day in court.

It emerged that the Spy Tapes consisted of sixty-three pages of thirty-five illegally intercepted phone conversations between November 2007 and April 2008, running into about ten hours of conversation. Approximately half of these were between Leonard

McCarthy and Bulelani Ngcuka. The rest were between McCarthy and such individuals as the minister of justice, Brigitte Mabandla (there were just three calls but they were fairly long conversations about legal matters), McCarthy's subordinate and close friend, Faiek Davids (Willie Hofmeyr's deputy in the Special Investigating Unit — SIU of the NPA), the businessman Mzi Khumalo (who was socially close to Ngcuka and his wife, Phumzile), and an initially unidentified man called 'Luciano', later revealed to be André Pienaar (a publicity-shy South African running a private intelligence company based in London).

Most of these were rambling conversations, interspersed with small talk and occasional expletives, but all essentially focused on the Scorpions' pending charges against Zuma and the question of their timing — when to act. This topic was the subject of McCarthy's conversations with Ngcuka and Khumalo, and it is clear they were earnestly hoping that Mbeki would be the victor at the Polokwane conference. Calls between McCarthy and 'Luciano' were brief. And so were five calls between McCarthy and me (none more than half a minute), which were not included in the thirty-five-page transcripts.[1] Since I had noted media speculation concerning a discussion between McCarthy and Ngcuka (on 7 November 2007) in the 2009 leaked intercepts, I publicly identified myself then as having interacted with McCarthy on the issue of the timing of the charges.

In meeting McCarthy in 2005 in connection with my support for retaining the Scorpions as an independent investigating unit, then the subject of the inquiry by the Khampepe Commission, and later when he approached me to seek my political counsel in the run-up to Polokwane, I had made one condition: I never discussed business on the phone: 'Not since I became involved in politics in 1960. Mr McCarthy, the first thing I was instructed then was don't trust the telephone. And I have remained true to that ever since. Only fools believe that they are not being overheard.' While he abided by my proviso in talking to me, he threw all caution to the wind in calls between himself and Ngcuka.

When I first read the leaked Spy Tape transcripts in 2009, and later the full sixty-three pages in 2015, I could scarcely believe that two experienced legal people like McCarthy and Ngcuka could have been so cavalier in their telephone discussions, although the exchanges need to be seen as taking place between a subordinate and his former chief whose advice he sought.

The McCarthy–Ngcuka telephone intercepts, unlike the 2005 Masetlha emails, certainly took place, but views on what they amounted to could differ. The NPA's top team of Mpshe and Willie Hofmeyr – who appears to have been tasked with evaluating the intercepts – interpreted them as clear evidence of conspiracy against Zuma on behalf of, and allegedly acting on the orders of, Mbeki. For their part, the courts would have their say on the matter for when they threw out the NPA's and Zuma's attempts to prevent the DA from getting hold of the tapes.

There undoubtedly is conspiracy in the world of politics, in business, in all manner of human affairs. My understanding of a conspiracy is that it involves an act of plotting between two or more persons to do something unlawful or harmful. In our benighted country the term has become a fit-for-purpose explanation twisted to conveniently suit any particular agenda or perverse imagination. It has become a favourite device of Jacob Zuma's. In May 2017, for example, the ANC's Integrity Commission suggested Zuma step down for the good of the movement, but received this reply from him, which it noted: 'The essence of the president's refusal to resign is his belief that there exists a conspiracy by Western governments to oust him as president of the ANC and of the country. Their objective is to replace him in order to capture the ANC.'[2]

The intercepts commenced with a banal conversation between the businessman Mzi Khumalo and McCarthy on 4 November 2007 and ended with a discussion between Bulelani Ngcuka and McCarthy on 7 April 2008. The first intercept concerned a long-winded arrangement about a dinner meeting with Mzi Khumalo, a member of the circle of Mbeki supporters. In the last intercept McCarthy sought a meeting with Mbeki. I happened to know that this had to do with McCarthy's plan to take up a top security post at the World Bank, for which he sought Mbeki's approval. Several intercepts involved four to eight pages of conversation, a duration of 30–45 minutes each. The average conversations, including chit-chat, amounted to 10–15 minutes.

What appeared to be at issue were discussions about the presidential election, both pre- and post-Polokwane: they revealed how hopeful McCarthy, Ngcuka and Mzi Khumalo were about Mbeki winning. There was nothing illegal in this. Ngcuka and Khumalo were ordinary citizens, but McCarthy, as an employee of the state, certainly was placing his reputation at risk for the perceptions that could be created. There were no conversations with others involving discussion about political factors other than the timing of the charges against Zuma. By way of insight into the intercepts I present a few samples, which I have greatly abbreviated for the convenience of the reader. The *Sunday Times* has posted the entire transcripts on its online website.[3]

Mzi Khumalo (MK) to Leonard McCarthy (LM), 4 November 2007:
MK: Howzit, I have just arrived ... You said you would be going to Cape Town today ...
LM: I must just see Rev. Chikane first, then I will go ...
MK: We can meet on Wednesday ...
LM: We can have dinner or early drinks, pick a place, just let me know ...

Bulelani Ngcuka (BN) to Leonard McCarthy (LM), 7 November 2007:
[Initially the discussion was about LM's request that BN assist in getting a job for his personal assistant – since LM was planning to take a job abroad with the World Bank – and references were made to a current Supreme Court of Appeal hearing into a High Court order that set aside search warrants in the Zuma case.]
LM: And then ... I met with the guy I mentioned, and you know his line is almost like that of Sam ... he says he will speak to the man ... he feels very strongly that I should not see the guy directly ...[4]
[The 'guy' was in fact me and I had previously volunteered that information to the media.]

Bulelani Ngcuka (BN) to Leonard McCarthy (LM), 26 November 2007:

[BN informing LM of the results of the ANC provincial nomination conferences]

BN: ... I have just been shocked, shocked, shocked ...

LM: Hm.

BN: ... I don't understand it, you know, I just don't understand it.

LM: Ja.

BN: I can't find that there are only nine people in the whole province of Natal [who voted for Mbeki] ... Twenty-six in Mpumalanga, it does not make sense ...

LM: Gauteng?

BN: Well, the Gauteng is fine ... Northern Cape we would have won, but those guys cheated ...

LM: Hm.

Bulelani Ngcuka (BN) to Leonard McCarthy (LM), 6 December 2007:

[BN called to congratulate LM about the prosecution of the gangster Glenn Agliotti before turning to the election of ANC delegates.]

BN: You know we were very complacent, Leonard.

LM: Hm.

BN: We did not understand the inroads the fool [Zuma] has made. He has just about bought everybody.

LM: With money from whom?

BN: Hey man, from everywhere, boet ...

LM: Hm.

Leonard McCarthy (LM) to Bulelani Ngcuka (BN), 12 December 2007:

[A discussion of the NPA's filing of court papers concerning Zuma's appeal to the Constitutional Court about the legality of the search warrant used against him.]

BN: ... It can be a devastating one for them and it will cause people to wake up [if the papers are filed] ... without you making any arrests ...

people will wake up and say, Look, let us think what are we doing ...

LM: Ja, I think, you know, by Friday, by Friday people are packing their bags [for Polokwane], they won't even read the fucking newspapers ...

BN: That is the thing ... that is why it would have been good if it could come out today [i.e. Wednesday].

LM: Today it is difficult ... we finalise this tomorrow morning, and file by lunchtime and give it to the media ...

Brigitte Mabandla (BM) to Leonard McCarthy (LM), 14 December 2007:

BM: Oo, there is so much panic ... that you are about to arrest the old man ...?

LM: The old man as in JS or JZ [Jackie Selebi or Jacob Zuma]?

BM: Zuma.

LM: No, no, all that is happening is ... we have to file today our opposition at the Constitutional Court to his application for a review of the search warrants ...

[BM expressed unhappiness about rumours of an imminent arrest or any action that might even fan such fears.]

LM: Well, I was completely unaware of that ... minister ... I won't send affidavit then. I will wait to hear from you when you are back [in Pretoria] next week ...

BM: Yes, but I think dispel all these rumours, please.

LM: We will do that ...

Leonard McCarthy (LM) to Faiek Davids (FD), 16 December 2007:

[FD, Willie Hofmeyr's deputy in the NPA, recounts a chat with him at an airport lounge and his disgust with Hofmeyr for gossiping with another person about Mbeki's alleged protection of Jackie Selebi.]

FD: Willie sê to this other person: Wat is verkeerd met die president? Hoekom staan hy in onse pad as ons vir Selebi will prosecute?

[FD goes on to recount to LM how he remonstrated with Hofmeyr.]

FD: Ek sê, Willie, waar kan jy soos 'n poes wees om die man [the other man] daai te vra? Hy sê, Ja, hy het a mistake gemaak.

LM: Hy praat met die verkeerde mense en hy praat uit sy beurt uit.

FD: Kyk, ek en hy het 'n weddenskap … ek het gesê Thabo gaan wen. Hy was so confident, hy gee vir die ander kant … odds van 20 to 1 … maar daai is nou tussen kollegas in lighter way … En hy praat al klaar van hoe Zuma dinge bymekaar sit. En hoe Zuma dinge gaan doen.

Bulelani Ngcuka (BN) to Leonard McCarthy (LM), 16 December 2007:

[The two discuss the start of the ANC's Polokwane conference.]

BN: The conference is very bad, hey, it is extremely divisive. The people [Zuma] have bused thugs and hooligans.

LM: I saw this morning [on television at home] and switched off.

Mzi Khumalo (MK) to Leonard McCarthy (LM), 18 December 2007:

[The two discuss Zuma's election victory at Polokwane.]

MK: It is a bad day for the whole country, but we should all just … sit and reflect on what next?

LM: I am shocked …

MK: … the level of hatred against Bulelani and the whole newer establishment [Mbeki and company] …

MK: I went and told Phumzile [Bulelani Ngcuka's wife and the country's deputy president], I said, You know, my sister, I love you so much … but this Thabo camp has a big liability. It is you and Terror Lekota. With you two we are going to lose … I told the president, you know, having Phumzile in the top list, people believed it was because Thabo Mbeki wanted her to be the next president.

LM: Yeah.

MK: And they just said we will show him.

LM: Yeah.

MK: It's never going to happen …

LM: What happens next?

MK: … first Kgalema [Motlanthe], who is a guy really they claim is not Zuma … has always accepted that Zuma is going to be charged and convicted … so he has positioned this thing and used Zuma as a Trojan horse … so then Kgalema will step onto the podium and become the next president … the question is does Kgalema try and stay a middle line or ... continue on this Zuma ticket ... surrounding himself with thugs or ... be a reasonable person ... and stay in the middle line ... I think Kgalema will dump Zuma but remain with those guys who put him in power ... He may even say that Zuma would be tried, convicted and he will then pardon him ...

LM: Are you serious?

MK: Everyone expects that Zuma will be charged ...

[They discuss plans for the festive season.]

LM: Ja no, enjoy it as you say. Let's be merry and festive and regroup another day. Let's wipe the blood off our faces. Hey, I feel bad about it. My wife says to me you look like you lost your mother ...

Bulelani Ngcuka (BN) to Leonard McCarthy (LM), 19 December 2007:

[BN declares that he is not afraid of threats or action against him by the new grouping.]

BN: ... [because they believe] there was a conspiracy hatched by Mbeki and he used me to implement that for which he compensated me by giving ... my wife Zuma's job. They needed that, and the masses, the poor gullible masses, believed that ... so that's where we are ... it is important that you sort out where you are going immediately. [about taking a job at the World Bank]

LM: Ja.

BN: And I think that the sooner you get out of that place [his current job] the better for you.

LM: Um.

BN: Let them sort out their mess, this is not your responsibility ... there is nobody out there who is going to be out there covering your back ...

LM: Yeah, OK ...

Leonard McCarthy (LM) to Bulelani Ngcuka (BN), 19 December 2007:

LM: We want to move on Friday, man [intending to serve a summons on Zuma].

BN: OK.

LM: I don't know whether that other call you referred to will ever come. I think these guys feel humiliated, and the longer we delay, the worse it becomes, we make it impossible for ourselves to act, if the guy wants us to meet and um ... just do it.

BN: Hm, ja.

Brigitte Mabandla (BM) to Leonard McCarthy (LM), 19 December 2007

[BM discusses some business issues with LM and then hands the phone to President Mbeki, who had just lost the Polokwane election.]

Mbeki: Advocate, how are you?

LM: I am well, I am well, thank you.

Mbeki: Do you know who is speaking?

LM: It sounds like the president?

Mbeki: Yes.

LM: How are you, president?

Mbeki: OK, thanks ... you have to choose, Leonard, whether you say president or former president.

LM: (*laughs*) You will always be my president ...

Mbeki: The minister told me some time back that you had asked to see me.

[They make arrangements to meet.]

McCarthy had wished to inform Mbeki that he would be departing to take up a post at the World Bank. I had advised him that he needed to formally take his leave of the president. The fact that McCarthy declared Mbeki would always be his president was considered as sinister, by some, although it was quite an innocent declaration. In fact, Mbeki was still the president of South Africa. It is also possible, judging by the previous discussion with Ngcuka, that McCarthy wanted to inform Mbeki formally that the Scorpions were proceeding to charge Zuma.

CHAPTER 24

Mastermind

Olympia Café, Kalk Bay, 7 September 2014

Sᴜɴᴅᴀʏs ᴀᴛ ᴍʏ ᴏɴᴇ-ᴛɪᴍᴇ retirement haven[1] of Kalk Bay, overlooking
False Bay, could be varied: anything from damp mist or driving rain
to balmy sunshine, with or without the 'Cape doctor' – the powerful
south-easter wind that blew in the purest Antarctic air. Those gusts
cleansed the lungs but rattled windowpanes for days on end. Whatever
the weather, Sunday was always a blessed relief from the week's toil.

I awoke to a fine spring day, thinking of my regular early morning
coffee at the Olympia Café, followed by a refreshing dip in the local
tidal pool. But I also had a feeling of anxiety. My thoughts were on the
Sunday papers, which I would ritually read over coffee and croissants
baked on the premises. That morning I was tense in anticipation of yet
another front-page story to freak my mind.

For at precisely six o'clock the evening before I had got a call on the
phone. A hesitant voice asked: 'Eh, is that – eh – Mr Kasrils?'

'This is he,' I answered rather abruptly, as I was expecting my wife
Amina, who worked in Johannesburg.

The caller introduced himself as Sam Mkokeli, a reporter from
the *Sunday Times*, and tentatively proceeded to inform me of a story he
had written that was coming out the next morning. 'It's about the Spy

Tapes,' he explained, 'and I am just informing that you feature, sir.'

It transpired that anonymous sources in government had identified me as a key player in the saga, in fact 'the guy' who was linked with 'the man' from whom the Scorpions boss, Leonard McCarthy, had sought guidance about charging Jacob Zuma ahead of the Polokwane conference in 2007. And that 'man' was none other than President Mbeki.

'Oh, really,' I answered, wanting to expunge what had become a smirking tone in his voice, 'but as a journalist writing this story, you ought to be aware that when the initial leaks about the so-called Spy Tapes were reported, I was open about "the guy" being me and "the man" being Mbeki. And I had been open about my association with McCarthy.'

The Smirk, as I had come to think of him, was now faltering, and attempted to add something, but I was not finished and added: 'I would have expected that you did your research and even at this late hour make mention of that fact?'

'Well, I was just alerting you about tomorrow's story.'

'At 6 p.m. on Saturday night, your presses are probably rolling. What about my rights in this matter?'

'Yes,' he cut in quickly, 'that's why I am phoning, to get your side of the story.'

That was a laugh. He had written his piece and the news editor, at the very last moment, must have reminded him of the obligation to alert me to the allegations and give me the benefit of responding. That should have been done in good time, but it was not.

'Well, we will mention what you say in a second edition,' he responded.

'Let's see about that.'

By the time I reached the Olympia, the café was buzzing with early morning customers. The artist Beezy Bailey, my friend and neighbour, was at a table, enjoying his favourite dish of kippers and poached eggs. A superb cook and host, he often invited me to share a meal with family and friends, but never indulged in kippers at home owing to the stench that lingered in the kitchen.

'Wooo, *broer*,' he greeted me, his face a mix of mischief and a touch of anxiety, 'front-page man in the Sunday Slimes', tapping the newspaper face-up with its prominent headline: 'Spy Tapes "illegal" and expose Kasrils'.[2]

Kenneth, the proprietor, was at my elbow, with a cup of my ritual double espresso and a couple of hot croissants. 'You'll need this, dude,' he said, glancing down at the newspaper and then raising his eyes to the ceiling in a 'stuff them' way.

The café was bustling with its regular patrons, mainly locals at that time, ahead of those who would later stream in from further afield. There was the retired bishop and his wife, both environmental activists, a number of resident poets and artists who had been around for decades, a cousin of Pallo Jordan's and partner with whom I often dined, all giving me thumbs-up signs.

Under the by-line Sam Mkokeli, the man who had called me the evening before, the report outlined by way of introduction the context of the interception of the phone calls, and the release of the 'Spy Tapes' to the Democratic Alliance (DA) the previous week, referring to 'already known allegations of political interference in the running of both the police and the prosecuting authority'.

'However, they reveal what a senior government source referred to as a "deep" manipulation of the prosecuting body by a web of politicians and business people who were associated with the then President Thabo Mbeki's bid for a third term as head of the ANC.'

Then came my role: 'Former intelligence minister Ronnie Kasrils is allegedly identified through the latest transcripts and tapes given to the DA as the mastermind behind most of the political manoeuvring at the height of the Polokwane battle, sources who have knowledge of the tapes said yesterday.'

There was much more about the Mbeki group, and the way the evidence of the tapes had justified the head of the NPA, Mokotedi Mpshe, in dropping the corruption charges against Zuma, clearing the way for him to become the country's president. The report confirmed that the DA leader, Helen Zille, who successfully led the court application for access to the tapes, had already read the transcripts, but could not comment as she was prevented from doing so by legal constraints. The report referred to edited transcripts that had been released in 2009, shortly before Mpshe announced the dropping of charges against Zuma, and then added another bombshell: 'The new transcript goes further, and allegedly unmasks Kasrils as the man identified only as "the guy" in the [previously released] 2009 transcript. In that transcript Ngcuka allegedly kept referring to "the guy", who it appeared was the link to Mbeki.'

The article contained some conjecture about McCarthy and his meeting with Mbeki; about the illegality of the handing over of the tapes to Zuma's lawyer, Hulley; an account of how McCarthy's phone came to be tapped; and then more about me: 'Some of the calls intercepted ... allegedly point to a Kasrils role as an "intermediary" between Mbeki and McCarthy. Some of the calls were between Kasrils and McCarthy and the political operators associated with Mbeki's political interests.'

Beezy, now joined by Kenneth, was watching me, the latter with another espresso, a touching act of support.

'We'll fight this,' I declared, melodramatically thumping the table, 'I'll sue!'

'Take them to the cleaners,' they both cried in jubilation as Kenneth saved my cup from clattering to the floor.

Kenneth was taking off his apron. 'Off then for a swim,' he suggested.

'Onward and into the breach. For Red Ron and the beautiful land,' Beezy proclaimed, as Kalk Bay's green bishop, Geoff Davies, grinned across his table at us.

CHAPTER 25

Complaint

Johannesburg, 9 September 2014

WHEN I GOT BACK FROM MY SWIM, Amina was on the phone from Joburg. She informed me that there were *Sunday Times* posters in the streets with the same message as the story: 'Spy Tapes expose Kasrils'. When I told her I would be suing, she suggested we discuss possibilities when I came to Joburg, where I was due to arrive within a day. We shared a small apartment in Killarney.

We talked about a response. Amina had been a media worker for years and we agreed I would grant interviews to the press, radio and television, who were all clamouring to get my side of the Spy Tapes story. Our main discussion centred on filing a law suit. I had three successful lawsuits against the mainstream media under my belt[1] and was gung-ho to teach a lesson to the *Sunday Times* and its sister daily, *The Times*, which carried a similar story on the Monday.[2]

Amina had, however, another suggestion, that I lodge a complaint with the Press Council's ombudsman. She had participated in the council's establishment, was a member in her capacity as a television and radio executive at the SABC, and explained that it was a watchdog over the print media, in the upholding of journalistic standards and in defence of the public interest. Notable judges assessed the ombudsman's findings in the case of appeals, the recourse to justice was swift, and the objective was to obtain apologies from any newspaper found to have infringed the regulations. It was an institution established in our democratic era and its opinions carried significant weight. Amina's explanation appealed to me, for what I most wanted was to get the *Sunday Times* and *The Times* to eat humble pie and apologise for what to me was a blatant untruth. Proceeding through the ordinary courts of the land was liable to be lengthy and costly. And I believed in striking while the iron was hot, while the issue was still fresh in the public mind.

Amina had a copy of the Press Council's Code Procedures and Constitution. This was a slim, user-friendly pamphlet. I noted from the foreword that the Press Council and its various entities, such as the ombudsman, public advocate (to assist complainants), appeals judge and appeals panel, formed 'an independent co-regulatory mechanism set up by the print media ... to provide impartial, expeditious and cost-effective adjudication to settle disputes over the editorial content of publications'. The Press Code was also meant 'to guide journalists in their daily practice of gathering and distributing news and opinion and to guide the Ombudsman and the Appeals Panel to reach decisions on complaints from the public'.

After a call to the public advocate, I received instruction as to how to go about filing my complaint on 9 September from the engaging Latiefa Mobara. I duly submitted my complaint to the ombudsman about 'reports that I believe have breached the Press Code generally and in numerous and serious respects:

'(a) by failing to obtain my views beforehand, and later only inadequately (2.5 of the Code);

'(b) through inaccurate and unfair reporting (2.1 of the Code);

'(c) by failing to clearly distinguish between fact and opinion (6.1 of the Code);

'(d) through relying solely and in an unbalanced way on anonymous sources whose allegations have been passed on as fact (11.2 of the Code);

'(e) by portraying me in a negative and unfair light to the detriment of my good name, dignity and reputation (4.7 of the Code). This relates in part to the content of the reports where I am referred to as the "mastermind" behind a political conspiracy to manipulate the National Prosecuting Authority (NPA); and

'(f) to the use of factually false and sensational headlines "Spy Tapes 'illegal' and expose Kasrils" (*Sunday Times*, 7 September 2014) and "I discussed NPA investigations – Kasrils" (*Times*, 8 September 2014).'

My complaint continued: 'To compound the unfair manner in which the *Sunday Times* conveyed its story, it used a profusion of posters in city streets proclaiming as fact: "Spy Tapes expose Kasrils" (a breach of items 10.1 and 10.2 of the Press Code relating to headlines and posters).'

I said I sought sanctions, 'which need to include equally prominent retraction and apologies from both publications, and with regard to the *Sunday Times* the use of street posters to carry their apology'.[3]

On 19 September 2014 – just ten days after I had submitted my complaint – the ombudsman, Johan Retief, presented his findings.[4] The gist of his ruling was: 'The [*Sunday Times*] headlines are in breach of Sect. 10.1 of the Press Code that reads "Headlines … shall give a reasonable reflection of the contents of the report … in question."

'The omission of Kasrils's comments in the first edition of the first story, and the fact that the article did not say that it was unable to include his views in time, were in breach of Section 2.5 of the Press Code's requirement that (a) publication shall seek the views of the subject of critical reportage in advance of publication … If the publication is unable to obtain such comment (in time), this shall be stated in the report.' A similar finding was recorded in respect of *The Times*.

Retief's sanctions against both newspapers were identical. The essential aspects were that they were directed to:[5]

- Apologise to Kasrils for stating as fact in the headlines that the 'Spy Tapes' exposed him as the mastermind behind the manipulation of the NPA, thereby unfairly and unnecessarily harming his reputation;
- Retract the 'mastermind' description;

- The *Sunday Times* to publish this apology on its front page; and *The Times* on an inside page where the story had appeared.

I was delighted and ready to accept the findings, although the ombudsman had not made reference to my request that the *Sunday Times* also declare its apology on its street posters. However, when the *Sunday Times* appealed against the findings, I decided to cross-appeal and request that my claim regarding the poster apology be upheld. The chairperson of the Press Adjudication Panel was Judge Bernard Ngoepe, a brisk and impressive jurist of many years standing.

The hearing was held in the conference room of the Press Council. The *Sunday Times* was represented by an eminent attorney, Ms Okyerebea Ampofo-Anti, a partner in the prestigious Webber Wentzel firm, and by its in-house attorney Susan Smuts. The public advocate, Latiefa Mobara, was at my side, but in terms of procedure it was up to me to argue my position for myself.

Judge Ngoepe provided his findings on 15 December 2014, in which he dismissed the application of the *Sunday Times* and *The Times*, and granted my application that the publication of the apology and retraction be on the street posters as well as on the front page of the *Sunday Times*. The judge noted that the ombudsman had declined to make a directive concerning the issue of the posters and questioned: 'Shouldn't the apology likewise be carried on posters?' He found that I had 'a reasonable chance of success and that the [Appeals] panel may adopt the view that each case should depend on its own facts and circumstances'.

I felt greatly boosted by this development and looked forward to the hearing concerning the poster issue. This was something the *Sunday Times* had fought strenuously against. It was unprecedented in South Africa for a newspaper to publish an apology on street posters, and it rankled with them.

As I prepared for the Appeals Panel hearing on the matter, Latiefa Mobara, with her ever-present air of good cheer, provided me with a most useful weapon. This consisted of a judgment in a Supreme Court of Swaziland defamation case, where Judge Phillip Levinsohn (the

South African Press Council chair, no less) had pronounced on the power of newspaper street posters. While the judgment in Swaziland did not apply to South Africa, and that case did not feature an apology of the kind I was seeking, Levinsohn's opinion would certainly carry weight. I carefully studied the sixty-four-page judgment and felt well prepared to face the redoubtable Ampofo-Anti in the second round.[6]

On 13 March we duly assembled before an impressive Press Council Appeals Panel chaired by Judge Ngoepe.[7] Once the hearing was under way, my opponent weighed in by arguing lack of precedent in the issue, and saying that the Appeals Panel did not have the power to order the publication of a poster apology. In citing several cases where the ombudsman had not ruled that apology should include posters, she argued that it was clear 'that sanction being requested by Kasrils is completely unheard of and contrary to common practice ... we note we can find no example of such a sanction being ordered in any comparable jurisdiction' and, if applied, would 'establish what ... will be a dangerous and chilling precedent'.

On the power of street posters, I quoted Judge Levinsohn's opinion in the Swaziland litigation: 'It is common knowledge that blazing headlines are regularly reproduced upon sizable posters and billboards which are prominently displayed at strategic locations ... The hoardings also help to propagate stories of doubtful accuracy.'[8]

I enlarged on this and stated: 'Countless people see street posters ... A person sees a poster ... and a message sinks in whether they purchase the newspaper or not. In such a case the message on the poster equates with the headline to a story ... I do believe that it is reasonable and correct that the poster should highlight the *Sunday Times* apology.'

I turned to the question of precedent: 'Why shirk from creating precedent? Does precedence not enrich the law ... there is always a first time in any legal procedure ... in evolving legal principles and procedures. Precedent makes law. It always has. It is an essential part of law.'

I turned to analyse the offensive poster 'Spy Tapes expose Kasrils', as my opponents had argued that it was noncommittal and on a par with the type of poster messages generally seen. Begging to differ, I argued that the message was a highly loaded phrase; and that, given the history of spying in our country, the reference to 'spy' had sinister connotations in the public mind. 'The term "Spy Tapes",' I explained, 'has been bandied around in a controversial manner for several years. It resonates with conjecture about spying, smear campaigns and disinformation from the apartheid era through to our democratic dispensation. In the media, political and public arena, government, parliament and the courts, the "Spy Tapes" saga since 2007 in particular has been clouded in fog, half-truth, distortion, character assassination, conspiracy theories and allegations often citing anonymous sources ...

'The word "expose" has a clear and strong meaning with reference to guilt and attempts at concealment of the truth by devious means. The *Oxford Dictionary* provides the following phrase to illustrate the meaning: "He has been exposed as a liar." That is a common understanding of the term "exposed", which is also defined as "uncover, unveil, unmask".

'Linking the three words in the poster "Spy Tapes expose" with "Kasrils" creates a deliberate, malicious and extremely disturbing connotation about my persona.

'Making amends by way of a poster apology,' I argued, 'would serve to restore my dignity and reputation maligned by the *Sunday Times*.'

To the assertion that allowing the apology would be 'dangerous and chilling', I retorted: 'How absurd that last remark ... what I would say is "dangerous and chilling" is a newspaper presenting allegations whispered by anonymous, faceless sources as fact, blared out on city streets in blazing headlines.'

Turning to the remedy, I explained that I would be quite satisfied if the poster simply stated: 'We apologise to Kasrils.'

Ending on a high note is important, and there is nothing like a good quote, so I stated: 'Daggers in the tongue and the pen — and on a street poster — can be just as injurious as a dagger in the hand or as Shakespeare would put it: "He that filches from me my good name, robs me ... makes me poor indeed."'[9]

Within ten days of the hearing the verdict was out, as reported in *The Star*: 'Kasrils wins *Sunday Times* spy tapes appeal'.[10]

The Appeals Panel stated in its ruling: 'It is a well-known principle of the Press Ombudsman and the appeals mechanism, including the Press Appeals Panel, that an apology or correction should be made with equal prominence to where the offence was committed, and on posters prominently displayed in the city streets where the offensive posters had been originally displayed.'[11]

CHAPTER 26

Unprecedented Apology
Johannesburg, 29 March 2015

ACCOMPANIED BY AMINA, I drove on a beautiful Sunday morning around Johannesburg, admiring the posters with the *Sunday Times* logo that said: 'SPY TAPES: WE APOLOGISE TO KASRILS'.

I was told I had made history. This was the first time an errant newspaper had been compelled to carry an apology on its street posters, to reflect an apology within the newspaper itself. After a jubilant drive around the city we settled down for coffee and croissants with my son Andrew and chums at a favourite pavement café in Parkhurst. We topped that off with a celebratory round of Buck's Fizz (sparkling wine with orange juice) including several other patrons as well, who had joined in the congratulations.

The *Sunday Times* apology was prominently displayed under the masthead on the top right and announced: 'Spy Tapes: apology to Ronnie Kasrils'.[1]

'The *Sunday Times* apologises to former Intelligence Minister Ronnie Kasrils for stating as fact in a headline that the "spy tapes" exposed him as the mastermind behind the manipulation of the National Prosecuting Authority ahead of the ANC's Polokwane conference in 2007 concerning President Jacob Zuma's corruption charges.

'Press Ombudsman Johan Retief said the headline "Spy Tapes 'illegal' and expose Kasrils", published on September 7 2014, inaccurately, unfairly and unnecessarily harmed Kasrils' reputation.

'He found that, at the time of publication, we were justified in reporting the allegations as allegations – but added that the headline went too far by stating them as fact.

'However, after having studied the transcripts of the "spy tapes" (which were revealed after the publication of our story), Retief said our sources incorrectly and unjustifiably identified Kasrils as the mastermind behind the "manipulation of the NPA".

'He said: "Kasrils is mentioned in the tapes only a few times, and then mainly in passing – these are not nearly sufficient to "unmask" him as the "mastermind" behind it all.

'We hereby retract the "mastermind" statement, and also apologise for failing to include comment from Kasrils in the first edition of the *Sunday Times*.

'Go to www.presscouncil.org.za for the full finding.'

I might add that the *Sunday Times* had attempted to get me to approve a watered-down version of this statement. I had rejected the attempt and had drafted the above-mentioned apology with the ombudsman.

Elated with victory and the bubbly, we mischievously filched a poster off a pole as a trophy of the saga. This reminded me of my chums in Kalk Bay, to whom I promptly sent an SMS: 'Dear Beezy and Ken, Check the Sunday Times and Poster! Thanks dudes for your support!'

CHAPTER 27

Informant Unmasked

Pretoria, March 2015

Notwithstanding the Press Council having cleared my name, a one-time comrade-in-arms made negative allegations about me. Willie Hofmeyr, clearly the pointsman for the National Prosecuting Authority (NPA) on the issue of the Spy Tapes, and one of only two officials who by admission had listened to all of them, submitted a last-minute affidavit to the courts, on 31 March, 2015 in an effort to thwart the Democratic Alliance's attempt to set aside Mpshe's decision not to prosecute Zuma, and reinstate corruption charges against him.[1] His affidavit appeared to indicate that Hofmeyr was possibly one of the anonymous informants in the *Sunday Times* story alleging I was the mastermind in the conspiracy against Zuma.[2]

This aspect of Hofmeyr's submission of concern to me was his allegation that 'from the tone of conversation' between myself and McCarthy it was clear that I had functioned as a 'conduit' between McCarthy[3] and Mbeki. To illustrate his allegations Hofmeyr cited calls between McCarthy and me over a six-month period; argued that there was no valid reasons for our interaction since I was not his line manager; claimed we spoke in 'guarded terms'; that we met more than five times in the run-up to the ANC's Polokwane conference; that

together with Bulelani Ngcuka I was a 'middle man' for Mbeki; that he
had worked out that I was 'the guy' and Mbeki was 'the man' referred
to by Leonard McCarthy in one of the phone intercepts; and said that
he was troubled by my stating in a radio interview that I had only met
McCarthy once when in fact I was close to the man. He cited a lunch
which he claimed had taken place at my home in Johannesburg in
2003, to which I had invited McCarthy, Nic Rowell (who had worked
for a while with the Scorpions), several others and himself.[4]

This reference was factually incorrect. The luncheon did not take
place at my home. Rather, we were all hosted at the Parkview residence
of the British author Tim Butcher and his journalist wife, Jane
Flanagan, as a farewell for his friend Nic Rowell. Nic had asked them
to invite me, my wife Eleanor and son Andrew. When we arrived, we
were introduced to Leonard McCarthy and his associate Faiek Davids.
Hofmeyr arrived soon thereafter. Coincidentally, another guest
present was Phylicia Oppelt, who was editor of the *Sunday Times* when I
had my dispute with the paper over its Spy Tapes story.

If I had not publicly identified myself as 'the guy' in 2009, when the
initial Spy Tape intercepts were leaked to the media, I very much doubt
if Hofmeyr or anyone else for that matter would have deduced it was
me. My approach has always been to state my case before conjecture gets
out of hand. I had indicated many times over the years that I had known
McCarthy from the time of Judge Sisi Khampepe's commission, and
explained the reasons why I had been willing to meet him in the run-
up to the Polokwane conference. It was false to conclude that I had
been trying to conceal the association. As for Hofmeyr's conclusion
that my interaction with McCarthy was 'suspicious', what would have
been odd was if the minister of intelligence had had nothing to do with
the head of the Scorpions. On several occasions I had made it clear
that I had dealings with McCarthy so mentioning I had only met him
once in a radio interview depended on what period I was referencing.[5]

The constitutional law expert Pierre de Vos said of Hofmeyr's
intervention: 'Hofmeyr's affidavit is, in fact, a lot of hearsay and
conjecture. I'm not sure how helpful it will be to the NPA, which
wants to stop the judicial review of the decision not to prosecute Zuma

... the NPA is completely politically compromised, has been for a long time and that won't change.'[6] In the event, the Pretoria High Court rejected Hofmeyr's argument and found in favour of the DA.

With the help of Hofmeyr's affidavit, I finally could connect the rest of the dots and work out what was going on in that murky world of emails, Spy Tapes and all the other puzzles taking place in the house of smoke and mirrors that South Africa had become. The vexed mystery of who at least one of the anonymous informants was – often referred to as senior government sources, anxious to provide their version of events from behind a curtain of secrecy – had become clearer.

A letter to the press from someone who had worked with Hofmeyr in the NPA in earlier years, and had then regarded him 'as a man of integrity, moral courage and a keen mind' wrote how subsequently they became 'disgusted at [his] role ... in the withdrawal of the charges against Zuma' in 2009. The writer expressed disappointment at Hofmeyr's being 'susceptible to political pressure in performing his constitutionally mandated legal duties' and being 'so ambition driven' in his quest for more senior positions.[7]

I bump into Willie Hofmeyr on and off at funerals of struggle friends and at book launches, and interact with him without rancour. What happened between him and me was minor compared with other disappointments. At times I am vexed but I have long learnt not to be consumed by personal disappointment. It is the corruption of a whole movement that really troubles me – the darkness that has descended on many in the liberation struggle, which they once served with courage and commitment. We have seen comrade turning against comrade; witnessed so many betrayals, seen, too, how the cancer spreads, depending often simply on the leader served; how integrity and principles could become eroded; how ego and ambition overrode the foremost principle of all that we had grown up with – the principle of service to the people and not to one's self.

This is, on a personal, individual level, what I have called a Faustian pact. Very often, underlying our behaviour are economic interests, as well as social, cultural and psychological factors, and ego, all bound together in wondrous and often unfathomable complexity. To understand the actions of so many of our compatriots, the answer is to follow the money trail. With others, perhaps those comfortably off, the driving force may be ego fulfilment and position. All this, however, falls within a bigger picture. To understand the plague that has become rife in the land, one needs to examine the political and economic forces at play within the context of the compromises and trade-offs made at the time of the negotiated settlement, and the enormous challenges these pose for the future.

CHAPTER 28

Of Spooks, Mules and Moles

Intelligence affairs, 2006–2017

SPYING OR, MORE POLITELY, the gathering of intelligence is said to be the world's second oldest profession. The bible refers to Moses sending his spies into the land of Canaan to gather information about the people living there. All leaders and countries require to know what is happening in the world, what opportunities and threats exist, for security is essential. Given the enormous powers and resources that intelligence agencies often possess and the secretive nature of their work, much can go awry. This is why regulations governing their activities are so necessary. Unless security and intelligence practices in government and the state are open to sensible transparency, operating in a mature and professional manner, they become more of a threat to society than an asset.

Already in 2006, arising out of the Masetlha affair I titled my parliamentary budget speech 'Quis custodiet ipsos custodes? Who will guard the guardians', in which I dealt with the need to strengthen oversight and keep the intelligence services to their professional mandate.[1] My speech was handed out with a small gift – a fridge magnet with the wording of my five rules of intelligence. One such magnet remains on my refrigerator to this day.

In the same year I also appointed a ministerial review commission on intelligence, the Matthews Commission, whose report, as I have mentioned, was tabled at the last Mbeki cabinet in 2008. Its main finding was that the institutional culture of intelligence agencies in South Africa was not sufficiently respectful of the rule of law or of lawful political opposition to the government. Instead, the intelligence services had been politicised and thus 'drawn into the realm of party politics, requiring them to monitor and investigate legal political activity and, as a result, undermining political rights that were entrenched in the constitution'. The commission also found that accountability to the public was weak, a 'consequence of excessive secrecy, which is inconsistent with the constitutional tenet that all spheres of government must be transparent and accountable'. More specifically, it found that the National Communications Centre (NCC) 'appears to be engaged in signals monitoring that is unlawful and unconstitutional' and that 'some senior officials believe that it is legitimate to break the rules when dealing with serious security threats'. The conclusion of the report crucially argued that 'the right of access to information lies at the heart of democratic accountability and an open and free society. Secrecy should therefore be regarded as an exception ... the intelligence organisations have not shed sufficiently the apartheid-era security obsession with secrecy.'[2]

After I resigned as minister, Zuma appointed as my successor a close confidant of his at the time, Dr Siyabonga Cwele. Gibson Njenje was re-employed as head of NIA and Moe Shaik was appointed head of SASS, a step I applauded in the media as I had always respected his abilities. Jeff Maqetuka, who I regarded as a person of intergrity, was made director-general overseeing both services in a new structure called the State Security Agency. The new appointments did not last long and ended with the resignation of all three. Shortly before this came the sensational discovery that Cwele's wife has run a drug mule to Latin America. She was found guilty and received a fifteen-year sentence. Dr Cwele claimed he was ignorant of his wife's racketeering.

In time Zuma transferred Cwele to head the post and telecommunications ministry, but before then Cwele introduced a

Protection of State Information Bill in parliament, which amounted in my view to the retention of apartheid-era security arrangements. After resigning from government I became an active supporter of the Right2Know campaign, fighting against government secrecy and corruption. I consequently took issue with the new Secrecy Bill, particularly as Cwele alleged in parliament that opponents of the bill were 'agents of foreign spies'.[3] As I stated at the time: 'Consider the impact of such inflammatory statements on members of the intelligence services ... [who] will be encouraged to adopt a mindset already noted for excessive secrecy, exaggerated fears and paranoia. And they are the very officials whom the Bill entrusts with all the tasks [of implementation] once it becomes law.'

The irony was that I had introduced a first draft of a bill, relating to the classification of information, when I was minister. At that time new legislation was required because the government still operated under a 1982 apartheid law with a regressive classification of information system and heavy penalties for anyone revealing such information.[4] I had an impressive team of human rights lawyers help produce my new draft. When journalists suggested the addition of a public interest clause, giving protection to whistleblowers revealing classified information pointing to corruption who otherwise might be prosecuted under the law, we were ready to oblige. However, by that stage my term as minister came to an end, and the draft was discarded by the incoming minister, Cwele, and replaced with his much tougher version. The public interest clause did not survive the parliamentary process. As Howard Varney, the lawyer who led the drafting team, has said to me: 'I don't know when it was removed or perhaps, following your departure, the new ministry reverted to an earlier version.' Varney also pointed out that the Cwele Bill 'denuded the former [draft] of its main safeguards'.[5] Cwele's Protection of State Information Bill was eventually passed by parliament in 2011 but by mid-2017 was still to be signed into law by President Zuma for undisclosed reasons.

After Cwele's departure in 2009, Zuma replaced him with a man with virtually no intelligence background whatsoever as minister of state security. This was David Mahlobo, who had worked for the premier of Mpumalanga, David Mabuza, said to be another Zuma acolyte. Mahlobo's behaviour was soon publicly ridiculed.

He startled the country with his antics, such as ordering the blocking of parliament's media signals in anticipation of the pandemonium that would be created by Economic Freedom Front (EFF) protests during Zuma's 2015 State of the Nation parliamentary address;[6] his allegations about the counter-revolutionary activities of foreign agencies and their internal agents; and his ridiculous appearances with walkie-talkie apparatus in hand on public platforms, presumably directing his spooks. Where else could the world see an inexperienced interpreter for the deaf, without a security clearance, officially provided for President Obama at the Mandela memorial event; or a founder of the so-called Anti-State Capture Death Squad Alliance arraigned with much fanfare in a court of law in early 2017 instead of being placed under observation in a mental institution?[7] Who other than Monty Python could have invented a script as side-splittingly insane? However we dare not be dismissive. These people have enormous power and are not shy to use it.

When Mahlobo refused to answer two parliamentary questions because the information was supposedly classified, I blasted the 'idiotic levels of secrecy'.[8] The one question enquired how much his department had spent on flowers for the ministry since 2009; the other was whether he and his colleagues had attended the World Cup in Brazil. 'That secrecy was the world of Big Brother,' I declared: 'For heaven's sake, we are living in the 21st century. It is terribly wrong ... to reply to questions in this way and it is not the case that everything to do with safety and security should be confidential.'

This kind of behaviour fitted in well with the manipulative use of intelligence by his president. When Zuma dramatically dismissed the finance minister, Pravin Gordhan, and his deputy, Mcebisi Jonas, in March 2017, he excitedly waved an intelligence report in the air and claimed they had been abroad with the intention of conspiring with foreign agents to overthrow him. Gordhan, who had seen the report, described it as a crude, poorly written, semi-literate smear.[9] Zuma has withheld the report from public scrutiny and will not reveal its origin. He has evaded questions about whether the report was provided by his intelligence service or simply came from an anonymous source. Without appearing to have learnt anything from the litany of bogus reports circulating through the years, he accepted a document that appeared to make Masetlha's phoney emails by comparison a sophisticated masterpiece of deception. His use of unsubstantiated intelligence has become synonymous with his rule and has seemingly been passed on to his offspring. If reports published by the *Sunday Times* are true, a 'devious' intelligence report compiled by his son Duduzane enabled him to have removed four top Eskom executives. If, again, the *Sunday Times* report is true, then, according to the newspaper, this paved the way for the appointment of his and the Guptas' man, Brian Molefe, as CEO of Eskom in 2015.[10] Given the history of Zuma's accession to power and his rule since then, I don't believe his behaviour to get his way by fair means or foul should be surprising. His clumsy but dangerous methods bring into doubt whether he was ever a skilled intelligence operative during the struggle years.

Zuma's penchant for directly controlling the police, and particularly security and intelligence, has proved disastrous for the services. The appointment of men like David Mahlobo was in keeping with his need to put in place pliable loyalists whom he could dominate and instruct. They were unlike the more senior officials he once installed, such as Moe Shaik, Gibson Njenje and Jeff Maqetuka, with the experience to question his decisions. At the same time, cabinet reshuffles, most notoriously in the mining, energy, communications and finance sector, and executive appointments in state-operated entities such as at Eskom, the SABC and South African Airways, ensured that almost all strategic posts came under his thumb.

Rumours gained ground that Zuma directly ran internal intelligence units, particularly of the political and surveillance type, which reported directly to him. I had often warned the SACP to watch out for Zuma's inclinations regarding the gathering and control of information, and the drift towards a security state.

Under Zuma, the intelligence services were transformed into a restructured security establishment, with Mahlobo designated minister of state security. Then followed the surprising appointment in September 2016 of Arthur Fraser as a new 'super' director general of the restructured State Security Agency incorporating NIA, SASS etc. I had followed Fraser's career with interest after my departure, particularly the controversies aired in the media about his appointment.

For Fraser it took a long time to come in from the cold. He had been under investigation within the department for the alleged improper utilisation of funds, but the case apparently disappeared. Then his surprising recall took place and his appointment at the highest possible level. Nevertheless, a cloud still hangs over him. A security company partly owned by Arthur Fraser stands accused of flouting tender processes and submitting a false tax certificate in order to score a R90 million contract from PRASA (the Passenger Rail Agency of South Africa), a National Treasury investigation has found. Resurgent Risk Managers, a company co-founded by Fraser and the former NIA chief Manala Manzini, may also have bribed their way into the contract, investigators concluded.[11] One wonders whether there is anyone in South Africa's security and intelligence community immune to the lure of power and wealth. Not, it seems, when the cancer is allowed to spread unchecked by leaders who appear to reward those ready to sell their souls. Corruption becomes endemic infecting once decent people who succumb as resistance is depleted as with any disease. That is why it is so difficult to eradicate.

One of the most interesting examples of the intelligence sagas that characterised Zuma's ascent to power was the so-called Browse Mole report. This strange-sounding animal appeared to lie low during much of the Masetlha email and Spy Tapes sagas. But when the intelligence report came to light in 2007, it was, to mix metaphors, akin to the proverbial cat tossed among the pigeons, for it caused terror among Zuma's inner circle who campaigned for him in the period leading to the Polokwane conference. Huge amounts of funds were said to have been acquired for Zuma's stunning comeback, for campaigning and for ever-rising legal fees, and there were suggestions that his most ardent supporters, top politicians in the country, were illegally bringing in the money from Colonel Gaddafi, the Libyan

'Brother Leader', as well as from the Angolan president, Eduardo dos Santos, both of whom admired Zuma and were hostile to Mbeki.

The name Browse Mole was coined by a journalist-turned-investigator for the National Prosecuting Authority (NPA), Ivor Powell. An all-out campaign to smear and intimidate him was mounted by the Zuma circle and included investigations by the security sector and the parliamentary Joint Standing Committee on Intelligence, which sadly, im my experience, had leant itself to Zuma's cause.

In an article published in the *Mail & Guardian*, the harassed Powell explained how he came up with the name Browse Mole.[12] He said it was a name for a report he was compiling, in the main from open sources. The phrase related to already published and available material from the media, research papers, speeches and so on. 'Mole,' Powell explained, 'is an arbitrary codename – the result, no doubt, of my reading of too many spy novels in my impressionable youth.' 'Browse,' he continued, 'is an open source exercise, a collection of information already in the public domain – or at most semi-public domain, as the rules of the game allow one to talk to sources on a confidential and voluntary basis. You, the browser, then sift it all and try to make sense of it. At the end of the day, you make recommendations in respect of follow-ups by empowered investigators.' Powell explained that 'Mole was an internal briefing and nothing more'. But Powell's role was sensationalised and this clearly caused him much hurt and embarrassment. In the *Mail & Guardian* he explained: 'I've kept faith with my former bosses in the NPA and what I hope was a dignified silence in the face of misrepresentations for almost exactly two years now, since 7 May 2007.'

I believe the author was uninvolved in the sensational additions or possibly manipulations to the report, which, as I have remarked, certainly set the cat among the pigeons. And I believe there were a few curious cats involved and possibly quite a few stool pigeons in a flock of doubtful reliability. Those strange creatures were on both sides of the square-off.

What made the Browse Mole so sensational and dangerous stemmed from reports 'filtering through in the media', as Ivor Powell noted in his *Mail & Guardian* article, 'that [Jacob] Zuma received money from Libya's Muammar Gaddafi to aid him in his struggle against Mbeki'. How those funds were syphoned into the country was a matter of conjecture, which made Browse Mole a feared document.

Up to May 2007, Browse Mole appeared to have been lying low, apparently hibernating in its hole, but it suddenly made a startling appearance when a copy was faxed anonymously, or so was the claim, to the Cosatu general secretary, Zwelinzima Vavi.[13] Vavi was particularly disturbed by the contents of the report, which associated him and the SACP's Blade Nzimande, among others, with activities to assist the Zuma campaign achieve its goals. What must have particularly worried them, so I learnt from Vavi himself, who later broke ranks with Zuma and Nzimande, was that the report raised queries about how the Zuma campaign was funded by sources at home and abroad. Rumours abounded about huge sums changing hands to 'buy' the votes of delegates to the forthcoming Polokwane conference of the ANC. This raised eyebrows, given the allegations being raised in the media that not only Libya's Colonel Gaddafi but also Angola's President Dos Santos were seeking to fund Zuma's ambitions. The upshot was that Vavi wrote to President Mbeki, and to me, copying the report to us both, and demanding that the police and NIA investigate what he regarded as an attempt to frame him. Blade Nzimande likewise anxiously reacted by requesting parliament's Joint Standing Committee on Intelligence to investigate as well. They were crying foul and protesting loudly, too loudly in my view.

President Mbeki set up a task team to investigate the origins of the document and the motivation behind the leak. The parliamentary committee received that report and carried out its own inquiries. Its findings were conveniently published shortly before the May 2009 general elections, which saw Jacob Zuma becoming the country's new president.

The committee found the Browse Mole document 'extremely inciteful [*sic*] and provocative', containing unsubstantiated statements about prominent political figures. It also noted that, according to the task team's investigation, 'the leaked document originated from Mr

Ivor Powell, and thereafter found its way to the public through (so-called) peddlers[14] and the media'.

Powell strenuously denied that allegation, stating: 'Curiously, neither the [task] team nor the [parliamentary] committee sought to speak to me before reaching their conclusions.' He made repeated attempts to contact the committee's chairman, Siyabonga Cwele at the time, as he (Powell) was willing 'to assist with any queries ... To no avail. Nobody seemed to give a tinker's for what I had to say.'

That was really strange given the near hysteria with which the Browse Mole document was attacked, and the anger that mounted against 'peddlers', allegedly sowing confusion with contentious information for sale. One would have expected that Powell's eagerness to be interviewed would have been welcomed. But inexplicably not. After all the fuss and noise, once the document's allegations were neutralised, no further interest followed from those who supported Zuma's campaign.

I have no doubt that had the funding allegations been adequately investigated, well-known political figures might very well have landed in prison. I do not think any of us in the once-proud liberation movement would have been happy to see that. But then again the only way to put an end to corruption is to deal firmly and openly with those involved without fear or favour. Like so much spy sensationalism in South Africa, it appears that once a story has served its purpose, it is swiftly forgotten by those who originally cried foul.

PART SIX

Saying No!

April 2014 to March 2017

Thank you for prising open this door.
— Njabulo Ndebele

CHAPTER 29

Sidikiwe

National election, 7 May 2014

As Zuma's presidency unrolled, the signs of the rot marking the decline of the ANC became ever more frequent. All of this fuelled the daily diet of anger and ridicule among South Africans. The abuse of power under Zuma was alarming: not least, the scandal of the upgrade of his Nkandla residence costing R247 million of taxpayers' money, and the blatant protection by ANC ministers and MPs; and the scapegoating of officials and cover-up of Zuma when the Gupta family were able to use the top-security Waterkloof air force base to fly in 200 wedding guests from India for a Bollywood-style function at Sun City. 'Guptakloof air base,' a pilot friend quipped to me.

But what raised anger to boiling point was the slaughter of mine workers by the police at Marikana on 16 August 2012. Zuma's lame media speech that evening, arguing 'this is not the time to point fingers', was that of a president of a country mealy-mouthing the claim of the police commissioner, Riah Phiyega, who had uttered those very words ahead of him. Zuma had plucked her from civilian obscurity and dressed her in a general's uniform. The militarisation of the police, reinstituting their ranking system among other things, by his administration after the civilian-type reforms of our new democracy was a reflection of the apartheid-style *kragdadiheid* (reliance on force) that typified that mentality. Consequently, the country had seen such shocking killings on television as the gunning down of the popular teacher Andries Tatane during a peaceful but militant protest in Fiksburg;[1] the shocking case of a Mozambican taxi driver being roped to the back of a police van and dragged to his death; increasing media reports and civil society concerns about torture in police cells; and then, the nightmare scenario of Marikana with the merciless slaying of the strike leader, Mgcineni 'Mambush' Noki, the man in the green blanket, and thirty-three others, half of whom were executed while seeking to hide behind the rocky landscape that made the location so iconic.[2]

Like so many, I was incensed by the Marikana massacre.[3] I had thrown Zuma's statement back in his face at the time, emphasising: 'Now precisely is the time to point fingers!' I declared that there was a need to look beyond the foot soldiers who squeezed the triggers, not stopping at those higher up in police ranks, but reaching to the very politicians and mine owners, including the one-time National Union of Mineworkers leader, Cyril Ramaphosa, who as a member of the Lonmin board, the London-listed platinum mining company, had been in close touch with government ministers, urging firm action, and even higher – all the way up to 'Number One', as the sycophants had taken to referring to Zuma. At the Farlam Commission of Inquiry it appears that everything was done by the state to shield the police minister, Nathi Mthethwa, and the mining minister, Susan Shabangu, herself a former union leader, from accountability. I well knew from my own ministerial experience that there was no way that the ministers and the president himself could not have been involved in decision making as the stand-off developed into a national crisis.

One of my last pieces of advice, before I retired, to my Communist Party comrades in parliament – Blade Nzimande, Jeremy Cronin, Yunus Carrim, Ben Martins and Buti Manamela among them – was a warning that they needed to be extra vigilant under Zuma, who would increase the powers of the police and the security and intelligence agencies. I had forecast that we were moving into a police state. It took ten years for the SACP to begin to raise criticism, and that appeared to be hastened by the increasing outspokenness of the second deputy general secretary, Solly Mapaila.

It was with all these burning issues in mind that I gave a commemorative lecture on Chris Hani in mid-April 2014 in Port Elizabeth, having been invited there by the district branch of the National Union of Metalworkers of South Africa (Numsa). The country's national general election was due in May, and I was expected to touch on that matter as well.

There was a clear air of expectation from the serried ranks of workers, tough as bolts of steel, sporting the T-shirts of the union. Being with workers was always an antidote to inclinations to depression. The strength and spirit they exuded, the disciplined and serious manner of their debates, were uplifting. They invariably follow statements and speeches with thoughtful focus, and provide a stirring example of good discipline. Before and after speeches their enthusiasm is unbounded and inspiring.

I sketched the life of Hani, who hailed from a poverty-stricken rural village in the region, pointing out his commendable virtues and dealing with the necessary qualities of leadership, from courage to commitment, and, above all, willingness to serve the people. Drawing on the relevance of his life in present-day South Africa, I pointed out how he had been ready to criticise a leadership that was going astray in the difficult exile years of the late 1960s. That drew big applause.

I built on this to remark how in 1991, when he became general secretary of the Communist Party, he had stated that if an ANC government failed to deliver to the people, he would be ready to march against them. That drew even louder applause.

With the backdrop of the police shooting of striking miners at Marikana — many from the Pondoland area of the region — there was a tense silence when I remarked that Chris had added that, of course, we would never expect our government to use batons or tear gas on our people. 'But they went even further,' I said, 'They use hard-nosed bullets and slaughtered our people like dogs.' It took quite a time for the din to die down and I then noted: 'How shocked Chris would have been. How angry. He would not have been silent.'

The energy seething through the Port Elizabeth hall was electric. 'So how shall we vote in the coming elections?' I enquired.

Many shouted out that they would not be voting. Others yelled that they would stay at home. A roar broke out of 'Phansi ANC! [Down with the ANC!] Phansi Zuma!'

I was not surprised at the anger but was troubled by the indication that many would not bother to vote. In eloquent or ribald expressions from the floor, it all came down to the failures and corruption of the Zuma government; the fact that the ANC took their vote for granted; the growing poverty, unemployment and brutality.

In addition to the commemorative lecture, Numsa had organised an extensive programme for me in the area. I spoke to students at the city university, to workers in the nearby motor assembly town of Uitenhage, and to smaller groups of motor industry organisers. Everywhere I encountered the same mood of indifference to the upcoming general elections. Engaging with Numsa workers in the Ekurhuleni area of the East Rand, a vast union stronghold, drew the same responses.

I had much to reflect on. Going against the ANC in such an open manner, as I had done, represented a radical parting of the ways, and much personal grief. Yet I thought of the stand I had been projecting as an act of 'tough love'. This implied that if one's family member was a public disgrace, then firm, even hurtful action was needed. Acts of denialism, simply papering over the cracks, or sweeping things under the carpet just compounded the problem. An 'act of love' meant shaking the ANC out of its stupor before things got much worse.

I began consulting comrades who, like myself, had become extremely disappointed with the dangerous mess the ANC and our government were creating; comrades who did not just wish to complain endlessly at dinner tables and street corners but were action-orientated and wanted to do something before we passed the point of no return. This, I might add, was spurred on by many Numsa members, once loyal to the ANC and the Communist Party, saying that the rot in the ANC was too far gone to save it from within. As for the SACP, it was widely considered to have sold out, having been a major supporter of Zuma, covering for his many scandals, including the shootings at Marikana and the Nkandlagate outrage. There was an initiative within Numsa, in particular on the part of its general secretary, Irvin Jim, his deputy Karl Cloete and others, in cooperation with the sacked Cosatu leader, Zwelinzima Vavi, as well as with disaffected leftists in the political wilderness, towards the formation of a new workers' party. I had been involved in these talks, but the process was moving very slowly.

I initially had discussions with Nosiviwe Madlala-Routledge, a deputy minister of health and of defence in the Mbeki government, and Louise Colvin, a social activist, who had served MK in exile. We soon brought together several other former MK and ANC members. Among these were the activist Mazibuko Jara and the academic Vish Satgar, both of whom had been expelled from the SACP. On board with us was Barney Pityana, an eminent academic and ANC member, who famously had inspired the Black Consciousness Movement in 1969 along with Steve Biko. They all had experiences similar to mine or had come to similar conclusions. I had taken to travelling around Johannesburg and Pretoria by bus, startling the almost all-African passengers, who soon recognised me and would get into passionate discussions. I was amazed at how many said they would not vote ANC and were even considering voting for the Democratic Alliance (DA).[4] In Cape Town I was long accustomed to the so-called coloured people making outrageous jokes about Jacob Zuma; they had been deserting the ANC in droves. And I joined in with the imaginative if ribald way in which they ridiculed 'shower-kop' (Zuma) who couldn't keep his hands off 'die dogtertjies van sy vriende' (his friends' young daughters).

So clumsy had the ANC's approach been in the Western Cape, needlessly giving the impression that black African needs had to be attended to at the expense of the 'coloureds', that the latter had become alienated. This was a vibrant community, the largest demographically in the province, which initially had voted the ANC into power. Not only had they suffered much pain and discrimination under apartheid, and during the centuries of slavery and colonial rule, but they had produced outstanding heroes and heroines of the liberation struggle, many of whom had been martyred. ANC errors had virtually handed the province on a silver platter to the DA.

We convened workshops and exchanged emails to canvas views and work out a collective approach. We had no illusions about making much of a difference, since we had no structures or membership, no possibility of seriously mobilising forces on the ground, and it was already late in the day. However, we spread our forces and managed to meet with grassroots movements: the Mining Affected Communities United in Action of Mpumalanga, the miners of the platinum belt such as at Marikana, the Housing Assembly in Cape Town, the Unemployed People's Movement in Botshabelo and Grahamstown, and Numsa members in various centres. Most significantly, we felt we could provoke a national debate, and rattle the ANC's cage for its benefit, for among its other deficiencies was an arrogance, an intolerance of criticism, a denialism about its faults, the withering away of internal democracy.

We launched our election appeal at a well-attended media conference at Witwatersrand University and received front-page coverage in many newspapers.[5] The name we chose for our campaign was Sidikiwe/Vukani, translated as We Are Fed Up/Rise Up. We prepared a statement with more than a hundred signatures of struggle activists as well as endorsements from civic organisations, and placed it on our website and distributed it in print form.

The statement in part ran: 'We are South Africans who played a part in the struggle against apartheid and who have contributed to the building of a democratic South Africa. We want a just, fair and egalitarian society as promised in the Freedom Charter and clarified in the Constitution and the Bill of Rights.

'It is a profound tragedy that these ideals and prospects are being sacrificed on the altar of self-enrichment and power mongering. Corruption, cronyism, control over the public debate have spread like a cancer through the ANC and, because of this, through government and state ...'

The declaration ended: 'As South Africans committed to democracy and social justice, we appeal to all of you who have registered to come out and vote on May 7th ... either spoil your ballot [paper] in protest or [vote] in ways that will challenge the huge power and hold of the ANC over the electorate.'

The intervention was welcomed by many who praised us for 'having the guts to raise issues head on which so many thought of but were nervous of expressing publicly'. Jay Naidoo, the veteran activist and former government minister, lauded us for the guts to confront the ANC.

As anticipated, we encountered hostility and spite from the usual suspects in government and the ANC, such as Lindiwe Sisulu,[6] who threatened to criminally charge me for encouraging voters to destroy electoral property, meaning the ballot paper. Her erudite reasoning? Kasrils by encouraging voters 'to deliberately spoil their ballot papers ... is urging ordinary South Africans to commit a criminal offence'.[7]

She was joined in her fury by Minister Nosiviwe Mapisa-Nqakula, who accused me of being a traitor, as though in a democracy one could not change parties, especially when your former home had deserted the policy and programme that drew you in the first place. Never shy of publicity, Kebby Maphatsoe, a one-time deserter from an MK camp, who nonetheless became chairperson of the MK Military Veterans Association (MKMVA), accused me of being a counter-revolutionary agent, among other sins. I shrugged that off at the time but it was defamatory vitriol that I would deal with later.

An article by Barney Pityana, in defence of our campaign, was published in several newspapers. Pityana wrote: 'The Sidikiwe/Vukani Campaign has caused waves. It has touched and rattled the South African political landscape just on the eve of what is likely to be the most contested general election to date ... The Sidikiwe Campaign is essentially a conversation within the ANC about the ANC. It is introspective. The champions of the Campaign have not given up on the ANC, and have not formed a political party. The purpose of the Campaign is to challenge the ANC about its faults and shortcomings, and in the end to clean up the organization. It happens outside of the structures of the ANC because the ANC has in fact been captured by a clique that has turned it into an instrument of self-enrichment, and for the control of the state — not for the common good, but for personal benefit.'[8]

The fifth national democratic election in South African history, which took place on 7 May 2014, went off without a hitch in an exceptionally calm and peaceful manner. There was barely a crime recorded in the police statistics that day. This reflected, whatever the outrageous scandals in which the Zuma government indulged, the outstanding democratic standards of the people of South Africa. And they sent a resounding wake-up call to the government.

The ANC's share of the vote dropped to 62.15 per cent — the lowest percentage in all five elections. This was the wake-up call, the message of 'tough love', we had hoped the electorate would signal to a complacent and arrogant party in denial.

The ANC needed to acknowledge that the 11,437,000 votes they obtained were a mere 36.4 per cent of the voting age public (all those eligible to vote), which stood in total at about 31.4 million. A further 41 per cent chose not to vote at all. We had said in our launch statement: 'Given the lack of participatory democracy and unacceptable levels of corruption in the ruling party and government, there is little wonder then that millions of voters have abandoned their faith in the ballot box.' What future was there for our country if the ANC continued its dominance on the basis of ever dwindling numbers of voters?

The Campaign put tactical voting squarely on the table, which led to much reflection and discussion. By choosing a party that would best hold the ruling party and government to account, voters contributed to the rise of the Economic Freedom Fighters (EFF), the DA and, in small measure, the United Democratic Movement of Bantu Holomisa, and to the demise of minority parties whose capacity did not allow for a strong opposition. The EFF was to bring an energetic voice to fill the void created by the absence of any strong left opposition in parliament. On many unforgettable occasions from then on, with twenty-five red-clad MPs, they pressured Zuma in particular during his parliamentary addresses and during question time, exposing his shallowness on TV screens to a spellbound country. The 2014 elections proved a turning point for parliament and for the country, and paved the way for the delivery of a far more terrifying shock for the ANC two years later in the 2016 local government elections. Their share of the total votes cast fell to under 54 per cent and they lost the three major metros of Johannesburg, Tswane and Nelson Mandela Bay (Port Elizabeth).

In a small but important way, with no resources and very few members in number, the Sidikiwe campaigners had contributed to an opening in the political debate. Njabulo Ndebele, the eminent writer, teacher and academic, congratulated the Sidikiwe activists: 'Thank YOU for prising open this door. May it never close again.'

CHAPTER 30

Kebby's Comeuppance

Pretoria High Court, 23 August 2016

WHEN KEBBY MAPHATSOE, the deputy minister of defence and military veterans, slandered me in April 2014, during the Sidikiwe campaign, he was echoing the diatribes by government ministers such as Lindiwe Sisulu and Nosiviwe Mapisa-Nqakula, that I was a traitor for daring to call on the electorate not to vote for the ANC.

Maphatsoe went much further. He alleged that I was 'an agent of counter-revolution' and 'an enemy of the people'; that I had 'purged the intelligence agencies of MK cadres for purposes of selling our secrets to imperialism'; and that I had 'hand-picked' the young woman referred to as 'Khwezi' to claim that Zuma had raped her; and that he could prove it.

At that point I was so involved in the Sidikiwe campaign that I initially ignored what I regarded as the ravings of a big mouth who craved publicity. However, when Maphatsoe launched a tirade against the public protector, Thuli Madonsela, alleging she was a CIA agent, and was forced to issue a humiliating apology,[1] it occurred to me that what was sauce for the goose was sauce for the gander. I decided it was time for me too to seek an apology.

The twists of life can bring shock but also delightful surprises.

As I was considering what to do about Maphatsoe, I bumped by chance into a long-lost cousin of mine, Jenny Friedman, in the Killarney Mall. We went for coffee to catch up on old times, she being the youngest daughter of Rowley and Jacqueline Arenstein, heroic communist mentors of mine back in Durban in 1960–3.[2] She had become a successful attorney in her late father's footsteps, practising in offices in that mall. When I got around to the Kebby Maphatsoe matter, she was of the opinion that I had been clearly defamed and had a very good case.

I accordingly wrote an open letter to Maphatsoe. I challenged him to prove his accusations so they could be tested in court, or to retract them. I said they were 'cowardly and false allegations', which I categorically denied. This was widely published in the press.[3] Jenny formally commenced the legal process by sending Maphatsoe a letter of complaint, requesting he retract his defamatory statement and apologise. He was tardy in his responses, delaying these until the last minute, and refusing to retract either in person or then through his attorneys. I sued him for R1 million in damages for defamation and insisted on a retraction of his statements, with a full apology. I had not wanted to include the MK Military Veterans Association (MKMVA) in the lawsuit, but the association insisted on being coupled with Maphatsoe. Owing to endless delays in Maphatsoe's communications, it was 18 months after my initial letter of demand that I had my day in court.

The case was heard in the Pretoria High Court. I was first in the witness box and for an entire morning was taken through my complaint, and the history of the matter, by my resolute advocate, Dali Mpofu.[4] He had become something of a terrifying figure for the Zuma ANC because of his alignment with Julius Malema's EFF, of which he was chairman.[5] Mpofu was keen to establish my record over thirty years as a commander in Umkhonto weSizwe (MK), and the fact that I had received numerous national and international medals and decorations, including a presentation from President Zuma himself in 2013.[6]

In contrast, it was brought out that the man who had defamed me was publicly known as a deserter from an MK camp and had been shot and lost his arm in his escape bid. Mpofu asked me whether I could recall the MK regulations for desertion. I informed the court that in fact I had largely written those regulations in the 1980s; that a deserter was regarded as the lowest form of life, akin to an informer; and that such a culprit in any army would face severe disciplinary punishment and, during wartime, the firing squad.

It was shown that I had not purged MK cadres working in the intelligence services when I was minister and that my singular disagreement had been with Masetlha, Mhlanga and Njenje: Masetlha having been dismissed on good grounds by President Mbeki; Njenje having resigned; and Mhlanga having sought a transfer to the police.[7]

There was no way Maphatsoe, or anyone else, could support the claim that I had personally handpicked the young woman known as Khwezi and lured Zuma into a 'honey trap' by setting up a sexual encounter, whether it was rape or sex by mutual consent. I was gratified to have my say in an open court on the matter, and found it a therapeutic experience to fully express myself so publicly, freeing myself of much pent-up anger and frustration. I immediately felt the benefit of getting that weight off my shoulders. I had not realised how much I had suffered emotionally in more than a decade, given the extent to which Zuma's supporters had sought to defame me in the way Maphatsoe also had.

It was Maphatsoe's turn to take the stand, but with lunch approaching, his defence requested an early break. As I relaxed with Amina over a refreshing cup of tea, I became aware of a flurry of activity between my legal team and that of the defendant's.

Jenny Friedman came over to inform me that Maphatsoe was throwing in the towel and wanted to settle. The offer was an apology from both Kebby and the MKMVA. Of course, we were not going to simply accept that. There was the matter of the R1 million damages to my reputation and the legal fees, which, with two advocates and eighteen months of my attorney's fees, would be considerable. The question she relayed to me from Dali Mpofu was how much I would be prepared to accept in relation to the damages. After some discussion we arrived at a minimum figure.

Just before 2 p.m. when the court was due to restart, Dali came over with Jenny grinning like a Cheshire cat. He inevitably brought into anything he did an air of levity and *joie de vivre*. 'They've put in an offer of R500,000,' he chuckled, 'but are requesting they pay that and our legal costs with a down payment of R200,000 and the rest in instalments over twelve months.'

That was music to my ears. 'We will write the apology we expect from them,' Jenny said. 'We won't let them get away with something toothless.'

With the proceedings resuming, the judge was informed of the settlement agreement and accordingly had this entered as an order of the court. With that, the case was over.

Advocate Mpofu had read out the agreed statement. Kebby Maphatsoe and the MKMVA agreed that the statements that were made about Kasrils were 'false, offensive and unacceptable'. Their statement read: 'The first and second defendants [Maphatsoe and the MKMVA] hereby retract the statements, and irrevocably and unconditionally apologise to the plaintiff.'

The statement also said that the MKMVA wished to record that it associated itself with the struggle against women's oppression. 'In the extent that the defendants have not always shown enough sensitivity to this issue, they do not believe that it is too late to start doing so.' They went on to declare that many women were justifiably offended by Maphatsoe's statement. 'The apology is also hereby extended to all women of South Africa.'[8]

The proceedings were attended by a considerable media contingent. Journalists clamoured around Kebby and me for statements, but he backed off, leaving his legal team to field questions for him.

I went over to Kebby, shook his hand, and suggested we make a joint statement declaring that I was 'pleased we could find each other in a spirit of reconciliation after the country had seen so much name calling and finger pointing'.[9] And I added that I wished to see the ANC pick itself up and show the country that it was committed to real democracy.[10]

Karyn Maughan, the eNCA television legal reporter, asked whether Maphatsoe would apologise directly to Khwezi on air, but his attorney shepherded him away.

'Oh well, Kebby,' I announced, as he backed off, 'let me be clear, that it was never the money I was after, but a retraction of your statement and an apology. It has become the order of the day for people to be maligned as enemy agents and that has to stop. And I hope your friends in government and the ANC take serious note of this. But I want to state further that the money you are paying will be given to Khwezi to help her recreate her life.' I added: 'This is to help her with her education and to help her ailing mother. They deserve this and I hope the MKMVA will also extend a hand of friendship to her.'[II]

It had been a good day in court where we had seen Kebby Maphatsoe receive his comeuppance.

CHAPTER 31

Girl in a Green Scarf

Johannesburg–Pretoria–Durban,
April–October 2016

A GAGGLE OF STRUGGLE VETERANS had gathered on the steps of the Constitutional Court in Braamfontein, Johannesburg, on an early April day in 2016, to raise their voices against corruption and the sorry state of government. There was Cheryl Carolus and Mavuso Msimang, the chairperson of Corruption Watch, and both senior ANC veterans; Zwelinzima Vavi, who had been expelled from Cosatu; the retired Constitutional Court judge Zak Yacoob; the Anglican bishop Jo Seoka; activist Mark Haywood of Section 27, the anti-corruption forum that had convened the assembly; and, among several others, an ageing, some would say grouchy, Ronnie Kasrils – two years short of his eightieth orbit of the sun. Several hundred supporters braved the cold rain to hear us pontificate.

There were fiery speeches calling for Jacob Zuma to stand down as president of the country, following that week's stunning Constitutional Court judgment that he had failed to abide by his oath of office and uphold the Constitution. I had listened intently to the live TV broadcast of Chief Justice Mogoeng Mogoeng delivering that opinion and thereby endearing himself to a worried populace, with tears running down my cheeks.

On the steps of that self-same court Zak Yacoob, warmly dressed against the weather, declared: 'Our president has acted miserably, dishonestly and horribly. I call on the ANC NWC [National Working Committee, which was about to meet on the question] and cabinet to look beyond the legality ... look into your conscience, my ex-comrades! Zuma, please go.'

He added that it was not Zuma alone who was to blame, and that the work ahead was bigger than one man: 'Our job is to make the ANC NWC aware of what they did by keeping Zuma. Our job is vast and it includes the whole movement ... the whole movement needs cleansing.'[1]

Vavi too made a forceful speech. I was seated next to Zak Yacoob with whom I had had a good personal rapport from underground days. Vavi, enumerating the many Zuma vices, said even a blind man could see them, forgetting the eminent retired judge next to me who had been thus disabled all his life. Zak is a great wit, and leant over to me with a wide grin, his mouth cupped by his hand, as he whispered: 'Ah, but you can see with your mind. And even with eyes you might not see.'

There were so many good speeches ahead of me, taking up all the points I would have made, that I began thinking of opting out when my turn came.

A declaration was read out listing all of Zuma's disgraces: the Gupta wedding party landing at Waterkloof air base; the cost to the taxpayer of his Nkandla residence; the firing of the finance minister Nhanhla Nene and his replacement by the unknown Des van Rooyen; and so on. It was seemingly all-encompassing, but there was a particular scandal not mentioned. With my turn next, I strode forward and said a single word: 'Khwezi'. I paused, then continued: 'Let's not forget the young woman called Khwezi who suffered so dreadfully for daring to accuse Jacob Zuma of having raped her.' There was a collective gasp and then a round of applause. At that point in time Khwezi's real name, Fezeka Kuzwayo, had not been revealed.

I reminded the crowd of the torment she had endured in and

outside the courtroom; of Zuma's disgraceful behaviour; of her second life in exile; of the fate of women in our country; and Zuma's hypocrisy, which had to be brought to an end.

After the event the radio talk-show host and author Redi Tlhabi, renowned for taking up the plight of abused women, phoned to congratulate me. She spoke of the stream of delighted messages she had received about my speech. Around that time she had been in touch with me about a book she was writing about Khwezi after I had connected the two, at Redi's request.

Four months later, a particularly spectacular event took place showing that Khwezi was not forgotten.

The television cameras and the eyes of the country were focused on President Zuma as he rose to speak at the Independent Electoral Commission (IEC) announcement of the results of the August 2016 local government elections. Present in their finest regalia were the country's political elite. ANC ministers and officials were trying to put on a brave face because of the disastrous showing of the party.[2]

The crowd, impatient for the lavish banquet to follow, was bored and hungry after lengthy preliminary speeches by IEC officials. As Zuma began his address on an elevated stage, four young women, in elegant black evening dress, strode quietly and with dignity to the front. With their backs to Zuma, they faced the bemused audience, each one holding aloft a simple hand-drawn placard. Neither Zuma nor the IEC officials on the stage could see the messages. The attention of the audience, and viewers at home, where I watched with Amina, stared either in consternation or in delight. All who witnessed the spectacle were amazed.

The posters read: 'I am 1 in 3', '10 years later', 'Kanga' and 'Remember Khwezi'.

The first poster indicated that one in three women in South Africa were sexually abused in their lifetimes. The name 'Khwezi' would have jolted many people's memories of the rape trial ten years previously and Zuma's inglorious references at the time to how he had been aroused by her wearing a 'kanga'. Those who were confused about the meaning of the posters certainly received an education by what appeared to have been an impromptu and creative protest.

As Zuma concluded his speech, still oblivious to what the commotion was about, security personnel pounced on the young women and unceremoniously hustled them out. Scenes of infuriated ANC women, such as Bathabile Dlamini and Lindiwe Zulu, berating Minister Nosiviwe Mapisa-Nqakula, who was apparently responsible for security arrangements that evening, simply added to the confusion.[3]

The entire country was agog at the spectacle and wanted to know who the remarkable young women were and what had motivated them.

Speaking to eNCA, Simamkele Dlakavu, a student and one of the protesters, said she had attended a previous solidarity event in support of Khwezi, organised by the One in Nine campaign, a women's rights association that fights sexual abuse in South Africa. The occasion had received little attention, and the women, while at the results ceremony, decided on waking the country up.

'It wasn't planned, it was spontaneous. I said to my sisters: "How am I going to listen to this man, when a few weeks ago we were protesting this man?"' Dlakavu said.

The silent protest was a refusal, Dlakavu explained, to be silent when rape and gender-based violence had become widespread in the country. Although Zuma had been acquitted of the charges, the young protester said that an acquittal did not mean the president was innocent.

'We refuse not to name and shame rapists. We refuse to let the country forget, because it happened,' Dlakavu said.

They had made their protest in a creative and dignified way and the name Khwezi was once more on people's lips.

By mutual agreement, Fezeka Kuzwayo (Khwezi) and I had been keeping apart. Neither of us wished to stoke up the controversy around our association and she had wanted solitude. We were both aware that, given half a chance, the Zuma grouping would seek to stir up feelings around our connection to suit their purposes. From the time she fled the country I had received occasional messages from her. These were from the Netherlands or Dar es Salaam, where she had stayed with her mother, or Zimbabwe, where she went on an annual pilgrimage to visit her father's grave. They were caring messages, reminding me of her mother's birthday, so I could send a congratulatory message, or a salutation in memory of her father. She had been back in Durban for about a year and I had arranged for Louise Colvin, my Sidikiwe friend, to be in touch with her and her mother, to see how we could assist, and provide advice where necessary. It was in these circumstances that I had linked Redi to Fezeka, for her to consider whether it was time for someone sympathetic and reliable to tell her side of the story.

Louise Colvin lived in Durban and, with her experience and wisdom, I believed she would be just the type of confidante Fezeka and her mother, Beauty, required. I had been receiving encouraging reports from Louise about the new life she was making for herself; the care she gave her mother; her job as an intern at a children's school on the Durban Berea; the house nearby which went with the job.

Through Louise I arranged a meeting early in August, a fortnight prior to the Kebby Maphatsoe court hearing, and invited Fezeka and Beauty to dinner. There were five of us, for Louise and Amina were present as well. It was the first time I had seen Fezeka since she came to my ministry early in 2005 before the rape issue. I had last seen Beauty in Swaziland, when Jacob Zuma and I were looked after by her and her husband, Judson Kuzwayo, before they fled to the safety of Zimbabwe in 1985 with their young daughter.

Fezeka entered the restaurant, which had been chosen by Louise to give us space and anonymity. Her mother was on her arm. She looked proud and well. A mature, attractive woman of forty, with a beautiful complexion, open-faced with lively eyes, strong white teeth, and a lively smile sitting above a determined jaw. She carried herself with an air of cool confidence: a person who stood out in a crowd.

She was smartly attired with an attractive green scarf around her neck, which suited her. After we hugged, she stepped back, giving a discreet flick of her wrist to the scarf, and asked whether I recognised it. I hesitated.

'This is the scarf you sent me that Christmas when I went into hiding. You sent a card which I still have.'

'Ten years ago, my dear Fezekile. I am deeply touched.'

We turned to Beauty, who was showing the strain of the difficult years she had endured since her husband's tragic death and the second, more recent exile following the rape trial. Louise had told me her memory was not good.

Fezeka was full of good humour and was clearly enjoying her work. She and her mother had never lived in such a 'cool leafy neighbourhood', as she put it, and certainly not in such a comfortable house. Beauty, however, far preferred the community life in the township of KwaMashu, with its neighbourliness and social network, which she missed. But that was a shared family home, with an unemployed nephew. The house was small and in a state of disrepair. In the usual ambiguous extended family arrangements, Beauty had claim to only part of the property.

Over dinner we listened intently to Fezeka speak of the years abroad, how happy she had been in Tanzania, but how her mother pined for life back in Durban — and specifically KwaMashu. We turned to the IEC poster demonstration in solidarity with her. She was pleased and saw this as a sign of the growing consciousness of young women in the country. That gave her cause for optimism. 'Wow, those gals must have been nine or ten years old when the trial took place,' she chortled. 'Some good things are happening around this country now.'

'Well, you have become a powerful symbol to women around the country', Louise and Amina told her in so many ways.

We discussed her future and our concern for her mom. She was in no hurry for assistance and said she would be pleased to have further discussions. I mentioned the forthcoming court encounter with Maphatsoe and told her I was determined to extract an apology for her and myself. She said she was following that with interest.

There had been some questions I had wanted to discuss with her privately. She had telephoned me on that fateful day in 2005, two days after the 'rape', she said, because the women accompanying her to the police station to lay the charge, knowing the law, had encouraged her to inform anyone, preferably someone in a position of authority, about the incident.

I heard how Zuma's coterie had aggressively pressed her and

her mother to drop the rape charge. One of her 'aunties', and she contemptuously revealed exactly who, had tried to pressure her 'to understand the big picture', which was not about her trauma, but about Jacob Zuma becoming the president of the country. Enormous pressure had also been applied on her mother, which had simply served to confuse Beauty even more, about so-called Zulu custom and promises of material benefit. *Inhlawalo* (a compensatory fine in cattle) would be paid, among other inducements. Recollecting the tawdry behaviour, and the leading ANC 'uncles and aunties', some of whom she had known as a child and who had since attained positions in government, turned her countenance into a pained mask of revulsion. That betrayal by people whom she regarded as 'family' and who had been her parents' comrades, still pained her ten years later, as if it had been yesterday.

I asked her about contradictory statements she had made to the press, the *Sunday Times* and *Sunday Independent* to be specific, the week after she laid charges against Zuma, when she was in a so-called safe house provided by the prosecution. She told me she had been in the company of three police officers, one a woman, and after the Sunday papers had got wind of the charge against Zuma, they had told her she should deny that she had levelled charges against him. She was confused and coerced by them, believing her and her mother's lives were under threat. Consequently, under duress she denied she had done so but had every intention of carrying on with the charges. Jeremy Gordin[4] was the *Sunday Independent* journalist, regarded by some as Zuma's spin doctor, who consequently got things wrong after being given the line that there was no charge, and was left red-faced, while Mondli Makhanya of the *Sunday Times*, with evidence to the contrary, got the scoop.[5]

Despite the serious discussion, we made sure there was ample time to relax and chill out. As the evening wound down and I helped Fezeka to put on her coat to leave, she said to me in a firm tone: 'He did rape me.'

Those were the last words I heard from her face to face. Everything she confided to me that evening had been confirmed to me, verbatim, by her close friend from childhood, Kimmy Msibi, who had given evidence in the trial. Much has been made by Zuma supporters, and those like his attorney, Michael Hulley, of the 'coincidence' that Kimmy had worked for me when I was intelligence minister. Such coincidences are common in the ANC, for we were a close-knit community, especially the small exile grouping – although this applies as well to those who had always been inside the country – and such relationships are frequently encountered within government circles.

The victory over Maphatsoe, and the apology from him and the MKMVA, were another notch in the vindication of Fezekile Kuzwayo alias Khwezi. It came less than a fortnight after our dinner, and with it my announcement in court that she would be the beneficiary of the R500,000 damages Maphatsoe would have to pay by court order. I phoned her to convey the news, which she had already heard on radio and through well-wishers. She was extremely appreciative and yet not wildly delighted about the prospect of receiving funds. As tough as life had been for her and her mother, she was never the type of person who craved money. I explained to her that the cash could take a year or more to materialise and depended on Kebby and the MKMVA keeping to the court order. The initial amount would have to go to paying the legal costs of the two advocates, and all of this would be in the hands of my attorneys. Jenny Friedman and Dali Mpofu were quite prepared to set aside some of the funds due to the legal team, which they agreed could be diverted to Fezeka for any immediate needs. She was quite patient, however, and accepted my suggestion that we consult with Louise Colvin and Ivan Pillay, who had remained very close to the family since the underground days in Swaziland. I arranged for all the funds to be handled by Jenny, once money became available.

No sooner had this been arranged than I received disturbing news through a concerned Louise that Fezeka had been admitted to hospital and was not well at all. We discussed getting her into a private ward and covering the payment. But she signed herself out and travelled to Gauteng with her mother to stay with a friend. This was worrying and I began enquiries to track her down.

Before I got anywhere, I received a sudden call that Fezeka had died, from Kerensa Millard, my legal adviser when I was minister. 'No, that can't be true,' I responded with a sinking feeling in my gut. She said she'd follow up to obtain more concrete news.

I hoped against hope that there was a mistake. I phoned Louise and Ivan. Neither had heard such news. I felt relieved. It seemed there was an error. Then Kerensa got back to me with details: 'It's true'. A notice was already out from Fezeka's friends on behalf of her mother. She had been complaining of aches in her legs and had suddenly collapsed. She was gone.

It felt as though my own daughter had died. And yet I had spent barely six or seven hours in her company when she was an adult: a couple of hours in my office in 2005 and some four hours at dinner in Durban just a few weeks previously. Other than that, there had been half-a-dozen overnight visits at her parents' Swaziland home thirty-five years previously. Yet she had affected me deeply and I felt a huge gap in my life. We had been thrown together by the actions of Zuma and the smear campaign against us. Just as things were looking so promising for my dear young friend, her life was tragically cut short, seemingly by the effects of her illness.

The media were in touch with me and I had to find the strength for an immediate response. They carried front-page banner headlines: 'Khwezi hailed as a heroine'.[6] I had stated: 'She was just getting her life together, I am devastated; she was a heroine of our struggle.'

I declared in full: 'As symbolic as the name Khwezi became, so her true identity, Fezekile Ntsukela Kuzwayo, emerges as a martyred woman of our liberation struggle. We must now all honour Khwezi by her real name, Fezekile Kuzwayo. She struggled for truth, equity and justice in a society where paternalism, patriarchy, male chauvinism and violence against women in many forms, hidden and obvious, have become such a cancerous disease, which must be defeated by the unity of women and men of all generations together.

'Let us honour Fezeka Kuzwayo by standing with the women of our country in this vital struggle.'

I homed in on Zuma's responsibility, a man seemingly with no sense of shame: 'The country's president, Jacob Zuma, who took advantage of a vulnerable young woman, needs to offer his apology and pay his respects. He needs to offer financial compensation to Fezeka's mother, Beauty Sibongile, widow of his late comrade-in-arms, Judson Kuzwayo, with whom he shared 10 years' imprisonment on Robben Island and underground work in Swaziland. All those who participated in the witch hunt and intimidation of Fezekile during that rape trial are honour-bound to offer apology or hang their heads in everlasting shame.'[7]

'Kanga'
A poem by Fezikile Ntsukela Kuzwayo[8]

I am Kanga
I wrap myself around the curvaceous bodies of women all over Africa
I am the perfect nightdress on those hot African nights
The ideal attire for household chores
I secure babies happily on their mother's backs
Am the perfect gift for new bride and new mother alike
Armed with proverbs, I am vehicle for communication between
    women
I exist for the comfort and convenience of a woman
But no no no make no mistake ...
I am not here to please a man
And I certainly am not a seductress
Please don't use me as an excuse to rape
Don't hide behind me when you choose to abuse.

PART SEVEN

Faustian Pact

1990–2017

What good will it be for a man if he gains the whole world;
yet forfeits his soul?
— MATTHEW 16:26

The decisions that were taken during the transformation
process in the early 1990s to exonerate the Mining Energy Complex …
were treacherous decisions that are going to haunt South Africa
for generations to come.
— SAMPIE TERREBLANCHE

The sincere, indeed naïve, belief in the value of freedom, equality, solidarity
and democracy that drove all of us at the time, has been systematically eroded
by the eruption of the narcissistic dog-eat-dog virus that is spreading across the
globe in the current era of the hegemony of neo-liberal capitalism.
— NEVILLE ALEXANDER

CHAPTER 32

The Corridors to Corruption

1991

WHERE AND HOW DID the rot all start? And who can we say was responsible? Do we blame individuals, the liberation movement, South African society, capitalism, the world we live in, human nature, an unfathomable enigma? Is there something innate about the human condition which makes people susceptible to greed, the lust for wealth and power? Can such flaws be overcome, can temptation be resisted or at least contained by mere appeals to conscience, by whistleblowing, by tough regulations and penalties? The Chinese resort to the death sentence in cases of extreme corruption, never mind betrayal. In many countries, corruption is simply accepted as a way of life. Are measures and regulations, even extreme combative penalties sufficient, without eradicating the root causes of the problem? For these surely lie in the rotten environment in which the disease germinates and flourishes and out of which the perverse values and behaviour are generated.

It is illuminating to examine a prophetic article written by Rusty Bernstein, in 1991,[1] three years prior to the ANC attaining political power. The article was titled 'The corridors to corruption', and its warnings about the pitfalls that lay ahead for the struggle generation were prescient and uncanny if we consider today's South Africa.

Bernstein, a luminary of the Communist Party and liberation movement, key drafter of the Freedom Charter, and co-accused with Mandela in the Rivonia Trial, died in 2002. He was well placed to formulate his observations and concerns. Writing under his pen name 'Toussaint', Bernstein reflected on the failure of East European communism, and the role that creeping corruption had played in undermining the integrity of former dedicated revolutionaries in Africa and elsewhere. 'I want to try to examine some of the forces that shape the behaviour of leaders of socialism,' he wrote, 'and try to establish whether it is their characters and personalities which determine the system – or, on the contrary, whether there are factors in the system which create their character and behaviour.' He was able to spot the hazards as the ANC Alliance prepared to take power and wrote: 'I want to draw on factors which can be seen in embryo in our own South African liberation movement ... the subtle process by which the foretaste of power that corrupts seems to be creeping upon us unnoticed. We ignore the warning signals at our peril. Unless we can identify and eliminate the factors which have corrupted good honest leaders and organisations elsewhere, we could well repeat the experience of their decline and fall.'

Bernstein considered how a process that had corroded the moral integrity of revolutionaries after power was achieved could well be repeated in South Africa. He considered the metamorphosis from comrade to minister of the typical respected People's Leader whose life had formerly been devoted to serving the poor and oppressed in an exemplary way. He imagined, sensitively and not without sympathy, how the new lifestyle – fashionable clothes; limousine with chauffeur and bodyguards; ministerial residence with a retinue of servants; champagne and smoked salmon; the demands of 'protocol' and 'security' – could come to take charge.

Despite these radical changes, the 'Comrade Minister', in Bernstein's example, was determined not to be seduced and diverted from the desire to represent the interests of the ordinary people. The trouble, Bernstein continued, was that he or she no longer would really interact with the people: 'He meets only other officials, or diplomats and businessmen wanting special favours from the government. He sees ordinary people from the windows of his car, and from the platforms of public meetings. But he no longer hears what they say or think or want.'

As for the aides in the ministerial office, only a few could be called 'veterans of the struggle'. Most were former young activists, bright and specially trained for the posts, and supporters of the new government. But few of them were motivated, like their minister, by selfless idealism. They developed a style of work suited to a regular civil service career, where it was better to do nothing than make a mistake. Publicly they must be seen to toe the official line, and where they were not prepared to do so, they could resign from their jobs, or conspire secretly in order not to lose the confidence of the party leadership.

Bernstein, basing his storyline on the upheavals of East European communism, contemplated, along with the growth of corruption and failure to redress the needs of the people, a scenario of rising popular discontent. 'Things are not going well for the new government,' he wrote in 1991 about an imagined near-future. 'The opposition has reorganised, and is obstructing the new government's policies. There are even rumours of sabotage. Foreign investors are withdrawing. Prices are rising and jobs are being lost. The servants of state want to combat discontent and bolster the government. They want to show the world that things are not as bad as the gossip suggests. They have the best of intentions — to encourage investors, improve the morale of the government's supporters, and dismay its opponents. Gradually they develop the habit of hiding the bad news, or "massaging the statistics" to make things look better than they really are. Only the good news must be allowed to get out.'

Rusty Bernstein believed that the East European experience, first of crisis then of fall, could happen in the new South Africa. We South Africans, he wrote, need to learn from what had happened in Eastern Europe. Those events of 1989–90 could provide several different storylines, all ending in much the same way. From his close experience and study of the socialist bloc up to the time of dramatic collapse in one country after another, he offered the following scenario as a possible example: 'The opposition to the government grows stronger and more active. Some people are said by "Security" to be planning a coup or uprising. The Security chiefs might be right, or they may be exaggerating the danger. They may just be building up a case for demanding a larger departmental budget and wider powers. Who knows? Who, even in the government, can any longer distinguish between what is being alleged by officials and what is actually happening in the country? Dare any Minister oppose the Security Department's demand for a State of Emergency? Detention without trial? Suppression of opposition parties or newspapers? Should public meetings be prohibited and new elections postponed indefinitely? Should strikes be made illegal to protect the supplies of food and power? The Ministers are not reckless men. They know the whole future of the country depends on their decision. If they could trust their own instincts against the whole weight of "Security's" assessments, they might turn down the demand for emergency powers. But if their judgement should be wrong, all will end in disaster. They decide to be safe rather than sorry. Reluctantly they decide to accept special security measures. Democracy is buried, and replaced with rule by emergency decree. This marks the end of all the high idealism with which the people's government set out.'

Bernstein stressed: 'My story is not either totally factual or totally fictional. It is not the story of a particular country or a particular party. But I believe it is a fair example of the real tragic story of socialism's decline and fall almost everywhere in Eastern Europe. It contains within it ... the separation of the leaders from the people ... that separation lays open even the most honest and dedicated comrade to irresistible pressures in high office. It explains, in part at least, what they do – and what they fail to do.'

Bernstein did not hold the view that power must inevitably corrupt, but he argued that we must understand that the 'trappings of power', passed on from generation to generation, from system to system – if unchanged – kept the policymakers separate from the people, underpinned existing power relations and insulated them from the forces of change. In reference to the Freedom Charter, he reminded us that 'the ending of white supremacy ... requires the total overturn of the status quo' of which the existing apparatus of the state was an essential part. 'Since the trappings of state power serve to uphold the status quo,' he argued, 'the trappings of protocol and privilege which surround apartheid power must be essentially hostile to our cause.' And he continued: 'They are incompatible with our aim of transforming society to ensure equal rights for all, and contradict the democratic spirit of our programme.'

While not wishing to suggest that the only cause of failure should be ascribed to such mechanisms of power, Bernstein averred that the case studies provided much evidence for the conclusion that the existing trappings of power were incompatible with the social transformation of society. 'In Eastern Europe,' he continued, 'attempts were made to take over the trappings of capitalist power, complete with all their diplomatic usages and privileges, and use them to serve the cause of socialist power. The results have been too disastrous for us to ignore.'

As a dedicated Marxist, Bernstein subscribed to the fundamental proposition that every social system divided into classes rests on a material base or foundation, consisting of the means of production of goods and all other forms of wealth and the production relations between the classes involved. The objective of a social revolution was to transform the economic foundation of society, but he went on to stress 'that it is equally necessary to change the whole superstructure of the system' arising from that base.[2]

Bernstein explained: 'Eastern European socialists generally followed that teaching. They made sweeping changes on a wide canvas – some critics say too wide. They changed institutions and customs of all kinds – parliaments, administrations, armies, factory managements, schooling, religion and social relations. They acted on the conviction that all former social institutions had to be changed if they were to serve the building of socialism. But surprisingly not in respect of the trappings of power and its diplomatic modalities. These were simply left unchanged. Whether this was because they were simply overlooked, or whether they were given a low priority until they were too well established to be altered, or whether they were deliberately preserved is unclear ... Whatever the reason, the fact is that the trappings were not changed ... they kept the old trappings, worked within them, and were undermined by them.'

Bernstein concluded: 'We can benefit now from the examples of those who have not tackled the problem in Eastern Europe, and in newly independent Africa. Their experience demonstrates the corrupting consequence of simply taking the trappings of capitalist power over into a new social order ... we have the chance to seal off in advance the Corridors of Corruption, where others tried and failed ... It demands that we debate the matter openly ... it also demands that we measure ourselves against the standards of honesty, incorruptibility and dedication which we expect – and generally get – from our leaders; and that we understand the pressures that they will be subject to if we cannot find the right answers. The task is nothing less than setting the world of liberation and socialism on a new path, where dreams of power without the corrupting restraints of the old order can be made real. Real people's power!'

It is worth repeating that these words were written in 1991, three years short of South Africa's first democratic election which voted the ANC into power and at a time when Bernstein assumed that all potential ANC government ministers would aim to be selfless servants of the people.

What Bernstein did not focus on, or perhaps expect of the ANC, was the role of sheer greed and patronage, the immense desire for acquisitive wealth at all costs which quickly came to consume so many people, and which can spread like a cancer of corruption among those holding power or seeking it. Neither did he contemplate the extent to which a disease of corruption was already embedded within the apartheid state and the private business sector flourishing within the dark recesses of secrecy. Without sweeping radical changes and an open democratic system, the weak and susceptible were bound to fall prey to the virus that the activist Neville Alexander warned about. I have no doubt Bernstein would have been shocked at the level of predatory acquisition and theft that has become so prevalent within ANC circles and beyond. And would we not all be tested and tempted as we came to wield power granted to us by appointments to government office – by salary, by comfort, by gratification, by ego?

Soon after the ANC won power, President Mandela established a commission to consider the extent to which cabinet ministers' salaries and perks should be reduced. Joe Slovo was his enthusiastic supporter. A group of veterans were, however, disturbed by this possibility. They approached me and requested I get Joe to back down. They pointed out that he should not talk since they believed he was well-off. They had nothing and needed similar salaries to those of the former apartheid political hierarchy. I spoke to my dear friend Joe and pointed out that the comrades, whether from exile or newly released from the prisons, had no property whatsoever; had never had a bank account in their lives; and had no savings to speak of. In the twilight of their lives, they generally had large extended families, all expecting to be assisted in one way or another. In the end Mandela thought better of reducing ministers' salaries and the subject was never raised again. On the contrary, those salaries continued to rise and apply to a young generation that had barely served in the struggle: it was not as though they needed to be compensated for an entire life spent in the trenches. Those were the realities of life in South Africa. The initial pressure to acquire wealth in the new situation was simply to live adequately. But the opportunities arising for further enrichment were immense and for some became an irresistible temptation. No doubt this was similar to what had taken place elsewhere, in Africa, in Eastern Europe, and in fact historically all over the world.

As Rusty Bernstein contemplated the dangers facing our movement and country in 1991, he asked what could be done at that transformative stage, with its opportunities and dangers. His suggestion was: 'A public campaign by our movement against the entrenched trappings of power.'

We did not take notice when he urged: 'We dare not wait until our leaders occupy the seats of power before we find alternative ways. We have the opportunity now to debate and reach consensus about alternative modes of behaviour and conduct which would be suitable for our own leaders in high places. Such alternatives might well offend against the existing behavioural codes of the hidebound ranks of today's great and powerful. No matter. The offence given by such alternatives is less important than our need for new ways which will be appropriate to a new society based on social justice and equal rights. And inimical to corruption in high places.'

CHAPTER 33

Faust and Mephistopheles

A timeless scenario

I first used the term 'Faustian pact' in 2013, prompted by the escalating corruption and creeping securitisation of the state under Jacob Zuma's presidency. I questioned what had spawned this unwelcome development and looked back at the critical decade of the 1990s, when the traps were laid that Rusty Bernstein had warned about in 1991. My view was that it was precisely in that period that 'the battle for the soul of the African National Congress was lost to corporate power and influence ... We readily accepted that devil's pact and are damned in the process. It has bequeathed to our country an economy so tied into the neo-liberal global formula and market fundamentalism that there is very little room to alleviate the dire plight of the masses of our people.'[1] I believed that untrammelled greed emerged unchecked among the political elite from that time on.

The salient economic concessions that were made in the Mandela era and that bedevil his legacy can be summarised in point form in a list that is more comprehensive than the one I provided in 2013.

- The repayment of the US$25 billion apartheid-era foreign debt. This denied Mandela money to pay for the basic needs of apartheid's victims.

- Giving the South African Reserve Bank formal independence. This resulted in the insulation of the central bank's officials from democratic accountability. It led to high interest rates and the deregulation of exchange controls.
- Borrowing $850 million from the International Monetary Fund in December 1993, with tough conditions persisting for years. These included rapid scrapping of import surcharges that had protected local industries, state spending cuts, lower public sector salaries and a decrease in wages across the board. Although not a huge amount, the loan indicated that the ANC was prepared to play by IMF and World Bank rules.
- Reappointing apartheid's finance minister, Derek Keys, and the Reserve Bank governor, Chris Stals, who retained neo-liberal policies.
- Joining the World Trade Organisation on adverse terms, as a 'transitional', not a developing, economy. This led to the destruction of many clothing, textiles, appliances and other labour-intensive firms.
- Lowering primary corporate taxes from 48 per cent to 29 per cent and maintaining the privileges of countless white people and corporates.
- Privatising parts of the state, such as Telkom, the state-owned telecommunications company.
- Relaxing exchange controls. This led to sustained outflows to rich people's overseas accounts and a persistent current account deficit even during periods of trade surplus, and raising interest rates to unprecedented levels.
- Adopting the neo-liberal macroeconomic policy of Gear. This policy not only failed on its own terms, it also caused developmental austerity.
- Giving property rights dominance in the Constitution, thereby limiting its usefulness for redress.
- Approving the 'demutualisation' of the two mega-insurers, Old Mutual and Sanlam. This was the privatisation of historical mutual wealth for current share-owners.

- Permitting most of South Africa's ten biggest companies to move their headquarters and primary listings abroad in the late 1990s. The results were a permanent balance of payments deficit and corporate disloyalty to society.[2]

I do not intend to lay all the blame at Mandela's door. There were in fact several overlapping Faustian pacts, entered into by various groups and individuals not all motivated by the primitive scramble to accumulate personal wealth and power. Mephistopheles, the devil's agent, comes in various forms and guises. In the case of the Mandela government, the choices arrived at were adopted with the best of intentions and not for personal gain. The Mandela choice focused on the need to make compromises that were not radical in order to allow for a peaceful transition from apartheid to democracy, more particularly in the context of the instability and violence of the time. This meant allaying the fears of the powerful white minority and economic elite by not fundamentally changing land and property ownership. As a result of making the economic, financial and property concessions arrived at in the early 1990s, ANC negotiators in effect succumbed to the fundamental requirements and pressures of hegemonic domestic and international capital. In short, we sacrificed the needs of the poor of our country in a trade-off for political office. It was this deal – or set of compromises – arrived at under Mandela's leadership that led to unforeseen consequences and that, I believe, could and should have been avoided, given what we had promised our people.

My strictures apply to the leadership of our entire liberation alliance – ANC, SACP and Cosatu – and certainly do not excuse my own responsibility as a senior member of that collective. At the same time, I do not believe that the pact that was made involved a 'sell-out', akin to that of the Faustian Zuma to the Mephistophelian Guptas. The belief of Mandela and the other negotiators of the settlement that there was no option, no other possibility, but to agree to the compromises arrived at may well constitute an error of judgement but it was not a conscious betrayal. Nonetheless, it was a monumental trade-off that many critics have come to regard as a catastrophic chain of errors.

In all struggles of national liberation and independence, and any form of revolutionary struggle, the question of seizing political power is primary. However, for social change that aims at overcoming inequalities, rather than simply achieving freedom and national independence, fundamental forms of economic change are absolutely necessary. The interconnection of the two has long occupied the attention of revolutionaries. This was a central theme within our movement, and came to the fore at the time of the adoption of the Freedom Charter in 1955. From that time on, the Freedom Charter was accepted as articulating the broad objectives of the struggle.

The emphasis on economic issues was evident in the ANC's milestone Morogoro Conference declaration of 1969, elaborating on the clauses of the Freedom Charter. In a prescient manner it stated: '[It] is inconceivable for liberation to have meaning without a return of the wealth of the land to the people as a whole ... To allow the existing economic forces to retain their interests intact is to feed the root of racial supremacy and does not represent even the shadow of liberation. Our drive towards national emancipation is therefore ... bound up with economic emancipation ... We do not underestimate the complexities which will face a people's government during the transformation period nor the enormity of the problems of meeting economic needs of the mass of the oppressed people. But one thing is certain ... this cannot be effectively tackled unless the basic wealth and the basic resources are at the disposal of the people as a whole and are not manipulated by sections of individuals, be they White or Black.'[3]

This was the consistent position of the ANC throughout the next two decades and through to the initial negotiation phase in the 1990s. In 1981 the ANC president, Oliver Tambo, stated emphatically in a public meeting: 'The objective of our struggle in South Africa, as set out in the Freedom Charter, encompasses economic emancipation ... It is therefore a fundamental feature of our strategy that victory must embrace more than formal political democracy; and our drive towards national emancipation must include economic emancipation.'[4] The failure of the movement to stick to those strictures has led to the mess that has engulfed South Africa. Those defending the fateful decisions of the time will claim there are no visible alternatives, no other possible way, but to proceed cautiously in dangerous circumstances. In fact, the damage that had been wrought to the liberation movement, economy and country compels us to fearlessly re-consider the choices that were arrived at.

Formal political independence without economic emancipation of the masses provided a stepping stone for all manner of predatory rogues to use power for self-enrichment and the devil to take the hindmost.

CHAPTER 34

Flight of the Flamingos

Shell House, Johannesburg, early 1992

JUST HOW EXACTLY THE CHOICES were made, and how quickly the leaders of the ANC came to agree to them, deserves examination. For me, the buy-in can be encapsulated in a meeting of the National Working Committee (NWC) in the ANC's boardroom at Shell House on a sunny day in 1992. The NWC had been convened to hear a presentation on the 'Mont Fleur scenarios' concerning options for the country's future. Nelson Mandela was present and looked sombre. His face was an expressionless mask. To me, that was a sign he was gearing himself to oppose something or anxious that what was being presented to us should be agreed to without fuss.

Trevor Manuel smoothly introduced the presentation, which took its title from a workshop at a fancy Cape retreat some months previously.[1] At issue was the choice the ANC should make from a set of future scenarios. The technique of scenario planning was introduced in South Africa by Anglo American Corporation guru, Clem Sunter. The point of such narratives is to massage protagonists onto a common ground.

First of these was the 'Ostrich' scenario, which pointed out the risk and futility of the white government trying to avoid a negotiated settlement with the black majority. A second scenario, 'Lame Duck', envisioned a prolonged transition with a constitutionally weakened government. Because the government 'purports to respond to all, but satisfies none', investors hold back, and growth and development languish amid a mood of long uncertainty. Another scenario, 'Icarus', suggested that a black government could come to power on a wave of public support, embark on a huge, unsustainable public spending programme, and consequently wreck the economy. Finally, the 'Flight of the Flamingos' outlined the broad parameters of a measured and sustainable transition that was to everyone's benefit. According to the consultants, the discussions at Mont Fleur involved the recognition that a successful move away from apartheid would require navigating not only the political, military and constitutional transitions, which were receiving most of the attention at the time, but also an economic one, which was not. Furthermore, the obvious economic solution — quickly redistributing wealth from rich whites to poor blacks — could not work.[2]

Manuel evoked chuckles with his wry sense of humour and the quirky titles of the four scenarios presented. He was a likeable comrade and I respected him as a brave freedom fighter, but I came to realise we differed widely with regard to the path of economic development that South Africa needed to follow.

Those wise enough to corporate presentations, crafted to lead listeners to predetermined outcomes, knew from the negative titles of the first two scenarios that those were just straw men (to mix metaphors), which were not meant for serious debate. What about 'Icarus', then, who in legend had fashioned himself a pair of wings to fly near the sun? He paid dearly for his rashness when the sun's rays melted the wax of his wings and he plummeted to earth. This was a warning that anything daring and bold was inevitably doomed. It was explained that 'Icarus' could come to power on a wave of public support, embark on a huge, unsustainable public spending programme, and consequently destroy the economy.

Trevor cleared his throat, I thought a tad nervously, for he is not without sensitivity, and breezed into the world of the exotic 'Flight of the Flamingos'. He described how these large birds set off from a lagoon in low flight, skimming the water and, as they built up speed and power, began their slow, gradual but sustainable 'take-off' until they soared powerfully and gracefully into the air … up, up and away!

Our Trevor could be smooth and convincing even when using US state department modernisation theory terminology popularised by W.W. Rostow.

At the conclusion of the presentation there were only two dissenting voices: Pallo Jordan and me. Pallo mocked the idea of the 'Flight of the Flamingos', comparing it to 'the flight of the Fish Eagle', a predatory bird. (A dig too at Trevor, who drank 'Fish Eagle' brandy.)

Joe Slovo, who was also present, gave the presentation a very polite hearing and was actually angry with Pallo for the roughness of his response. Slovo, who was then showing himself to be extremely pragmatic, had taken to accepting that there was one man driving the bus and that was Mandela. He in all likelihood would have found the opportunity to whisper privately in the bus driver's ear.

Chris Hani was not present and in any case he tended to be silent on issues of economic policy during the rare debates that arose. Pallo Jordan has remarked to me that he supposed Chris was confident that the ANC would adopt the more progressive economic policy of the ANC's own economics think tank, the Macroeconomic Research Group (MERG), when it took office. However, he was assassinated in April 1993 before MERG could report.

Mandela was not amused at our reaction. He tore strips off us and at the conclusion stalked out.

Both Pallo and I saw the presentation for what we believed it was: a public relations session to gear our minds for jettisoning anything that could decisively alter the plight of the masses short of an exceedingly long period of time. They would be the very last in the queue. The 'Flight of the Flamingos' greatly prettified the consequences of economic policy for the masses. As the trendy pink birds soared to the heavens, the poorest would be left mired in the mud.

What were we up against? What forces induced our economic drivers under Mandela to turn their backs on the Freedom Charter and on the economic liberation of the people we had dedicated ourselves to serve? Without a doubt Trevor believed in his presentation and its formula for the country's economic development. Along with Mandela and Thabo Mbeki, he believed this was the only possible way forward. By no means do I write off Trevor's commitment or his hard work. But as he himself has said, the government's neo-liberal Gear policy, introduced in 1996 and declared by Trevor himself as 'non-negotiable', had its roots in the Mont Fleur scenario exercise. 'It's not a straight line [from Mont Fleur to Gear]. It meanders through, but there's a fair amount in all of that going back to Mont Fleur.'[3]

Ironically, the title of Trevor's biography is *Choice Not Fate*, yet the term for the non-negotiable nature of his economic trajectory is 'Tina', the acronym for 'there is no alternative' – in other words, there was 'no choice'. Those were the words frequently repeated by the British prime minister Margaret Thatcher, whose abiding mantra was that the free market economy was the only system that worked and debate about the matter was a waste of time, for 'there is no alternative'. Indeed, at the public launch of the Gear policy, which replaced the more social-democratic Reconstruction and Development Programme (RDP), Thabo Mbeki, then deputy president, said to the media, perhaps sarcastically but perhaps ominously: 'Just call me a Thatcherite.'

If the Mont Fleur presentation to the National Working Committee hadn't already shown which way the party was heading in its economic trajectory, then the ANC's response to a major report of its own economics think tank left no one in any doubt.

MERG had been established in November 1991 and fell under the ANC's Department of Economic Planning, headed by Trevor Manuel. MERG brought together a formidable network of leading progressive economists from all over the country and abroad with detailed and practical experience. It was headed by the London-based struggle veteran and economist, Vella Pillay, who for almost thirty years had worked in the banking sector.[4] In two years of dedicated work MERG drew up a landmark report on transforming the South African colonial-style economy to meet the country's modern needs. It tactically avoided hard socialist formulae given the context of the times and in essence was a Keynesian-style social-democratic blueprint. This was in line with current global constraints but it did also correspond to the ANC's objective of uplifting the poor and setting the country on a realistic growth path with an emphasis on social and economic redistribution. MERG envisioned a two-phase approach to South Africa's development, a state-led social and physical infrastructural investment programme focusing on housing, education and health (comprehensive and realistic details of which were provided), which would provide the 'growth drivers' of the first phase. This would lay the basis for a second phase of sustainable growth when private sector investment would kick in more forcefully as growth picked up.[5]

Such an approach was the direct opposite of what the emergent neo-liberal global economic order preached. Had South Africa adopted the MERG programme, it might very well have attracted other developing countries to follow suit. This would have constituted a serious challenge to what is sometimes described as market fundamentalism or neo-liberalism. Far from being successful, the free market formula has had a disastrous effect around the world, ruining domestic economies and creating massive unemployment, poverty and misery. The other side of that coin has been enormous profits for global corporations, the all-engulfing financial system and the very wealthy.

Such was the silo-style activity of the ANC that those operating in its other departments barely knew of MERG's work or did not bother to enquire. Moeletsi Mbeki, who worked at Shell House in Pallo Jordan's research and communications department, has told me how economic planning reports would be sent up the line to the National Executive Committee (NEC) but received no response. I cannot recall any such reports ever reaching the NEC, at least the meetings I attended.

Those who worked with MERG, such as the South African economist Vishnu Padayachee and Ben Fine, a leading Marxist academic based at the London School of Oriental and African Studies, have related to me how all along their understanding was that MERG's economic policy was in accord with the ANC leadership's wishes and they were confident that they were generally on the right track. However, a *Business Day* editorial later on 8 November 1993 signalled the contrary, lauding the stance of the ANC's Department of Economic Planning (DEP) in rejecting one of MERG's suggestions that the Reserve Bank should be brought under government control — presumably through an inspired leak. *Business Day*'s comments were not simply confined to the newspaper's understanding of the DEP's stance but went further with special praise for the DEP's leaders as follows: 'the fact that the ANC's Department of Economic Planning unanimously rejected [MERG's] suggestion indicates that members of the organisation who count are aware of economic policies necessary if the economy is to grow and create jobs. It also indicates an understanding that South Africa cannot afford experiments in socialist economics.'[6]

When the MERG team had completed their mammoth task and Vella Pillay came to present their report to Trevor Manuel at a packed meeting at a hotel in Rosebank, Johannesburg, on 3 December 1993, they received an astonishing rebuff and were axed, just as the RDP would be two years later. Ben Fine has told me how taken aback he was when those who had formerly lauded MERG's efforts tore strips off him and his colleagues for subjecting the ANC's sectoral work to their macroeconomic model. Manuel formally thanked them and then imperiously consigned them to a footnote in history. He virtually told them to go to hell.

MERG's authors did not claim they had all the answers, but to this day they wonder what prevented the ANC from debating their recommendations. My educated guess is that those calling the ANC's economic shots had a big corporate finger wagged in their faces, which coincided with their own fears and with Mandela's concern to maintain the blessing and confidence of big business.

In stark contrast to the treatment of the MERG team was the warm relationship that had been growing in parallel with the World Bank in the same period. MERG was slapped down with one hand by Manuel, while the World Bank, on which he was later to serve in a top post, was embraced with wide-open arms. A 1995 World Bank report was effusive about its breakthrough with the ANC: 'The South African experiment undertaken by the Bank over the last four years has been quite successful, with the informal and client-driven approach followed by the staff having yielded clearly positive results. It enabled the Bank to establish a meaningful Bank–country relationship in the absence of a recognized Government and in the framework of a difficult process of political and social transition. It has improved substantially the Bank's image in South Africa. It has provided the country with the technical tools required for sound economic policies.'[7]

Whether those 'tools required for sound economic policies' have been advantageous to our people, and particularly the workers and the poor, is quite another matter. MERG or the Word Bank, Icarus or Flamingo? What the scenario planners failed to understand was that Icarus dared believe man could fly. It appears the option we have bought into has turned into a very lame duck.

CHAPTER 35

Sleepwalking into the Future

The early 1990s

ONE CANNOT UNDERESTIMATE the pressures and forces, both physical and economic, that bore down on the ANC at the time of the negotiations and transition to democracy. Indeed, President F.W. de Klerk was not only struggling to save as much political power for the white minority as possible, within the context of unprecedented violence against the ANC support base, but also economic power for the traditional business elite in mining, industry and agriculture. As he says in his autobiography, *The Last Trek*, 'I was deeply aware of the fact that our challenge was not only to negotiate a new constitution, but also to ensure that, after the election, the ANC would implement the right economic and financial policies.'[1] Everything he did was aimed at ensuring that the final journey out of apartheid would not entail the dreaded farewell to an economic system from which the Afrikaners in particular and whites in general had benefitted so much.

Nor was De Klerk expressing the interests of his party alone. Afrikaner capital had long sought to become part of the global market economy. De Klerk had been in discussion with the country's economic elite, its financial institutions and the Western powers alike to safeguard common business interests. This entailed a conscious attempt, largely successful as it turned out, at weaning the ANC away from radical economic transformation. And in De Klerk's judgement, as a man who had accepted the need to hand over the political levers of power, 'the National Party's greatest contribution ... was to promote the adoption of a balanced economic policy framework which could assure growth and progress and which would steer a course away from the socialist tendencies which the ANC had espoused for the whole of its existence, as a result of its close alliance with the Congress of South African Trade Unions and the South African Communist Party.'[2]

De Klerk wrote of the need in particular to encourage the ANC's economic team: 'With this in mind, I gave Derek Keys [his finance minister, previously a leading figure in the mining company Gencor] the task of entering into discussions on the economy with key people in the ANC ... Derek Keys did wonderful work and succeeded in winning the confidence of the ANC.' This was before the 1994 election. De Klerk went on to state that Keys 'regularly reported back to the [National Party] Cabinet on his discussions with the ANC'.[3] Keys was briefly maintained by Mandela in the new Government of National Unity as minister of finance for continuity purposes and to maintain business confidence, with the ANC's Alec Erwin as his deputy. Chris Liebenberg[4] took over from him until 1996, when Trevor Manuel, now well prepared for the strategic portfolio, became finance minister.

I have learnt from Vishnu Padayachee how crucial Keys's role was, together with that of Chris Stals, Reserve Bank governor from 1989 to 1999, and later the equally affable and seasoned apartheid-era banker, Chris Liebenberg. Says Padayachee: '[Keys] won over the young and inexperienced ANC cadres – "God gave me the gift of this communist," he said of Alec Erwin ... [Keys] was charming, and he was always well armed with beautiful slides (he called them his "dirty pictures") and economic data, which were hard to challenge. For he was able to rely on Treasury and the Reserve Bank team, and I learnt that Rudolf Gouws of RMB [Rand Merchant Bank] also supplied Keys with economic data for the presentations he made. Keys adapted the Mont Fleur scenarios, using the fresh, in-depth data supplied to him by these sources. What chance did our guys have to really challenge all this impressive-looking stuff? Key to Keys (excuse the pun) was to prove the dire state of our public finances at the time. Once this could be "proven" to the ANC, any talk of redistribution etc. could be ruled out. And it worked like a charm.'⁵ No wonder that De Klerk could claim: 'We also made positive contributions to the development of the government's economic strategy — the Growth, Employment and Reconstruction [*sic*] strategy known as GEAR.'⁶

In fact, as Jay Naidoo, the minister in charge of the RDP programme in Mandela's Cabinet, makes clear, the new policy of Gear was completely unexpected and imposed from outside: 'In complete secrecy, a plot was devised by a cabal that operated outside traditional ANC structures, the Tripartite Alliance and even Cabinet and parliament, in order to terminate the RDP initiative. The RDP office was closed within weeks and a new strategy known as GEAR ... became the programme for advancing development in South Africa. In one Stalinist process, the entire social consensus between the alliance partners and the majority of citizens which we had been building for decades was destroyed. It was an event that still informs the broken trust between citizens and government today. I felt that this was one of those rare occasions when Mandela acted like an orthodox president, responding to false fears and giving in to the idea that we had to follow the rest of the world and adopt a neo-liberal economic policy.'⁷

As for Mandela, it has long been understood that it was his trip to Davos in 1992, for a meeting of the World Economic Forum, of the high and mighty of global capitalism, that changed his mind about the ANC's economic principles. Meeting the world's business and political elite, he reported, dissuaded him from pursuing radical economic policies. Unless South Africa joined the global free market economy and avoided the disasters of socialism, he came to believe, the country would suffer economically, investors would be frightened off, and South Africa would face isolation like Cuba or become a failed state like Zimbabwe. No doubt the collapse of the Soviet Union and, before that, signs of failure in the socialist East European bloc would have raised Mandela's concerns in prison. One may be inclined to think that he already had doubts on the road to Davos.

Soon after his prison release in February 1990, Mandela began engaging with South Africa's leading businessmen, Harry Oppenheimer in particular, Douw Steyn and others.[8] From that time ANC comrades began to complain that it was easier to obtain a meeting with Mandela if you were in business or a celebrity. That's easy to say. Mandela was arguably carrying a responsibility weightier than the rest of us put together, and he realised he had to meet with such people, particularly from the white community, to ensure that they were carried along for change.

This helps explain the anecdote told by Elias Masilela, a former member of the ANC underground, who met Mandela on an early visit of his to Swaziland. When Masilela in the presence of fellow exiles asked him about nationalisation and its feasibility, Mandela 'was visibly irritated by the question, to the extent that he felt it did not warrant a response. Not only that, he suddenly lost the appetite for the meeting and immediately stood up and walked out of the room.'[9] Masilela would probably have had in mind the statement Mandela made in January 1990, shortly before his release, when he wrote to the Mass Democratic Movement: 'The nationalisation of the mines, banks and monopoly industries is the policy of the ANC, and a change or modification of our views in this regard is inconceivable. Black economic empowerment is a goal we fully support and encourage, but in our situation state control of certain sectors of the economy is unavoidable.'[10]

In retrospect, it seems that most in the ANC leadership, except for those involved directly in the economic discussions behind closed doors with the National Party and big business, were virtually, sleepwalking into a disastrous accommodation with the powerful capitalist system. Our focus was on other battlegrounds, on tasks that included organising ANC structures, mobilising our forces behind mass action, confronting the sinister violence unleashed against our people, and preparing for the forthcoming election campaign. Those were dangerous and exciting challenges, and we turned our backs on the dismal science of economics as we contested for the prize of political power. It needs to be said, that lack of economic focus represents the Faustian pact of a collective leadership to which I belonged. For just as one cannot claim to have been ignorant of a law one infringes, neither can one claim innocence in having left the barn door open when the economic horse has bolted. There can be no excuses for what was a major irresponsibility and I personally regret having let my guard down or allowed myself to be seduced by the thought of political power when constant vigilance was required. We should have been aware. We should have put up a fight. Instead, we allowed the ANC to succumb to the neo-liberal, free market economic embrace because some of us were fast asleep. Perhaps it was akin to tip-toeing into the future.

Could we have decided on a different economic course or was there no alternative to the path we chose in the transition from apartheid to democracy? To judge the outcome, one needs to consider the context of the times and the balance of forces.

The ANC was a popular liberation movement with the might of the masses behind it. On the other hand, the De Klerk government had a formidable military and police force under its command and all the considerable resources of state power. In comparison MK was a far smaller, lightly equipped adversary. But the continuing state of civil war in South Africa demonstrated that the people of the country were not prepared to live under the old conditions, and the regime could no longer rule in the old way. The economy was in dire straits, and the campaign to boycott South Africa had resulted in foreign banks calling in the loans that had propped up the apartheid army and economy. It was in these circumstances that De Klerk sued for peace.

In this context, in which neither side could vanquish the other, negotiations got under way. To reach agreement on a new political and constitutional settlement was never going to be easy. Mandela's assessment of the situation was that it was vital to maintain stability and unity.

The ANC faced stubborn bargaining from the old order and violent destabilisation. Yet a universally acclaimed solution was reached. Key to the achievement was a willingness by both sides to compromise in attaining a new constitution based upon agreed principles. This agreement was achieved through undertakings by the ANC not to disrupt the economy by the adoption of radical policies. These undertakings became the glue that held the transition together, laying the foundation for the beginnings of a just and democratic society.[11] That was a truly tremendous achievement, and credit is due to Nelson Mandela's leadership.

It was in the area of the economic order that generous concessions to big business were agreed upon behind closed doors, outside the constitutional negotiations, between the ANC and the regime. It was judged that the fundamental measures required to transform the economy had to wait. Anything precipitate could jeopardise a fragile transitional process, risk opposition from the Western powers or the prospect of an investment boycott, or so it was thought.

Yet, in my view, those claiming at the time that there was no alternative were throwing away the strong cards in the hand of a movement that had won the support of the masses and the acclaim of the global community. It seems to me that those of us who negotiated at the economic level focused too much on how weak we were as a country and an economy, and did not factor in our strengths as a movement. I characterise their approach as preferring to tip-toe into the future when a more robust approach was necessary. The question is: how much more might we have gained if we had not reined in the Mass Democratic Movement, the trade unions and even MK, with the young lions swelling its ranks? One is left to imagine the leverage those forces could have given to the ANC at the negotiations table and beyond, particularly as watchdogs over government as part of a robust civil society in the years to follow. With their continued empowerment, they would have stiffened the ANC's backbone and helped counter corrupt forces. Our failure to hold a militant course for economic transformation at that time of mass activism in my view opened the gates to the disaster that has overtaken us.

CHAPTER 36

A People's Pact

South Africa, 2017

THE ENIGMATIC JACOB ZUMA is not the simple man of the people he enjoys potraying himself as. Astute and engaging from earlier days, along the way he has become driven by a lust for wealth and power. Whether he was lured by the unscrupulous or was the principal in engagement himself is a moot point.

Jacob Zuma — and the Gupta state-capture project — is a consequence of the economic choices made by the Faustian pact. He and many others have exploited the opportunities presented by the new form of socio-political relationships, emerging after the demise of apartheid, that favour predatory forces. The economic failures that arose as a result of the settlement, the collapse of revolutionary resolve, have allowed a pack of criminals and charlatans to hijack the ANC and masquerade as the proponents of radical economic transformation, which is a term they abuse to hide their nefarious business interests. They look like tin-pot Mussolinis strutting the stage in a comic opera but they are as dangerous as any brand of *Duce* ('leader'), from Idi Amin and Mobutu to Pinochet. They have considerable resources at their disposal and are able to wield influence within the security and intelligence services. All this emerges from a vacuum of leadership and from economic failure. Jacob Zuma has adroitly used the collapse of the ANC's revolutionary agenda as a stepping stone for his own goals.

The danger that all this poses to the ANC and to the country was highlighted by Blade Nzimande in his opening address to the South African Communist Party's national congress in July 2017. He said: 'It is an open secret ... the ANC is threatened with serious decline, buffeted as it is by factionalism, moneyed patronage networks, and corporate capture ... If the current trajectory is not reversed, the ANC is unlikely to pass the 50 per cent mark in the general elections scheduled for 2019 ... Much, but not all, of this popular decline is related to the almost daily revelations of scandals involving highly placed ANC politicians in government and particularly those who have been entangled within the notorious Gupta empire, including the president's own family. The phenomenon of "state capture" of critical and sensitive state organs and state-owned enterprises by a web of parasitic capitalists has created a parallel, shadow state, or even, as some leading academics have argued, a "silent coup".'[1]

Given my 2005 critique of Zuma to the SACP leadership, I listened as Nzimande confessed to the 'marriage of convenience' that had been formed to topple Mbeki and replace him with Zuma. He bitterly added: 'our trust has been broken and we have been betrayed'. I could take no joy in that. The situation was far too dire.

The fact that Zuma's term as the country's president is due to end with the national elections of 2019 – leaving aside the thought of some form of disguised coup to extend his term in office – does not mean the end of the nightmare. He is working night and day to ensure his dynasty is maintained, that whoever takes over – whether his faction or another – will keep him out of prison, that the shadow state he has established will continue to manipulate power on his behalf and multiply his wealth. He might even manouevre for a third term as ANC president.

'It was inevitable that it would get to this point. The great unravelling, the lacuna, the interregnum between one epoch and the next. Now is the time that all the President's men and women – those shifted into place since 2009 (and before) and who have survived and still lurk in the shadows — prepare to launch their final offensive to protect Jacob Zuma,' warns the journalist Marianne Thamm.[2]

Either way, Zuma or no Zuma, unless we reverse the Faustian pact that has made his rise to power possible, those 'treacherous decisions' of the early 1990s — as Sampie Terreblanche has termed them — will 'haunt South Africa for generations to come'.

A cornered Zuma cries 'havoc' and, if he can get away with it, would 'let slip the dogs of war'. Reasons, incidents and frame-ups can be manufactured. If we allow the far-from-simple man and his cabal to win, then beware the apocalypse.

Our benighted world faces the consequences of interminable, overlapping deals with the devil. International monopoly capitalism is wreaking unprecedented havoc in the quest for markets and resources, with invasion, war, destruction and reaction in its wake. As was stated a century ago by Rosa Luxemburg during a previous era of havoc, 'the outcome is either socialism or barbarism'.[3] The consequences today, including the ravages of pollution and climate change, threaten humanity and countless other species and the very capacity of our planet to maintain life as we know it.

Our people have suffered the consequences of decisions and trade-offs made by the political and economic elites, at home and abroad, who believe they know what is best for the masses. Those decisions have protected big business interests, devastated the lives of the workers, the poor, the unemployed, the rural, the women, youth, the marginalised; adversely affected land, water, food security[4] and the environment. Bad policies caused the rise of unprecedented unemployment (35 per cent counting those who have given up looking), inequality, crime, corruption, violence and xenophobia. The result has crippled the country's economy, undermined our democracy and benefitted the extremely wealthy.

We are not alone, for when we look at the world's most powerful country, the United States of America, we are reminded of Marx's observation about state capture: government is the executive committee of the bourgeoisie. We witness a worldwide phenomenon, which has seen 1 per cent of humanity hogging 50 per cent of wealth and running governments in their interests. Periodic financial chaos and bouts of austerity, worsening unemployment as a 'Fourth Industrial Revolution' threatens the majority of jobs, as well as growing evidence of climate meltdown, all reflect the irrational, self-destructive character of global capitalism.

In South Africa as we struggle with the consequences of disastrous errors and deals, the demagogic cries for radical economic transformation are hollow calls from a small rank of crony capitalists headed by the Zuptas, besotted by their own greedy interests, who do not state how their mantra is to benefit the majority. But likewise, the traditional capitalist elite have no answer to the claim that they refuse to invest more than a trillion in idle cash, and overpay their executives to the point that three white men now have as much wealth as half the 56 million population.

What is required to avert catastrophe is a pact, a People's Pact, to be arrived at through a national consultative process built from grassroots participation. No community or section of the people must be ignored in order to give democratic expression to the will of all who yearn for security and comfort. We have an example of such mobilisation in the Congress of the People, of 1955, which gave rise to the Freedom Charter. The 1992–94 Reconstruction and Development Programme process, similarly, gathered inputs from the Mass Democratic Movement and generated a popular programme based on decades of struggle demands.

Today we have a parliamentary democracy, resulting from that vision of liberation, which must be a part of the process of re-inventing true people's power through ground-up participation, which rose to heights during the 1980s in the form of the UDF and mass democratic movement. Today's polity, from municipal to national level, must be transformed by a system of direct accountability to the electorate with elected representatives subject to recall by their constituency rather than being rubber-stamp captives of a party list. Such measures must focus on a new beginning required to save our country from endemic crisis.

Tackling the economy must be fundamental to the solution. Which is why the approach must place the interests of the people before profits, and focus on the needs of the poor in order to eradicate poverty and unemployment. This will require turning away from the prescripts of a corporate-dominated economy, which have been disastrous. We could start by revisiting the product of the MERG group and subjecting their recommendations to consideration and debate.

Vital to economic turn-around and the growth required to create decent jobs for all and an effective industrial policy is to stem the flow of capital abroad and unlock the dormant billions of rand within the country. Increasing the corporate tax rate, which benefitted from the generosity of the cuts allowed since 1994, would create further funds for social and infrastructural investment, and for example provide for free university education for needy students and the long-delayed National Health Insurance. It is shocking that a poor woman is expected to rear the next generation on a meagre child support grant of R380 per month, with even the Democratic Alliance agreeing it should be doubled. It is as shocking as the Marikana deaths that upward of 100 mentally incapacitated patients should die because the Gauteng medical service had to outsource them into inadequate private care facilities where they were grossly neglected.

We do not have to believe that the only way to develop the economy is through bowing to elusive foreign investment and taking more foreign debt — since at $150 billion, we are over-borrowed to international financiers. (Some such loans, such as borrowed by Eskom and Transnet for corrupt projects, could technically be considered 'Odious Debt' and repudiated.) We have the resources, mineral and other, that must be utilised for economic and social development. Our human resource, the talent and energy of our people, must be fully realised and not left dormant. Cuba provides the example of how it eradicated illiteracy within one year in 1961, shortly after its revolution, by mobilising 200,000 students and teachers to fulfil the task, and how after the Soviet Union's patronage it moved to a relatively post-carbon economy. Its resources compared to ours are minimal apart from the turning of human resource into the most powerful weapons of change and development.

The blight of corruption can only be effectively tackled by transparency and competency in government, democratic controls and the involvement of an active civil society, which must be built and preserved as a necessary oversight watchdog of the state, public and private enterprises, and security agencies. That active civil society is integral to all the struggles and challenges we face and has served us well in the past. Instead of searching for so-called 'best practice' solutions from business practitioners and pricy consultants we are able to draw on the creativity of people's power from the examples of history.

The transformation of an economy and society is possible given the people's involvement. What is crucial is the building of that agency for change that was once fulfilled by the Tripartite Alliance now in the process of breaking apart. I am no clairvoyant and cannot predict whether the rot therein can be reversed; whether the efforts to establish a new united front, trade union federation and workers' party some are contemplating will succeed; and the extent to which the emergent EFF, or SACP standing in elections as an independent workers party will become part of that agency. If the SACP can truly shed itself of the Zuma legacy and play its independent role it could prove a decisive force in the process. The challenge is whether the convergence of left forces will succeed and provide the basis for the essential driving force for change; capable of responding to events often entirely unpredictable as they unfold. What it is not difficult to suggest is that without that organised agency of change there can be no fundamental transformation. The working class is the decisive driving force in this regard.

We must keep alive the belief that change can happen and will come if we are properly organised; that people will become again aware of the reality of their situation and seek to confront the perverse and corrupt world for what it is. Such a movement will strive to reconnect with its own history in order to re-establish a different version of humanity, in which human potential might be realised, freed from the stunted form dominated by greed and selfishness that is regarded by many as natural.

Once mobilised and inspired the masses who are the true creators of history have the creativity and strength to storm the heavens. They will do so in a democratic participatory system, where the basic wealth and resources benefit the people as a whole. Call this People's Power; give it the name of democratic socialism if you will. Another world is possible.

Glossary

Alliance	Political alliance of the ANC, SACP, Cosatu and the South African National Civic Organisation (Sanco)
ANC	African National Congress, South Africa's governing party since the achievement of democracy in 1994. Established on 8 January 1912. Outlawed 1960 and operating illegally from then to 2 February 1990
AFU	Asset Forfeiture Unit, which resides under the National Prosecuting Authority with a mandate to recover the proceeds of crime for which purpose it works closely with the Special Investigations Unit (SIU)
BRICS	Acronym for the association of five emerging major national economies of Brazil, Russia, India, China and South Africa, for mutual trade and cooperation. It was originally composed of the first four, with South Africa being inducted in 2010.

CC	Central Committee, the highest decision-making organ of the SACP between national congresses. Congresses elect thirty-five members to join the six office-bearers as the CC.
Cope	Congress of the People, a political party formed by former defence minister and ANC chairperson Mosiuoa 'Terror' Lekota in 2008 as a breakaway from the ANC following the ANC's decision to recall Thabo Mbeki as national president. Support has plummeted from 7 per cent of the national vote in 2009 to 0.48 per cent in 2016
Cosatu	Congress of South African Trade Unions: South Africa's largest trade union federation with 1.8 million members in twenty-one affiliated trade unions, established in 1985. In alliance with the ANC, SACP and the South African National Civic Organisation (Sanco)
DA	Democratic Alliance, the centre-right official opposition in parliament. The DA controls the Western Cape province and the Cape Town metropolitan council and, in 2016, took control, in coalition with the EFF and other minor parties, of Johannesburg, Tshwane (Pretoria), Nelson Mandela Bay (Port Elizabeth) and Mogale City.
DEP	Department of Economic Planning of the ANC headed by Trevor Manuel in 1991–4 before the ANC was elected to power. Was also referred to as the Department of Economic Policy.
DPCI	Directorate for Priority Crime Investigations (see Hawks)
DSO	Directorate of Special Operations (see Scorpions)

EFF   Economic Freedom Fighters, the third biggest
           political party in South Africa, with 8.3 per cent of
           the national vote in 2014. Established in 2013 under
           Julius Malema (the 'commander-in-chief') following
           his expulsion as president of the ANC Youth League

Hawks   The Hawks or DPCI, South African Police Service's
           Directorate for Priority Crime Investigation which
           targets organised crime, economic crime, corruption,
           and other serious crime referred to it by the president.
           Established in 2008 to replace the Scorpions. Shortly
           after its establishment, the Hawks unit terminated the
           Scorpions' investigation into corruption and bribery
           by Zuma associates in the multibillion-rand arms
           acquisition programme.

IEC   Independent Electoral Commission. Established in 1997
           as a constitutional body to manage free and fair elections
           of legitimate bodies and institutions in South Africa to
           deepen electoral democracy.

IFP   Inkatha Freedom Party, political party with its main
           base in KwaZulu-Natal

IG   Inspector General for Intelligence

Imbokodo   Grindstone in isiZulu; colloquial term among ANC
           exiles for the ANC security and intelligence organ, the
           latter section was headed by Jacob Zuma from 1987.
           See NAT.

MERG   Macroeconomic Research Group, established under
           the aegis of the ANC in the early 1990s to develop a
           costed, South African-appropriate economic policy
           for the incoming democratic administration. Its first
           report, rejected by the Mandela leadership of the
           ANC, was published in late 1993 as a 300-page book,
           *Making Democracy Work: A Framework for Macroeconomic Policy in
           South Africa*.

MK — Umkhonto weSizwe (the Spear of the Nation), established following the banning of the ANC in 1960. Undertook its first sabotage operations on 16 December 1961. It was responsible for the bulk of guerrilla and military operations against the apartheid government and contributed significantly to the semi-insurrectionary resistance to apartheid in the mid- to late 1980s that became a major factor in the F.W. de Klerk administration's decision to begin negotiating with the ANC. MK was formally disbanded on 16 December 1993. Many of its members were integrated into the SANDF.

MKMVA — Umkhonto weSizwe Military Veterans Association

Movement (or the Movement) — Colloquial reference to the African National Congress (ANC) or to the broader alliance, including the SACP and the South African Congress of Trade Unions (Sactu) of which the ANC was the dominant formation. Sactu was replaced in the alliance by the Congress of South African Trade Unions (Cosatu) in 1990.

NAT — National security organ of the ANC, primarily security and counter-intelligence in exile, referred to as 'imbokodo', meaning 'the grinding stone' in the Zulu language.

National Conference — Elective and policy-making gatherings of the ANC, which take place every four years

National Congress — Elective and policy-making gatherings of the SACP, which take place every four years

NCC — National Communication Centre. Arm of the State Security Agency, monitors electronic communcations, focussing on foreign signals intelligence. Has no explicit funding legislation and rules governing its activity are not public.

NDR   National Democratic Revolution. Strategic concept
           of the ANC and SACP, characterising the immediate
           phase and objectives of the movement seeking
           to overcome and transform the socio-economic
           manifestations of apartheid colonialism on behalf of
           the entire oppressed people, with the African majority
           and black working class as the central driving force.
           The SACP see the NDR as a necessary stage for the
           advance to a socialist society.

NEC   National Executive Committee, the highest decision-
           making organ of the ANC between national
           conferences, which elects eighty NEC members.
           These, plus the six elected office-bearers and two
           provincial representatives from each provincial
           executive committee, form the NEC. Meets quarterly

NGC   National General Council: gathering of ANC
           delegates, predominantly elected by branches,
           held every four years, usually midway between
           the organisations's four-yearly elective National
           Conference (NC). The agenda deals primarily
           with ANC strategy and policies, and reviews
           implementation of resolutions adopted at the
           immediately preceding NC.

NIA   National Intelligence Agency, South Africa's domestic
           intelligence-gathering agency from 1994 to 2009
           (when it was reorganised as the State Security Agency's
           Domestic Branch)

NICOC   National Intelligence Coordinating Committee,
           responsible for assessing reports submitted by the
           intelligence agencies and presenting a final product to
           Cabinet.

NPA	National Prosecuting Authority, established in terms of the 1996 Constitution as a central agency responsible for all prosecutions in South Africa. The NPA is formally accountable to parliament, but appointment of its senior executives has been highly contested, particularly under presidents Mbeki and Zuma.
NUM	National Union of Mineworkers, affiliated to Cosatu, which had variously been led by Cyril Ramaphosa, Kgalema Motlanthe and Gwede Mantashe.
Numsa	National Union of Metalworkers of South Africa. Founding affiliate of Cosatu and, with 330,000 members, its largest affiliate until its expulsion in November 2014. Main affiliate of the rival federation, Saftu, established in April 2017
NWC	National Working Committee of the ANC: comprises ANC office-bearers, one representative each from ANC Women's League, Youth League and Veterans' League, and an unspecified number (currently twenty) of additional members elected from among their number by the ANC NEC. Meets fortnightly
OIC	Office of Interception of Communcations, an arm of the State Security Agency, responsible for targeted interceptions approved by a designated judge; established in terms of the Regulation of Interception of Communcations Act (Rica)
PAC	Pan Africanist Congress, which broke away from the ANC in 1959 over the ANC's adoption of the Freedom Charter, which the PAC said opened the way for influence by communists
Party (the Party)	The South African Communist Party

PB   Political Bureau of the SACP (Politburo), comprises the general secretary, national chairperson and six members elected by the CC from among its number. Meets quarterly

SACP   South African Communist Party. Established on 30 July 1921 as the Communist Party of South Africa (CPSA) and outlawed under apartheid from 17 July 1950 to 2 February 1990

SADF   South African Defence Force, the military arm of the South African state from establishment of the Union in 1910 until 1994. During the apartheid era from 1948, and particularly under the P.W. Botha administration, the SADF played a directly political role in resisting the mounting, semi-insurrectionary opposition to apartheid led by the ANC.

Saftu   South Africa Federation of Trade Unions, launched in April 2017, with former Cosatu general secretary Zwelinzima Vavi as general secretary. It has 800,000 members in twenty affiliates.

SANDF   South African National Defence Force, formally established in 1994 to replace the apartheid-era SADF. Although most SANDF were drawn from the SADF, combatants from MK and other anti-apartheid military formations (notably the PAC's African People's Liberation Army) were integrated into it.

SAPS   South African Police Service, established as a national police service in 1994, replacing and demilitarising the apartheid-era South African Police (SAP), which had been described as a 'police force'.

SASS   South African Secret Service, South Africa's foreign intelligence-gathering agency, from 1994 to 2009 (when it was reorganised as the State Security Agency's foreign branch)

SCA — Supreme Court of Appeal, which sits in Bloemfontein, is the highest judicial authority, save for the Constitutional Court based in Johannesburg.

Scorpions — The Scorpions or DSO was an independent multidisciplinary agency established as a unit of the National Prosecuting Authority under President Thabo Mbeki in 2001 to investigate and prosecute organised crime and corruption, serious and complex financial crime; and racketeering and money laundering. It was disbanded in 2008 and replaced by a police unit, DPCI (the Hawks).

SIU — Special Investigatiosn Unit, of the NPA, with a primary mandate to prevent financial losses to the state caused by fraud, corruption and mismanagement. Works in tandem with the Asset Forfeiture Unit (see AFU).

SWAPO — South West African Peoples Organisation (of Namibia)

WMC — White Monopoly Capitalism. The term became an issue of contention within the ANC in 2017 as to whether it was necessary to characterise capital with a racial label. It raged around the so-called 'state capture' allegation and the argument that it was traditional white business that controlled the economy and the emergent black capital, including the Gupta family, were small fry by comparison and needed to be assisted by the State and not be the focus of criticism.

Notes

Dedication page

1. Academic activist, Robben Island prisoner, 1936–2012, address at the Strini Moodley Memorial Lecture, 2010.

Prologue: Crossing the Border

1. This is the vicinity where Samora Machel's plane mysteriously crashed on 19 October 1986 inside South African territory, at Mbuzini, possibly brought down by a decoy beacon placed by South African agents.
2. Lomahasha is the village on the Swaziland side.
3. Jeremy Gordin, in *Zuma: A Biography* (Cape Town, Jonathan Ball, 2008), p. 1, gives a formal and correct interpretation, possibly assisted by Zuma himself: 'I can't keep quiet when someone pretends to love me with a deceitful smile.' Perhaps by 2008 Zuma preferred this to the interpretation he gave me in the early 1980s, since by 2008 that meaning would have become too close to the mark.

Chapter 1: Update

1. This was codenamed 'Operation Marion' and led to the charging of General Magnus Malan and other apartheid-era generals in 1995 on murder charges in Natal in the 1980s. They were acquitted owing to lack of evidence.
2. Gwala was a veteran leader of the South African Communist Party (SACP) and had been imprisoned with Mandela on Roben Island. Nzimande later came to prominence as general secretary of the SACP.
3. The ANC did not at the time consider itself a political party but rather a national liberation movement.

Chapter 2: Spooks

1. Zulu and Xhosa terms
2. The more formal term is the South African War.

3   Parliamentary Budget Address, 25 May 2007, 'Emulating the African spies of yesteryear'.

Chapter 3: A Suitable Man
1   See Gordon, *Zuma: A Biography*, pp 67–8.
2   Nkosazana Dlamini-Zuma was minister of health and then minister of foreign affairs. Jacob Zuma was member of the Executive Council (MEC) for economic affairs and tourism in the KZN legislature, 1994–9.

Chapter 4: A Long Shadow
1   Whilst there was some talk of Zuma having been linked to Thami Zulu's sad fate, as the head of ANC intelligence, it was Thabo Mbeki who explained to the TRC that an internal ANC Commission of Inquiry had not made any conclusive findings about that (South African History online: biography of Jacob Zuma). But the Motsuenyane Commission, investigating abuses of detainees expressed unhappiness 'with Zuma's explanations of events that took place and condemned him for not exercising proper supervision' (ibid) and see TRC, Final Report, Ch. 6, p 242.
     There are many references to Thami Zulu's incarceration and Zuma's responsibility as the ANC's head of intelligence, which Zuma has never responded to. See: *David Beresford, Truth is a Strange Fruit* (Johannesburg, Jacana Media, 2010); Stephen Ellis, *External Mission: The ANC in Exile 1960–1990* (London, Hurst, 2012); Kenneth Good, 'How the killing of Thami Zulu contradicts Zuma's claims', *Politics Web*, 13 May 2013. Good places credibility on Beresford's assumptions that Zuma's silences 'justify an assumption, if not presumption of guilt', which I believe is justified in raising with regard to Thami Zulu's 14-month detention and incarceration in miserable conditions. See also: 'Jacob Zuma is by most accounts a useless manager', *Business Day*, 21 March 2009 (with the comment, 'Its time he [Zuma] felt the pain of Zulu's family and told them and the country what happened to their son.'); Paul Trewhela, 'Jacob Zuma, Mbokodo and the death of Thami Zulu', *MoneyWeb*, 13 February, 2009; Christi ven der Westhuizen, 'The Z factor: Is the real Jacob Zuma emerging?', *Mail & Guardian*, 25 November, 2009

Chapter 5: Working-Class Hero
1   With a changed policy on supplying the antiretroviral medicines in 2004 when life expectancy was 52, today it is 64. From a near zero of black south Africas getting the medication in 2004, nearly 4 million do today
2   Adriaan Basson, *Zuma Exposed* (Cape Town, Jonathan Ball, 2012), p. 139..

Chapter 6: A Question of Morality
1   According to Roger Southall writing in *The Conversation*, PricewaterhouseCoopers in 2014 and 2016 recorded the Sandton bourgeoisie as the world's most economically criminal, ahead of France and Kenya.
2   Shortly before his death in May 2005 Tony Holiday made an observation in the *Cape Times* under the heading 'Block Zuma, or SA courts disaster': 'If this country is to achieve its goal of permanent First World status and retain its rank as repository of Africa's hopes for economic and political renewal, then Jacob Zuma must not become our next president … Mbeki's chief difficulty is to find a way of stopping Zuma without doing irreparable damage to the ANC … As the drama unfolds, Mbeki may well find that he has to choose between party unity and national survival.'

See Neil Marais, 'On Tony Holiday', *Daily Maverick*, 27 September 2017.
3   Maharaj and Moe Shaik accused Ngcuka of being an apartheid-era agent, but the Harms Commission cleared Ngcuka of this charge.

Chapter 7: Wolf Boys
1   On 20 September, four days after I interviewed the trio, Inspector General Ngcakani began his investigation in terms of the Intelligence Services Oversight Act, 1994. The information I have recounted and later reveal appeared in the media and in a report Ngcakani placed in the public domain: *Executive Summary of Final Report of an Investigation into Operations Carried Out by NIA on Mr S Macozoma – Extended Terms of Reference on the Authenticity of the Allegedly Intercepted E-mails*, Media Release, 23 March 2006.

Chapter 8: A Long Night
1   These emails and others later cited are all in the public domain.
2   Sir Walter Scott's poem 'Marmion', which refers to a forged letter implicating an innocent person in treason.
3   David Beresford, *Ten Men Dead* (London, HarperCollins, 1987).

Chapter 9: On Billy's Trail
1   The initial 1976 group had trained in Angola while I was still in London, and he had moved on to Lusaka, Zambia, as part of the Youth League, when I transferred to Angola. Later he was based in London for ANC intelligence while I was in Maputo and, then, Lusaka with MK. And he was originally in government intelligence (first as deputy and then as chief of SASS) while I served in defence and then water and forestry.
2   *Mail & Guardian Online*, 14 October 2005.

Chapter 10: The Plot Thickens
1   Executive Summary of the IG's Final Report – Media Release, 23 March 2006.
2   On the information at hand I concluded it was necessary to ascertain whether Avani was linked to the Macozoma surveillance operation. Accordingly, I extended the IG's terms of reference to include this. It had been a quick check with President Mbeki to ascertain that he knew nothing of Avani.

Chapter 11: Services Day
1   Strategic Communications was a unit of the apartheid-era security agencies, specialising in disinformation, character assassination and smearing of opponents.
2   'Sinister e-mails slammed' and 'Spygate probe widens', *News24*, 23 October 2005.
3   Address by Minister Kasrils, Musanda, 21 October 2005.
4   Up to the termination of my term in office on 30 September 2008, the president's speech could be viewed on the website of the Ministry of Intelligence Services at www.intelligence.gov.za/Speeches.html, and also that of the Presidency.

Chapter 12: Knocked Down by a Feather
1   The NEC met at Esselen Park outside Johannesburg on the weekend of 18–20 November 2005.
2   Sam Sole and Nic Dawes, with Rapule Tabane, 'Why is Billy Masetlha still at

large?', *Mail & Guardian*, 31 March 2006.

3   The email extracts in this chapter have been sourced from a *Mail & Guardian* report, dated 15 December 2005 by Sam Sole and Nic Dawes. Their story included this caveat: 'The following are extracts from the alleged e-mail exchanges, with, in some instances, the names of the alleged senders deleted. In publishing them, the *Mail & Guardian* in no way implies that they are authentic communications.'

4   Vusi Pikoli, head of the NPA, and Manne Dipico, former ANC premier of Northern Cape province and a business associate of Kgalema Motlanthe.

5   Sandi Majali, a business associate who had featured in the media in connection with a notorious oil deal.

6   Joel Netshitenzhe, regarded as a loyal Mbeki intellectual, who headed the policy unit during the Mbeki Presidency.

7   The NPA's crack investigating prosecutor.

8   Mhlanga and Njenje.

9   This and the next email were in the Kgalema dossier but did not appear in the *Mail & Guardian* report of 15 December 2005. I was, however, able to obtain, in my personal capacity, all emails relevant to myself in order to analyse them for the IG's inquiry. These were not classified documents.

Chapter 13: Connecting the Dots

1   Caxton CTP Publishers and Printers fund the Caxton Chair of Journalism at the University of the Witwatersrand, held at the time by Harber.

2   I cannot recall whether I referred to Zuma at this or a subsequent NEC meeting when we discussed the IG's final report. The emails were discussed at two NEC meetings.

3   Executive Summary of the Final report, Media Release, 23 March 2006.

Chapter 14: Emails Unlocked

1   *Sunday Argus*, 31 May 2009. The two companies were Multi-Consult Technologies, a BEE (Black Economic Empowerment) information technology company in South Africa, and Paradyne Networks, based in the US.

2   The Kwasizabantu Mission, near Kranskop, KwaZulu-Natal. Interesting background on the mission, and its political positioning while Kunene was working there, can be found on www.ksb-alert.com/confession/ and www.ksb-alert.com/.

3   South West Africa People's Organisation.

4   *Sunday Argus*, 31 May 2009, reported Koos Greeff alleging the Kwasizabantu Mission was used for training self-defence units, and the existence of a close relationship between some church members and apartheid-era military intelligence.

5   From the IG's *Executive Summary of Final Report of an Investigation into Operations Carried Out by NIA on Mr S Macozoma — Extended Terms of Reference on the Authenticity of the Allegedly Intercepted E-mails*, Media Release, 23 March 2006, posted on www.orgi.gov.za.

6   'Dit gaan baie goed met my, General, ek hoop dit gaan ook goed met U ... ons het a groot problem die kant.' The correct Afrikaans would be: 'Dit gaan baie goed met my, *Generaal*, ek hoop dit gaan ook goed met *u* ... ons het *'n* groot *probleem* aan hierdie kant.' No literate Afrikaner would use the capital 'U' in addressing another person, for that is reserved for addressing God. The lower case 'u' is applied when addressing a person.

7   A hard copy because the emails were presented in print-out form.

8   Muzi Kunene's identity was not furnished in the *Executive Summary of the Final Report*

but became publicly known through media reports and when he stood trial.

9   Such as Njenje and Mhlanga.

10 *Executive Summary of Final Report of an Investigation into Operations Carried Out by NIA on Mr S Macozoma — Extended Terms of Reference on the Authenticity of the Allegedly Intercepted E-mails*, Media Release, 23 March 2006, posted on www.orgi.gov.za.

11 There were fourteen counts against Masetlha, such as failing to report to the minister on the surveillance of Saki Macozoma; misleading the minister and the investigative team; failing to exercise the required degree of management and oversight over the surveillance operation; sanctioning the unlawful surveillance of Macozoma, Tony Leon and Anton Harber; instructing the unlawful interception of voice communications without a judge's authorisation; outsourcing intelligence functions to a private entity (Kunene) without proper registration; participation with Muzi Kunene in the manufacturing and distribution of the allegedly intercepted emails; misrepresenting the authenticity of the emails and knowingly using fake emails to direct and inform intelligence projects; obtaining a financial benefit for a source (i.e. Kunene) from NIA based on an unlawful activity; and so on.

    Gravest among the charges were failure to inform the president and minister of the emails despite their gravity and impact on national security; and seeking to mislead the president and minister through the inclusion of knowingly fabricated emails in the Presidential Special Investigative Task Team Report.

    Charges against Bob Mhlanga centred on transgressions related to the Macozoma surveillance operation: misleading the investigative team; failure to exercise management and oversight; and failure to comply with mandatory operational and authorisation procedures.

    Charges against Funi Madlala related to his role concerning the emails and Kunene: as an accomplice of Masetlha in misrepresenting the authenticity of the emails; as an accomplice of Kunene in the fabrication of the emails; misleading the IG about his relationship with Kunene; and obtaining a financial benefit for Kunene based on an unlawful activity.

    The IG noted that his investigation provided sufficient prima facie evidence to warrant criminal charges against various individuals. He pointed out, however, that an outcome as to individual culpability would ultimately depend on further evidence obtained and gathered through criminal investigation. These criminal charges related to defrauding NIA of R152,000 paid to Kunene; instructing the unlawful interception of voice communications without proper authorisation of a designated judge (Masetlha); and unlawful interception of data communications (Kunene).

12 Unfortunately this was not followed through.

Chapter 15: Hook, Line and Sinker

1 *The Star*, 24 March 2006.

2 'Why is Billy Masetlha still at large?', *Mail & Guardian*, 26 March 2006.

3 Paul Vecchiatto, 'Zuma e-mails "the work of amateurs"', *ITWeb*, 29 March 2006.

4 'Hoax email saga far from over', *IOL Online*, 22 March 2007, www.iol.co.za/news/politics/hoax-email-saga-far-from-over-319935.

5 Announced at an NEC meeting on 25 March 2006, following the release of the IG's report and the dismissal of Masetlha.

6 Motlanthe insisted that the report be handed back at the end of proceedings.

7 'Spy-war emails: What they really say', *Mail & Guardian*, 15 December 2005.

Notes

Chapter 16: In Cold Blood

1 Madlala was NIA's cyber unit manager under Masetlha.
2 Hanti Otto, 'Kunene guilty of shooting son', *The Witness*, 17 October 2013.
3 'Kunene gets life for murder of estate agent', www.mg.co.za/article/2009-05-29-kunene-gets-life-for-murder-of-estate-agent; SAPA, 29 May 2009.
4 A murderous anti-Swapo police unit that served apartheid in Namibia. Koevoet literally translates from Afrikaans as 'crowbar'.
5 The Pamodzi group, established in 1979, is a South African investment company (although the name is imported – it means 'togetherness' in Zambia's dominant schiNyanja language). Although well established by 1990, as a construction company building two-rooms-and-a-garage township houses, it benefitted greatly from the achievement of political democracy.
6 'Meet Mr E', *Mail & Guardian*, 25 November 2005.
7 Inspector General's *Final Report of an Investigation into Operations Carried Out by NIA on Mr S Macozoma – Extended Terms of Reference on the Authenticity of the Allegedly Intercepted E-mails*, Finding and Recommendations, pp. 122–3, 8 March 2006.

Chapter 18: Kanga Man

1 Elizabeth Skeen, 'The rape of a trial: Jacob Zuma, Aids, conspiracy and tribalism in neo-liberal, post-apartheid South Africa' (BA thesis, 2007, Princeton University), www.amandlawonye.wikispaces.com/2007 and see also Jeremy Gordin, *Zuma: A Biography* (Cape Town, Jonathan Ball, 2008).
2 The term 'bunga bunga' was popularised by the Italian media during the 2011 judicial investigation into Silvio Berlusconi's underage prostitution charges.
3 Gordin, *Zuma*, pp. 154-5.
4 Originally an African garment worn by both men and women, similar to a sarong, and also known as a kitenge.
5 Jacques Depelchin, *Silences in African History* (Dar es Salaam, Mkuki na Nyota Publishers, 2005), pp. 4 and 21. I am grateful to the respected law academic and struggle veteran Raymond Suttner for his comprehensive review of the trial and for bringing Depelchin's work to my attention.
6 Wits Institute for Social and Economic Research workshop on 'The arts of human rights' on Thursday, 31 July 2014. Yacoob was answering a question and gave this answer.

Chapter 19: The Dogs of War

1 Fellow NEC members.
2 I believe I once challenged him in the *Mail & Guardian* but have failed to trace the item.
3 The so-called Meiring Report was drawn up by Defence Intelligence and passed on directly to President Mandela. It was slickly written and alleged that General Bantu Holomisa, Winnie Mandela and General Siphiwe Nyanda – next in line to succeed General Georg Meiring as head of the defence force – were plotting a violent revolution aimed at overthrowing Mandela. It was alleged that Robert McBride, formerly MK, was smuggling arms into the country from Mozambique for the rebels. The cunning nature of the report was that the authors had McBride under surveillance and had their Mozambican agent entice him into a meeting in Maputo. At the same time the report was handed to Mandela, the trap for McBride was sprung, and he was arrested by security personnel in that country, to whom 'evidence' had been leaked that he was looking for arms. A commission found that

the report was false and Meiring was removed from office, although there was no evidence that he was part of the plot, apart from handing the report to Mandela.

4   From Shakespeare's *Julius Caesar*. Actually, either I put this down incorrectly or she was wrong. The phrase is 'Cry "Havoc!", and let *slip* the dogs of war', delivered by Mark Antony in Act 3, Scene 1, line 273. In the scene, Antony is alone with Julius Caesar's bloody corpse, shortly after the assassination by Brutus and other senators.

Chapter 20: Polokwane Tsunami

1   Leonard McCarthy in a discussion with the author, December 2007, just prior to charges being laid against Jacob Zuma.
2   This cluster also included the ministers of correctional services (formerly prisons) and defence.
3   Vusi Pikoli, *My Second Initiation: The Memoir of Vusi Pikoli* (Johannesburg, Picador Africa, 2013).
4   Ibid., p. 274.
5   Pikoli was subsequently cleared by the Ginwala Commission.
6   Jacques Mallet du Pan, French journalist and monarchist during the 1789 revolution. The full quote, published in 1793, is: 'Like Saturn, the Revolution devours its children.'
7   The ANC's constitution allowed this, unlike the country's constitution which permitted only two terms in office. Mbeki's move was seen as wishing to control from Luthuli House whoever became the nation's president. A crucial argument against, apart from those who disliked him, was the need to avoid what the ANC termed 'two centres of power'. There were those among his supporters – I was one – who urged him to have a 'Plan B' – a dependable candidate in his place, but he refused to listen.
8   There were three-year intervals between national conferences until Mafeking, when it was resolved that from then on these would be five-yearly.
9   'Bring me my machine-gun'
10   Steven Friedman, 'The person may change, but the policy lingers on', *Mail & Guardian*, 11 December 2007: 'An analysis of audited ANC membership figures produced by … Idasa's Jonathan Faull shows that most of the growth in ANC membership since the last audit came from rural areas.'
11   See Kgalema's comment on the 53rd ANC National Conference in Mangaung, *Daily Maverick*, 8–9 April 2017, where he refers to inflated membership and problems with accurate audits prevailing even at that later date.
12   Mosibudi Mangena, 'Dead calm in the eye of the storm', *Cape Times*, 21 September 2009, described Mbeki being recalled as state president in September 2008.
13   Interviewed in the documentary *Behind the Rainbow*, produced by Egyptian filmmaker Jihan el-Tahri.
14   Pierre Barbancey to Ronnie Kasrils, email, 6 July 2017.
15   Khulu Mbatha, *Unmasked: Why the ANC Failed to Govern* (Johannesburg, KMM Review Publishing Company, 2017), p. 123.

Chapter 21: Exit Mbeki

1   28 December 2007.
2   www.justice.gov.za
3   Mosibudi Mangena, 'Dead calm in the eye of the storm', *Cape Times*, 21 September 2009.
4   The Ministerial Review Commission on Intelligence, informally known as the

Matthews Commission, after its chairperson, Joe Matthews. The other two commissioners were Frene Ginwala and Laurie Nathan. The report could be found on the *Mail & Guardian* website.

5 www.news24.com, 12 January, 2009
6 Adriaan Basson, *Mail & Guardian*, 12 January 2009.

Chapter 22: Fake News

1 Possibly on 12 August 2008. I saw it while working in my ministry when Lorna Daniels, my media officer, drew it to my attention.
2 Gordin, *Zuma*, p. 12.

Chapter 23: Intercepts

1 These were referred to in accompanying papers and affidavits later drawn up by Wille Hofmeyr, head of both the NPA's Asset Forfeiture Unit (AFU) and the aforementioned SIU, who was to later submit an affidavit opposing the DA's long-running application and making allegation about my role. See chapter 27.
2 www.news24.com/SouthAfrica/News/zuma-refuses-to-resign-saying-west-wants-me-out-20170709-2.
3 www.images.timeslive.co.za/pdf/Spytapes/transcript1.pdf.
4 This is apparently the basis on which Hofmeyr queried whether 'the man' was Kasrils and 'the guy' was Mbeki. I hadn't in fact tried to hide anything in 2009, when the media were speculating about Mbeki's role in the timing of the decision to prosecute Zuma. I explained in an interview with the *Mail & Guardian*'s Pearlie Joubert that McCarthy was quite probably talking about me when he referred to 'the guy I mentioned' (*Mail & Guardian*, 22–29 May 2009). I had in fact acknowledged this, after the first leak of a few 'Spy Tape' transcripts.

Chapter 24: Mastermind

1 I described my situation as 'refirement' not 'retirement'.
2 *Sunday Times*, 7 November 2014.

Chapter 25: Complaint

1 *Business Day* and Argus group (twice).
2 *The Times*, Johannesburg, 8 September 2014.
3 The public advocate strives, in the first place, to get the two sides to settle the dispute amicably, but it became apparent that the *Sunday Times* was not prepared to give any quarter, so my complaint went to the ombudsman for consideration.
4 All documents relevant to the issue can be downloaded from www.presscouncil.org.za.
5 See www.presscouncil.org.za for the full finding.
6 The Supreme Court of Swaziland, Civil Appeals Case No. 48/213 in the case of African Echo, owners of *The Times* of Swaziland, and I.G. Simelane, 23 November 2013.
7 With Mr Mahmood Sanglay (press member), and Dr Simphiwe Sesanti, Ms Carol Mohlala and Mr Peter Mann, all public members of the council.
8 The Supreme Court of Swaziland, Civil Appeals Case No. 48/213, paragraph 16, p. 13.
9 *Othello*, Act 3, Scene 3.
10 *The Star*, 23 March 2015.
11 I got my apology on the front page of the *Sunday Times*, 29 March 2015, above the

fold —that is, on the top half of the page, alongside the lead story.

This also proved to be a sore point owing to challenges I later made, as I felt that the newspaper had not completely fulfilled the appeals order. As a result, a further hearing on 14 May 2015 took place. I had erred in believing that the original poster had appeared in Cape Town, but this had not been the case. However, I was able to show that no posters had appeared in the Eastern Cape, which the *Sunday Times* conceded had been an error. The paper was subsequently ordered to place adverts carrying the apology in the regional newspapers. The *Sunday Times* had upped the ante for this final hearing and Ampofo-Anti and Smuts were reinforced by the redoubtable Dario Milo, regarded as South Africa's leading expert on media law. At tea prior to commencement of the hearing he genially reminded me that we had once been on a conference panel debating freedom of expression and secrecy. I recalled we had been in general agreement on that occasion.

Chapter 26: Unprecedented Apology
1   *Sunday Times*, 29 March 2015.

Chapter 27: Informant Unmasked
1   Hofmeyr was dual head of the NPAs AFU and SIU at the time. The other official was Sibongile Mzinyathi. The *Sunday Times* of 18 November 2012 had previously reported 'only Hofmeyr apparently believed McCarthy's "alleged prosecutorial misbehaviour" warranted dropping the charges ... Mzinyathi reportedly wanted Zuma's prosecution to go ahead'. From 1990 Hofmeyr was deputy secretary of the ANC in the Western Cape for a few years, and we organised many marches and rallies together.
2   Hofmeyr's affidavit as second respondent, in the High Court of South Africa, Gauteng Division, Pretoria in the matter between the Democratic Alliance as Applicant, Case No. 19577/2009. His affidavit was dated 31 March, 2015. Implications of discussion between Kasrils and McCarthy, paras 280–8, pp 88–90. See also para 213, p 67. Transcript of all conversations between the two, marked WHX. See also Sithembosi Msomi, 'Hofmeyr affidavit may rescue Zuma', *Sunday Times*, 5 April 2015. By 2014, McCarthy had been with the World Bank for six years, while the Scorpions had been dissolved and replaced by the Hawks, which resided under the police.
3   *The Times*, 2 April 2015.
4   Nic Rowell, who briefly worked as a researcher under Ngcuka in the NPA, was the son of Anthony Rowell, who was stationed at the British embassy in Pretoria from 1990–4, and later worked for Kroll and subsequently André Pienaar's G3 agency in London. Rowell Senior interacted with many key ministers in that earlier period, including Jacob Zuma, whom he met several times even after Zuma became the country's president. He also had participated in training South African intelligence officers in a Kroll programme in the 1990s after his retirement from British government service. I never hid my association with him. I had come to know and like the young Nic Rowell, who visited me at ANC HQ, Shell House, to learn about South African history. He was living with his father in Pretoria and was at school there at the time. He was an extremely bright youngster: Ngcuka employed him from 1999–2003 as a researcher for the NPA.
5   'Kasrils told SAPA that Hofmeyr had said nothing he had not explained before. "I knew him professionally, had a few meetings with him at his request in the

run up to Polokwanw and after!"' *PoliticsWeb*, 31 March 2015, by Emsie Ferreira 'Hofmeyr lifts lid.'

6   Graeme Hosken, 'Hofmeyr bombshell a dud', *The Times*, 2 April 2015.
7   Letters, *Mail and Guardian*, 15 May 2009. By August 2015 Hofmeyr was no longer head of the NPA's once-crack AFU but head of the Legal Affairs Division, well out of the public eye.

Chapter 28: Of Spooks, Mules and Moles

1   'Meeting the challenges for the 21st century: The importance of oversight – *Quis custodiet ipsos custodes? Who will guard the guards*?', National Assembly, Cape Town, 1 June 2006.
2   The Matthews Commission Report could be accessed on the *Mail & Guardian* website.
3   Gaye Davis, 'Kasrils: Info Bill must be withdrawn', *Pretoria News*, 20 August 2010. Minister Cwele's Protection of State Information Bill was passed by parliament in 2011 but President Zuma has not signed it into law.
4   The Protection of Information Act of 1982.
5   Howard Varney, email to the author, 5 July 2017.
6   This caused an uproar during Zuma's 2015 State of the Nation parliamentary address with protests by MP's delaying proceedings.
7   *City Press*, 30 April, 2017. The unfortunate young man, Elvis Ramosebudi, was arrested and charged with attempting to obtain funds quite openly as a hired assassin of Zuma, the Guptas and a variety of ministers he promised to bump off with guns he tried to buy on Twitter – while at the same time soliciting for assassination work from the Guptas.
8   'Ronnie Kasrils blasts "idiotic" levels of secrecy', *City Press*, 17 August 2014.
9   Gordhan rubbished allegations of 'secret' meetings held in London, a bogus intelligence report and the grounds for his dismissal in general. See *Daily Maverick*, 31 March 2017.
10   'Zuma used fake intel to cull Eskom execs', *Sunday Times*, 21 May 2017.
11   *Daily Maverick*, 20 June 2017. 'SA's spy boss implicated in massive tender fraud at Prasa', was the headline in the article about Arthur Fraser. The *Huffington Post*, 20 June 2017, featured a similar article about Fraser headed 'Spy boss' company in dodgy Prasa contract'. PRASA has been regarded as paralysed by systemic corruption, and the former CEO Lucky Montana, one-time active member of the SACP, is under investigation. He used to complain to me about perceived corruption in the SACP under Blade Nzimande and presented himself as a squeaky-clean whistleblower.
12   'Smoke and mirrors', *Mail & Guardian*, 1–7 May 2009.
13   Ibid. Cosatu received the fax on 6 May 2007, according to Powell.
14   Peddlers are private and anonymous intelligence sources touting information.

Chapter 29: Sidikiwe

1   A popular school teacher who led a protest demonstration for better municipal service delivery in Fiksburg, Free State, in April 2011. He was shot in the chest after being assaulted by police.
2   Greg Marinovich, *Murder at Small Koppie: The Real Story of the Marikana Massacre* (Johannesburg, Penguin Random House, 2016). Marinovich's stark and horrifying conclusions on how the police had tracked and killed the miners first appeared in *Daily Maverick* in September 2012 under the headline 'The cold murder

fields of Marikana', www.dailymaverick.co.za/article/2012-08-30-the-murder-fields-of-marikana-the-cold-murder-fields-of-marikana#.WR1Rk8b-vDc.

3 The terrible event has been brilliantly captured in a prize-winning documentary by Rehad Desai, *Miners Shot Down*. See www.minersshotdown.co.za.

4 'Kasrils unsure how to vote', *Mail & Guardian*, 14 March 2014.

5 *Business Day, The Star, Citizen* and *New Age*, 16 April 2014 and most of their counterparts in the smaller cities.

6 Lindiwe Sisulu and I have not had an easy relationship, which seems to have had its origins in my appointment in 2004 to take over her beloved intelligence services, where she had been minister from 2001 to 2004, when I succeeded her. She took umbrage at my first budget speech in June 2005 when I mentioned the urgent need to harmonise the expenditure ratios, which showed that since 1994 a worrying disjunction was evident: running costs (which included a growing salary bill) were eating into operational and capital costs. She complained about this to the deputy president, Jacob Zuma, and to the minister in the Presidency, Essop Pahad. The latter raised this in cabinet: I denied my remarks were meant personally as they covered former minister Nhlanhla's tenure as well, and I pointed out that I had recorded my appreciation to my predecessors, by name, for their fine work. In his office, Zuma was bovine-faced in raising the issue with me. 'Have you read the speech?' I enquired, knowing full well that he scarcely bothered reading anything. Since he had not, I told him I would provide him with a copy. I did, but I never heard from him again on the issue. However, the extent of Sisulu's feud with me became evident after Mandela's death. MK veterans (not the MKMVA of Maphatsoe, I hasten to add) were scheduled to meet at his Houghton home to pay respects to his widow, Graça Machel. The group, including Josiah Jele, Siphiwe Nyanda and a score of *mgwenya* (1960s MK veterans), were ushered into a reception area where Graça was seated on the floor in the traditional way, with numerous other female mourners. Sisulu is adept at performing the role of usher at such occasions. My wife Amina had accompanied me to the house and overheard Sisulu instructing Mandela's daughter, the temperamental Makaziwe, to inform Graça to cut me short as I 'tended to speak far too long'. I had in fact been honoured by the MK group's prior request that I be their spokesman in conveying our commiserations. As I was speaking to an attentive and clearly grateful Graça, Makaziwe had the effrontery to interrupt my speech by approaching Graça and whispering into her ear. I paused until she had completed her mission. Graça looked up at me, with her sympathetic eyes, motioning me to continue. After I concluded a five-minute address with a sentence or two in her native Portuguese she thanked us in a warm and appreciative way.

7 *The Star*, 7 May 2014.

8 'Barney Pityana on Vote No', www.defendingpopulardemocracy.blogspot.co.za/2014/05/barney-pityana-on-vote-no.html.

Chapter 30: Kebby's Comeuppance

1 The *Citizen*, 9 September 2014, and *Mail & Guardian*, 12 September 2014.

2 Ronnie Kasrils, *Armed and Dangerous* (Johannesburg, Jacana Media, 2013), pp. 13–43.

3 'Kasrils also wants apology', *New Age*, 17 September 2014.

4 His junior advocate was François Grobler, both briefed by Jenny Friedman Associates.

5 I had worked with Mpofu and Winnie Mandela in the undercover days and had

become a close friend of his in protesting against Zuma's corruption and slating the government over the Marikana massacre of striking miners on 12 August 2012. At the Farlam Commission hearings, Mpofu represented the widows and victims of those ghastly shootings.

6   1983: Chief of Brigade, Higher Officers' Course, Moscow; 1994: Unity Medal by Presidential Warrant (in the creation of SANDF); 1995: 10-, 20- and 30-Years' Service Medals in MK; 2002: Cuban International Friendship Medal; 2005: Russian Friendship Medal – 60th Anniversary 1945 Victory over Nazi Germany; 2005: Russian Veterans' Medal for Co-operation in Angola; 2012: Two Platinum Class (iii) Decorations, presented by President Zuma in 2013.

7   There was one case where I had insisted that one of our foreign service representatives be suspended for a year for having brought the SASS into disrepute owing to drunkenness but I subsequently had him reappointed after it was clear that he had reformed.

8   *Business Day*, 24 August 2016.

9   *The Star*, 24 August 2016.

10   Ibid.

11   *The Star*, 24 August 2016.

Chapter 31: Girl in a Green Scarf

1   *African News Agency*, 4 April 2016.

2   The ANC's vote was under 54 percent, and they lost power in the metros of Nelson Mandela Bay (Port Elizabeth), Johannesburg and Tshwane (Pretoria). The DA maintained its Cape Town stronghold with an increased majority.

3   eNCA and Ra'eesa Pather, 'Four women and the protest that shook the results ceremony', *Mail & Guardian*, 6 August 2016.

4   Author of a biography of Zuma.

5   See 'Robbed of her identity, Khwezi's humanity can finally be fully acknowledged', *City Press*, 16 October 2016. In this piece Makanya revisited and updated his November 2005 report in the *Sunday Times* and makes reference to 'a pliable journalist' who had been given access to Khwezi's phone number.

6   *The Star*, 10 October 2016.

7   *The Star*, 10 August 2016 and *Amandla*, November 2016.

8   Written while she was in exile and widely circulated following her death. She had performed it publicly while living in the Netherlands as an exile.

Chapter 32: The Corridors to Corruption

1   'The Corridors to Corruption', by 'Touissant' (Bernstein's pen name) *The African Communist*, No. 124, First Quarter, 1991.

2   Bernstein's reference to 'superstructure' encompasses the institutions of state, governance, law, finance, education, and the mainstream ideas, philosophy and culture dominant in society. These institutions and ideology emerge from the material base or foundation of society, which consists of the means of production (tools, factories, land, raw material, labour), distribution and exchange of goods and wealth produced. The dominant ideology of the ruling class strives to justify the social relations of production between social classes arising out of property relations.

Chapter 33: Faust and Mephistopheles

1   From the Introduction to the 2013 edition of *Armed and Dangerous* (Johannesburg,

Jacana Media, 2013).

2 I record my indebtedness in particular to Sampie Terreblanche, the retired Stellenbosch professor of economics, and Patrick Bond, activist and academic who was closely involved in the drafting of the ANC's Reconstruction and Development Programme White Paper, and again in drafting the aborted 1996 National Growth and Development Strategy.

3 *Strategy and Tactics of the ANC*, adopted at the Morogoro Conference, Tanzania, April 1969.

4 Oliver Tambo, Address to 60th anniversary meeting, SACP, London, 30 July 1981.

Chapter 34: Flight of the Flamingos

1 The scenarios had previously been presented to a score of economists from the ANC, trade unions, academia and business. The product was later adopted by Generon Consulting, a Texas-based firm that offered 'large-scale organisational renewal' and claimed to 'help our clients to change from a controlling management style to a cooperative decision-making management style which often includes re-shaping the organizational culture through adopting a more comprehensive world-view.'

2 See Pieter le Roux, 'The Mont Fleur scenarios', *Weekly Mail & Guardian*, July 1992, and Adam Kahane, 'Between a ostrich and a flamingo', *Mail & Guardian* online, 2 August 2007.

3 Pippa Green, *Choice Not Fate: The Life and Times of Trevor Manuel* (Johannesburg, Penguin Books, 2008).

4 At the Bank of China in London.

5 MERG Report, *Making Democracy Work: A Framework for Macro-economic Policy in South Africa*, 1993, Chapter 1.

6 *Business Day*, editorial comment, 'Left Bank', 8 November 1993.

7 R.G. Cofino, 'A successful approach to participation: The World Bank relationship with South Africa', July 1995.

Chapter 35: Sleepwalking into the Future

1 F.W. de Klerk, *The Last Trek: A New Beginning* (London, Pan Books, 1999), p. 344.

2 Ibid., p. 345. De Klerk was explaining his party's support for Gear in the Government of National Unity.

3 Ibid., p. 345.

4 Chris Liebenberg was CEO of Nedbank, one of South Africa's 'big four' financial institutions, from 1990 to 1994. He was minister of finance from 19 September 1994 to 4 April 1996, in the Government of National Unity.

5 Vishnu Padayachee in an email to the author, 27 May 2017.

6 De Klerk, *The Last Trek*, p. 343.

7 Jay Naidoo, *Change: Organising Tomorrow, Today* (Johannesburg, Penguin, 2017).

8 Steyn, South African billionaire founder and shareholder of the UK-based insurance and financial services company BGL Group, was an early wooer of the ANC leadership, opening his lavish, sprawling home in Hyde Park, Johannesburg, to them.

9 Elias Masilela, *Number 43 Trelawney Park* (Cape Town, David Philip, 2007), p. xviii. The address in the book's title was the humble home of his exiled parents and the venue had been central to ANC activity for many years. Masilela later went on to work in South Africa's finance department and as CEO of the strategic Public

Investment Corporation.

10 'We will nationalise — Mandela', *Weekly Mail & Guardian*, 26 January 1990, www.mg.co.za/article/1990-01-26-we-will-nationalise-mandela.

11 I am indebted to a reading of 'Transitional justice, criminal justice, and exceptionalism in South Africa' by Howard Varney in Michael Reed and Amanda Lyons (eds.), *Contested Transitions: Dilemmas of Transitional Justice in Colombia and Comparative Experience* (International Center for Transitional Justice, Bogota, and Ministry of Foreign Relations of Norway, 2010).

Chapter 36: A People's Pact

1 Blade Nzimande, Address to the SACP's 14th Congress, Boksburg, 11 July 2017.

2 Marianne Thamm, 'Corrupting the country's soul, Zupta style'. *Daily Maverick*, 12 July 2017.

3 Rosa Luxemburg, *The Crisis of German Social Democracy* (The 'Junius' Pamphlet) (1915): 'Bourgeois society stands at the crossroads: either transition to socialism or regression into barbarism.'

4 The term 'food security' should be understood as the concept of 'food sovereignty', being the right to healthy food produced through ecologically sound and sustainable methods, and their right to define and control their own food and agriculture systems. It is the alternative to the corporate food system. Refer: Peoples' Food Sovereignty Act No 1 of 2016, of the South African Food Sovereignty Campaign (SAFSC).

Index

Kasrils slams Cw

Above all,

Workers are wors

Spy tapes: apology to Ronnie Kasrils

Kasr 'idio of se

ANC left weak as

Kasrils: Zuma gov